Self and Society in Medieval France

Self and Society in Medieval France

The Memoirs of Abbot Guibert of Nogent (1064? - c. 1125)

Edited with an Introduction and Notes
by John F. Benton

The translation of C. C. Swinton Bland
revised by the editor

HARPER TORCHBOOKS
Harper & Row, Publishers
New York, Hagerstown, San Francisco, London

SELF AND SOCIETY IN MEDIEVAL FRANCE.

Printed in the United States of America.

First HARPER TORCHBOOK edition published 1970 by Harper & Row, Publishers, Incorporated, New York, N.Y. 10022.

Library of Congress Catalog Card Number: 75–97060.

80 81 82 10 9 8 7 6

HARPER TORCHBOOKS: Advisory Editor in the Humanities and Social Sciences: BENJAMIN NELSON

PATRI MATRIQUE

QUI ME HISTORIAM AMARE DOCUERUNT

Contents

Map and Illustrations

Preface

This translation rests on the work of a great many people. The Latin text of Guibert's book was first published by Dom Luc d'Achery in 1651, and since that date a series of distinguished scholars, beginning with Dom Jean Mabillon, has contributed to our understanding of it. Guizot brought Guibert's story to the attention of a wider audience by publishing a French translation in 1825, and in 1907 Georges Bourgin produced a modern edition of the Latin text.

Readers of English have known this work through a translation by C. C. Swinton Bland, published in the Broadway Translations in 1925. The unfortunate slowness of communications across the English Channel is shown by the fact that Bland did not make use of Bourgin's book, but based his translation on the outdated edition of d'Achery. Bland's version is also flawed in other ways. He showed a cavalier disregard for names (Rouen is rendered as Rome and Fly is consistently called Ely), made serious errors of translation, and sought to create a feeling of archaism by preserving much of Guibert's confusing sentence structure. And yet his English version has vigor and color and his understanding of the Latin was in places extremely perceptive.

The original plan for the republication of this work as a Harper Torchbook was that I should supply some annotation (since Bland had none) and that Michael Alexander and Andrew C. Kimmens would touch up Bland's translation. Alexander and Kimmens began their job in 1966 and made over a thousand corrections. But it soon became apparent that a more fundamental revision than they had time to make was needed, and I fell heir to the entire project. I have gone back over the text, making use of Bland's translation and the Alexander-Kimmens emendations where I could, but correcting and recasting as much as I thought necessary. The result is a translation for which much of the credit should go to others and the entire responsibility for error rests with me.

Mabillon wrote of Guibert that "multa ille scripsit non inerudite, sed scabroso stilo," and most readers have agreed with the judgment that his style is rough. The cause of some of our difficulties is that the only complete manuscript known at present is a seventeenth-century copy in serious need of emendation. But Guibert himself is responsible for the ambiguity and wandering complexity of his sentences, since he tells us with misplaced pride that he did not prepare his writings first in draft "but committed them to the written page in their final form as I thought them out."[1] He is particularly galling in his use of relative pronouns, which sometimes do not indicate which of several individuals Guibert had in mind. I have seen no advantage in faithfully preserving Guibert's diffuse and uncertain style, and have felt free to break up complex sentences and replace vague pronouns with proper names. The reader who regrets these alterations is welcome to read the Latin instead. This translation also uses more medieval terminology than did Guibert, who did his best to describe his world in classical vocabulary.

D'Achery's extensive annotation made his edition, reprinted by Migne in the *Patrologia latina,* a masterful work of scholarship. Bourgin added further useful annotation and wrote an introduction which summarized the information available in 1907, but unfortunately the quality of his work was not up to the high standards of the series in which the book appeared, the *Collection de textes pour servir à l'étude et à l'enseignement de l'histoire*. Surprisingly often erroneous translations are suggested, incorrect identifications are made, quotations are unidentified, and useful emendations by d'Achery are rejected.[2] The new scholarly edition being prepared by M. Edmond René Labande will be very welcome indeed.

The present translation is a compromise between a simple reissue and a thorough reworking of the quality the reader might hope for. Without a new Latin text based on the manuscripts, many difficulties are bound to remain unresolved. Guibert knew both the pagan and

[1] See below, p. 91.
[2] See Appendix II for critical reviews of the edition.

the Christian classics better than either Bourgin or I, and although I have been able to identify some 35 more allusions and quotations than my predecessor, I have no doubt that many more have gone unnoticed. The annotation has not been prepared for scholars, but is intended to make Guibert's book more understandable to the general reader. I have felt free to omit documentation available in Bourgin's edition, and have usually given supporting references only when the notes supplement or differ with Bourgin's.

The Introduction, which attempts a psychological study of Guibert's personality, is a departure from the usual view of the man. The reader is warned that there are distinguished medievalists who consider this approach highly questionable.

In the three years I have been studying Guibert, I have bored and bothered my friends with many questions. Some help must pass unacknowledged, but I wish to express my particular gratitude to Professors Frederic Amory, John W. Baldwin, Thomas N. Bisson, Elizabeth A. R. Brown, Giles Constable, Lloyd Daly, Norman Golb, William Roach, Eleanor Searle; Fr. Georges Folliet; Dom Jean Leclercq; Dr. William M. Newman; Mme. Jacqueline Le Braz; M. Denis Larquet of the Syndicat d'Initiative of Laon; and M. Georges Dumas of the Archives Départementales de l'Aisne. Miss Willow Roberts of Harper & Row drew the map.

I am grateful to the Penrose Fund of the American Philosophical Society for making possible a trip to France in the summer of 1968, and to the California Institute of Technology for other support. The facilities of the Institut de Recherche et d'Histoire des Textes greatly aided my investigation.

Though she eventually echoed Guibert's favorite comment—"Why say more?"—Mrs. Lucille Lozoya typed and retyped with great good will. My wife, bless her, gave me her critical reading, support, and understanding.

April, 1969
Pasadena, California

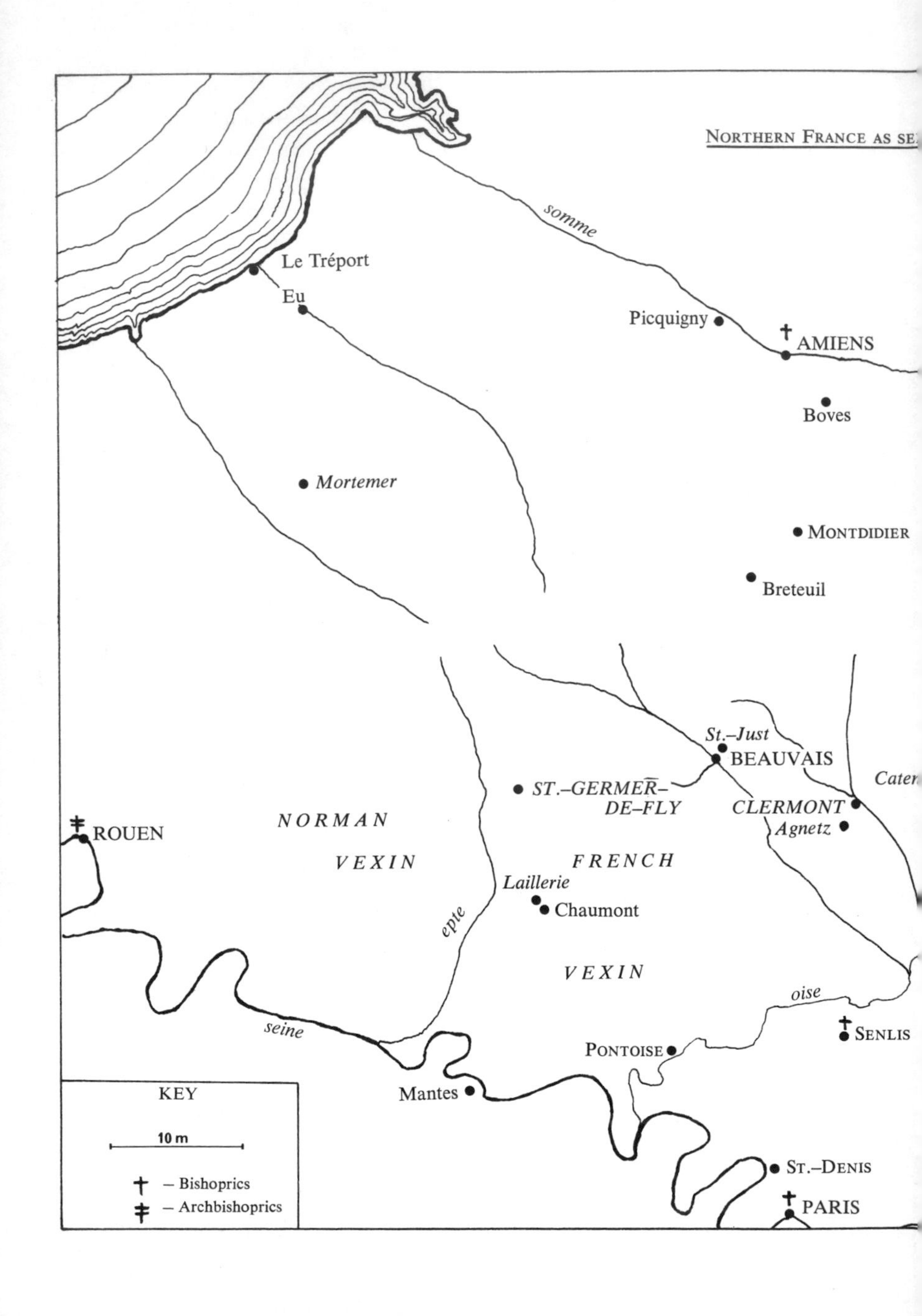
NORTHERN FRANCE AS SE
somme
Le Tréport
Eu
Picquigny
AMIENS
Boves
Mortemer
MONTDIDIER
Breteuil
St.-Just
BEAUVAIS
ST.-GERMER-
DE-FLY
CLERMONT
Caten
Agnetz
ROUEN
NORMAN
VEXIN
FRENCH
VEXIN
Laillerie
Chaumont
epte
oise
seine
SENLIS
PONTOISE
Mantes
ST.-DENIS
PARIS
KEY
10 m
– Bishoprics
– Archbishoprics

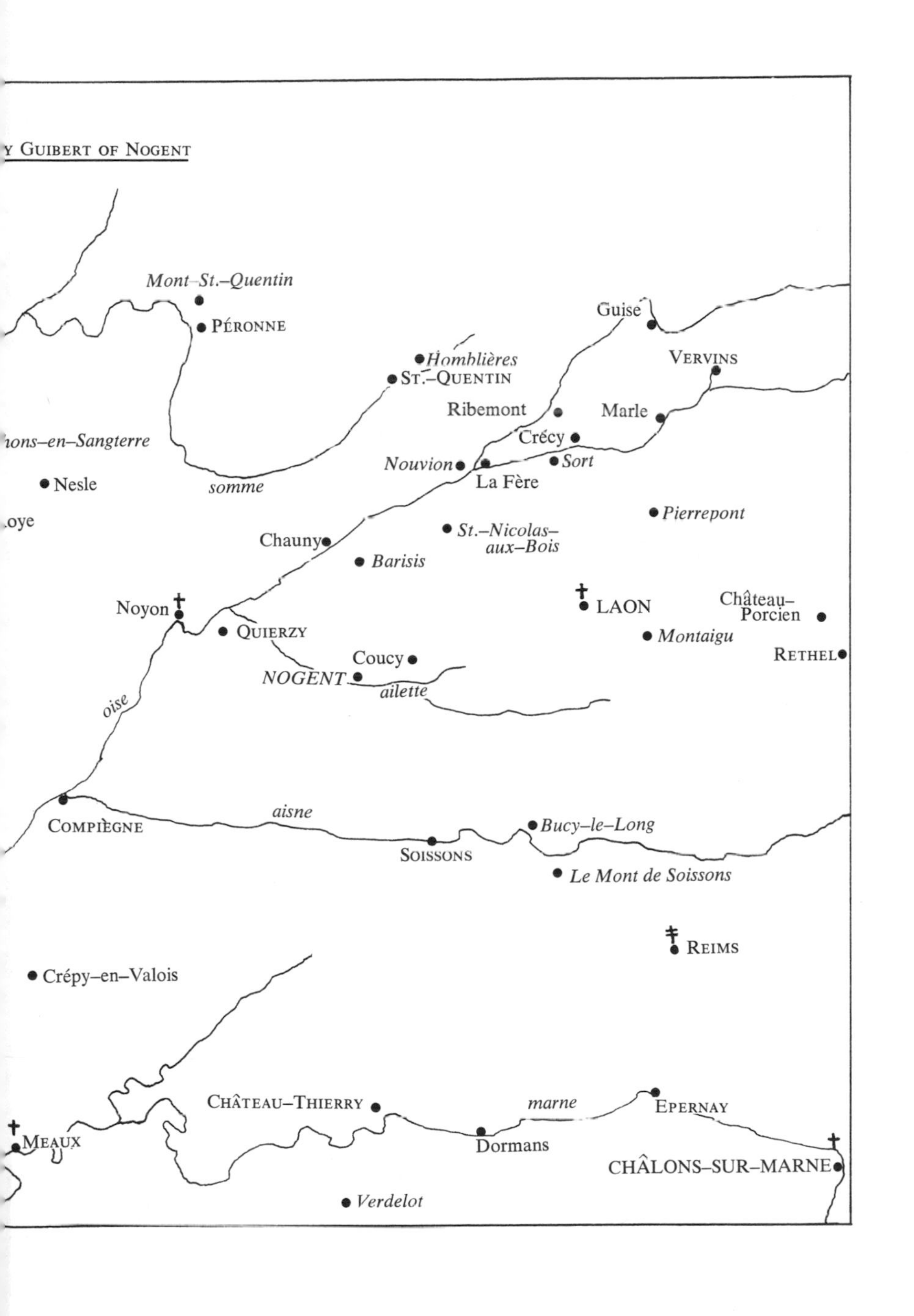

y Guibert of Nogent
Mont-St.-Quentin
Péronne
Guise
Hombliéres
St.-Quentin
Vervins
Ribemont
Marle
ons-en-Sangterre
Crécy
Nouvion
Sort
La Fère
Nesle
somme
Pierrepont
oye
Chauny
St.-Nicolas-
aux-Bois
Barisis
Noyon
Laon
Château-
Porcien
Quierzy
Montaigu
Rethel
Coucy
Nogent
ailette
oise
aisne
Compiègne
Bucy-le-Long
Soissons
Le Mont de Soissons
Reims
Crépy-en-Valois
Château-Thierry
marne
Epernay
Meaux
Dormans
Châlons-sur-Marne
Verdelot

Introduction

In the three books of his *Memoirs*, Guibert of Nogent wrote of his own childhood, career, aspirations, and dreams, of the two monasteries where he was a monk and abbot, and of the wider world about him, notably of the revolt of the commune of Laon in 1112. Among his other works are a vivid history of the First Crusade and a treatise critical of the cult of relics, as well as a series of Biblical commentaries and religious tracts. Because of his remarkable writings, Guibert has attracted the attention of historians as a critic, thinker, and observer, and some have acclaimed him for intellectual qualities they label unusual if not unmedieval. But as yet no one has attempted to show why or how Guibert became the unusual man he was, even though his story of his life provides an extremely intimate view of the formation of a medieval "personality." As an introduction to Guibert's book about himself and his world, let us look at his life from a viewpoint different from his own to see if we can find some explanation for his striking characteristics.

What has struck modern historians as unusual about this Benedictine monk who played only a minor role in his own day and is barely mentioned in the writings of his contemporaries? In the first place, he was the author of what the great historian of autobiographical writing Georg Misch calls the first "comprehensive" autobiography in medieval Latin.[1] The example of Augustine's *Confessions* lay behind it, but medieval authors seldom followed the demanding example of Augustine's great work of self-examination.[2] When Abelard wanted to write about himself, he wrote a

[1]*Geschichte der Autobiographie*, III, 2 (Frankfurt am Main, 1959), p. 109.
[2]Pierre Courcelle, *Les confessions de Saint Augustin dans la tradition littéraire* (Paris, 1963), esp. pp. 272-275.

letter (or at least used that form), and we know such men as Bernard of Clairvaux and Peter the Venerable as intimately as we do because of their letter collections. That Guibert was willing to invite a comparison with Augustine by beginning his work with the word *Confiteor* is indicative of the extraordinarily high standard of self-expression he set for himself.

Secondly, Guibert's treatise on relics, *De pignoribus sanctorum,* in which he attacked the alleged tooth of the Saviour venerated at the abbey of Saint-Médard of Soissons and more generally superstition and the cult of relics as practiced in his day, shows that he had marked critical abilities. Abel Lefranc, writing in 1896, was ecstatic about this treatise, which he called "absolutely unique," and about its author, "truly enamored with rationalism," whom he compared with Rabelais, Calvin, and Voltaire. "He was the first who tried to provide a total view, systematic and rational, on the questions of the cult of the saints and their relics."[3] Bernard Landry joined in calling Guibert's example "unique," and Charles Haskins said that he "showed striking skepticism." Marc Bloch thought that Lefranc had exaggerated Guibert's critical sense, but still called it "quite sharp, rare indeed in the twelfth century."[4]

Admiration for Guibert's critical mind has also been based on his history of the First Crusade, the *Gesta Dei per Francos.*[5] In this book Guibert cites his written sources, discusses the problem of not being an eyewitness, and is methodically critical of the validity (as well as the style) of his predecessors' work, among other things challenging some of the miracles reported by Fulcher of Chartres. Bernard Monod was so impressed by Guibert's historical

[3]"Le traité des reliques de Guibert de Nogent et les commencements de la critique historique au moyen âge," in *Études d'histoire du moyen âge dediées à Gabriel Monod* (Paris, 1896), pp. 285, 298, 304. For a modern study which shows Guibert's relationship to other medieval critics of relics, see Klaus Schreiner, "Discrimen veri ac falsi," *Archiv für Kulturgeschichte,* XLVIII (1966), 1-53.

[4]Landry, "Les idées morales du XIIe siècle. VII. Un chroniqueur: Guibert de Nogent," *Revue des cours et conférences,* année 1938-39, II, 350; Haskins, *The Renaissance of the Twelfth Century* (Cambridge, Mass., 1927), p. 235; Bloch, *Les rois thaumaturges* (new ed., Paris, 1961), pp. 29 and 30, n. 1.

[5]Critical edition in *Recueil des historiens des croisades. Historiens occidentaux,* IV (Paris, 1879), 115-263, hereafter cited as *Gesta Dei,* with page references to this edition.

method that he called him "the most intellectual man of his century" and came very close to suggesting that Guibert shared the virtues of the contemporary school of scientific history.[6] Lefranc had earlier come to the same conclusion, saying that Guibert was "better prepared than anyone of his time to glimpse some of the essential rules of historical criticism."[7] In 1965, Jacques Chaurand swept much of this praise away by arguing that Guibert shows the training not of a critical historian but of a moralizing Biblical exegete.[8] Chaurand's view is preferable, but while the anachronism of Lefranc and Monod should be qualified, still it is true that Guibert showed an unusual desire and ability to dispute with other authors on rational grounds.

A third facet of his thought which has struck historians as unusual or precocious is his patriotism. "At no time in the twelfth century was the pride of being French expressed so forcefully," Landry wrote in reference to a spirited defense of the French which Guibert made to the archdeacon of Mainz. Warming up to his subject as he thought later about his conversation with the archdeacon, Guibert had called his people "noble, wise, warlike, generous, and elegant." Their very name was a word of praise, so that "if we see Bretons, Englishmen, or Genoese behaving honorably, we call such men *frank.*"[9] Guibert had an eye for national differences—he was the first to describe for us a Scot wearing a kilt and sporran (p. 137)[10]—and he was sure that God had established the French to lead the rest of the world. He was also the first to record unequivocably that a French king could cure scrofula by touch. He added that he knew the English king had never had the audacity to try it.[11] With his patriotism Guibert combined a strong sense of modernity. Joining in the debate over the relative virtues of the ancients and moderns,

[6]"De la méthode historique chez Guibert de Nogent," *Revue historique,* LXXXIV (1904), 51-70, esp. p. 52.
[7]"Traité," p. 289.
[8]"La conception de l'histoire de Guibert de Nogent," *Cahiers de civilisation médiévale,* VIII (1965), 381-395.
[9]Landry, "Idées morales," p. 356; *Gesta Dei,* II, 1, p. 136.
[10]Page numbers in parentheses refer to the text which follows. For the kilt, see *Gesta Dei,* I, 1, p. 125.
[11]Bloch, *Rois thaumaturges,* pp. 29-32, 46.

Guibert stressed the superiority of his own time. Not for him dwarfs sitting on the shoulders of giants; instead he quoted King Roboam: "Our little fingers are thicker than the backs of our fathers."[12]

Nineteenth-century historians were drawn to Guibert by his rationalism, skepticism, and proto-nationalism. In that condescending fashion with which historians sometimes grant awards, Lefranc called him "practically a modern man."[13] But other commentators have noted a dark side to his character, expressed in his violent and scurrilous denunciations of his enemies. In the *Gesta Dei,* he announces that Mohammed preached "a new license of promiscuous intercourse," and tells a detailed story of his evil life and end. In the process he admits that his sources are questionable, but explains that "it is safe to speak evil of one whose malignity exceeds whatever ill can be spoken."[14] Throughout his history Guibert dwells immoderately on the lusts and sexual crimes, both natural and unnatural, of the Moslems. He was also among the first anti-Semitic writers to accuse the Jews of witchcraft and black magic. After relating Guibert's gross story (p. 115) of a monk tempted by the Devil, who had been conjured up by a Jewish physician, Joshua Trachtenberg commented in *The Devil and the Jews:* "To one who is familiar with the later accounts of the witches' and sorcerers' ritual the early appearance of the sperm libation and the act of communion with sperm [in this part of Guibert's book] must provide a particularly revealing insight into the development of witchcraft out of purported heretical practice."[15] In addition, Guibert provides one of the most vivid descriptions of the unnatural vices of the dualist heretics of his day (p. 212). And, besides what he says about Moslems, Jews, and heretics, he is a prime source for stories about the license, depravity, and violence of those with whom he was associated.

This survey of some of the ways Guibert has seemed unusual or

[12]*Gesta Dei,* I. 1, p. 123; cf. III Kings 12:10. The Vulgate or Douay-Rheims version of the Bible is used throughout.

[13]"Traité p. 286.

[14]These quotations are noted in Norman Daniel, *Islam and the West: The Making of an Image* (Edinburgh, 1960), p. 145, and Richard W. Southern, *Western Views of Islam in the Middle Ages* (Cambridge, Mass., 1962), p. 31.

[15]New York, 1966, p. 213.

precocious or simply interesting has drawn freely upon the words of others to make a point. The traditional comparative approach of intellectual history permits a critic to say that his subject is either "typical" or "owes his ideas to some other source," or, as in the case of Guibert, is "exceptional" or even "unique." But medievalists rarely discuss how or why their subjects became typical or unusual people, even when the materials for such an investigation are as readily available as they are in this instance. If we are to have a fuller understanding of this unusual man, our approach must be developmental as well as comparative.

Unfortunately for us, Guibert did not think of his personal reflections as a formal autobiography.[16] He addressed this book to God, Who "knoweth the secrets of the heart," and wrote it for the edification of his readers and to provide material for sermons. Modern readers more interested in history or personality than in Guibert's spiritual message may regret that the author buried the story of his life in the religious conclusions that gave it meaning to him. Digging is required, but with application it is possible to put together a reasonably coherent account of the course of his life.

Guibert fails to tell us three pieces of information with which modern biographical statements usually begin: when and where he was born and who his family were. Dom Mabillon, who was once a monk at Guibert's abbey of Nogent and studied him carefully, calculated that he was born in 1053, and, backed by the authority of the great seventeenth-century scholar, that date now appears as an established fact. It really is not soundly based, however, and my conclusion is that a date in the mid-1060's, perhaps 1064, is much more likely. The place of his birth has been disputed. Although Mabillon was confident that he was born in Clermont-en-Beauvaisis, others have argued for Beauvais or other places, or have left the matter up in the air. The weight of the evidence shows, however, that Mabillon was right about his birthplace. As for his family, Guibert gives us tantalizing hints which have suggested to

[16]Although both d'Achery and Bourgin called this book *De vita sua*, Guibert did not use this title or treat the book as an autobiography. He referred to the work as *Monodiae*, which literally means "songs for one voice" and may be translated as *Memoirs*. For this title, see Migne, *Patrologia latina*, t. 156, col. 622. This volume contains Guibert's collected works; it will be cited hereafter as Migne's edition (ed. Migne).

many that he was a scion of the baronage of Picardy. It is more likely, however, that he was descended from a family which guarded the castle of Clermont and who were vassals of the future counts of Clermont, and that he was therefore a member of a family which was noble and influential in a small locality, but was neither wealthy nor highly placed.[17]

What was more important to Guibert than the details of a biographical entry was his personal development. He was born on Holy Saturday, a day which seemed to him and his mother to involve a special dedication. The labor was difficult. Guibert was a tiny baby who seemed unlikely to live, and his mother almost died. The extreme danger of the labor led his father to dedicate the life of his unborn child to God, and Guibert had later to carry with him the knowledge that his birth had almost caused his mother's death.

Some eight months later, his father died. His mother never remarried, and Guibert remained forever her youngest child and her consolation in her widowhood. Guibert had older siblings, but he tells us so little of them that we do not even know how many were in the family. An elder brother, who was perhaps eight or ten years older, followed his father's military career and held an important position at Clermont as a young man. Guibert mentions in passing that at the time of their mother's death he and a brother had left the abbey of Saint-Germer, where they had been together, and were then busy at the abbey of Nogent (p. 133). This passage is our only indication that Guibert shared his monastic life at Saint-Germer with an older brother, who later placed himself under Guibert's authority at Nogent. Guibert expresses neither love nor warm feelings for any member of his family except his mother. Of his relations with his siblings he tells us only that he was his mother's favorite (p. 41) and that a brother had earned his punishment in hell (p. 95).

From his mother, Guibert received indulgent care if not warm love. The boy in turn loved and admired his mother and saw her as by far the most important human influence on his life. No uncle or other male relative took responsibility for bringing up this

[17]The evidence for these statements is discussed in Appendix I.

orphan, and since he was to be a cleric he was not sent to the court of a relative or feudal superior to be raised. What sort of woman was this widow left to mold her cherished son? From Guibert's description it appears that she was a person of beauty, pride, intelligence, and determination, able to stand up to her husband's relatives and to exercise authority, and vigorous in protecting her child and advancing his interests. But above all Guibert saw her as modest and virtuous, particularly in sexual matters. As a young girl, "she had learned to be terrified of sin, not from experience, but from dread of some sort of blow from on high, and—as she often told me herself—this dread had possessed her mind with the terror of sudden death" (p. 64). No doubt her dread affected her young husband, too, for at the beginning of his marriage Guibert's father was afflicted with impotence and could not consummate his marriage for years. During this troubled time, rich neighbors tried to seduce the virgin bride, but she resisted them all. Finally, Guibert's father was able to break the spell of impotence, seen by all as a knot of bewitchment, by conceiving a child with another woman, and only after this did Guibert's mother begin to have conjugal relations with her husband.

Guibert grew up with a sense of modesty and a determination to strive for absolute sexual self-control. His views can be seen most explicitly in a little statement on "Why the private parts of the body are covered," which he inserted in the tract on the Incarnation which he directed against the Jews. Here is the beginning of his comment:

"Certain people ask why we clothe those parts of the body so carefully, since we cover no other parts with such attention. Not only do we hide them, but also we scarcely permit the places near them, including the navel and the thighs, to be seen. And why? When my finger, my eyes, my lips move, they move at my direction, by my will, and since they act docilely under my authority, they occasion me no shame. But since those members we are considering are driven toward unbridled activity by a certain liberty acting against the rules of reason, it is as if there were a separate law in our members, as St. Paul puts it, fighting against the law of our mind and leading us captive in the law of sin that is in our members (Romans 7:23). Therefore quite properly we blush, since whether we like it or not, we appear to be shamefully erected out of passionate desire."[18]

The influence of a censorious mother who had nearly destroyed the potency of her husband and who we are told remained strictly celibate after his death became a part of Guibert's being. His writing abounds with denunciations of the sexual depravity of his male relatives, of nobles whom he disliked, of monks and church officials with whom he came in contact, of practically all women of his own generation in contrast to those of his mother's time. Revulsion from sexuality is also a major theme of his religious writing. His commentary on the first verse of Genesis, written when he was under twenty, took as its theme the struggle of spirit and flesh. Before the Fall, spirit and flesh were in perfect harmony, but now, he says, "the disobedience of concupiscence is in control, calling us against our wills to indecent movement."[19]

And so Guibert looked back to his childhood with nostalgia as a time when he was free of the torment of sexuality. As he went on to say in the tract on the Incarnation: "We see infants and often boys short of puberty displaying themselves naked without shame. If they suffered any excitement, they would surely embarrass themselves or those who happened to meet them. How blessed was the primal condition of Adam and Eve! How happy the ignorance of childhood, since while it is protected by incapacity, it enjoys the security of the angels."[20]

We may also see the influence of Guibert's childhood in his fastidiousness about bodily cleanliness and his association of excrement with punishment. The reader will note that Guibert goes out of his way to tell stories which involve privies, sewers, and excrement; for instance, he relates a pair of tales in which men who defy religion are struck down with a loosening of the bowels (pp. 216-217). In the *Gesta Dei,* we even have a chance to see how

[18]Ed. Migne, cols. 496-497. The thought is thoroughly Augustinian; cf. *The City of God,* XIII, 13, and *Marriage and Concupiscence,* I, 6, 7, ed. Corpus Scriptorum Ecclesiasticorum Latinorum, XLII (Vienna, 1902), 218-219.
[19]Ed. Migne, col. 33. Guibert's theme is in the tradition of Augustine and Gregory the Great. These comments on Guibert's personal outlook are not meant to minimize the importance of his sources, but to add to our understanding of the vitality of the tradition.
[20]*Ibid.,* col. 497.

Guibert reshaped his sources. The *Gesta Francorum* which Guibert used reported simply that Guillaume of Grandmesnil and his companions deserted from the army at Antioch by climbing down the wall, but Guibert composed a little poem saying that they had crawled out through filthy sewers, after which the skin fell off their hands and feet, leaving the bare bones exposed.[21]

After Guibert had mastered his alphabet, his mother engaged a local grammarian on the striking condition that he give up his other teaching and tutor her son alone. And so as a boy Guibert was denied a chance for rough play or for companionship with other boys in which he could measure himself and his abilities directly against others. Instead, he saw his peers through the moralizing comments of his mother and his tutor. Consider this description of his cousin, whose instruction his teacher had given up to take employment in Guibert's household. He "was handsome and of good birth, but he was so eager to avoid proper studies and unsteady under all instruction, a liar and a thief, as far as his age would allow, that he never could be found in productive activity and hardly ever in school, but almost every day played truant in the vineyards" (p. 46). Nothing in his book suggests that Guibert ever had any close friends.

From six to twelve, his mother and tutor saw to it that his future calling as a monk set Guibert apart. He had to find satisfaction in discipline and virtue, for other pleasures were not permitted. He was forbidden to play childish games, to leave his tutor's company, to eat away from home, to accept presents without permission, or to have a holiday even on Sundays or festivals. "In everything," he says, "I had to show self-control in word, look, and deed" (p. 46).

As was usual at the time, Guibert was severely beaten if he was unable to satisfy his demanding teacher. After an infancy of indulgence came a boyhood which he remembered as a time of fre-

[21]*Gesta Dei*, V, 14, p. 194; cf. *Gesta Francorum*, ed. Rosalind Hill (London, 1962), pp. 56-57. Since the family of Grandmesnil was bound to his by ties of friendship, Guibert suppressed the name in his account. The anonymous author of the *Gesta Francorum* also informed Guibert in a straightforward manner that the Italians besieged in the castle of Xerigordo were reduced to drinking their urine; Guibert passes on the story, adding that it was "horrible to relate." See *Gesta Dei*, II, 10, p. 144, and *Gesta Francorum*, pp. 3-4.

quent and unjustified punishment. How could he bear it? In desperation, he found two lines of internal defense. The first was that his teacher truly loved him and meant the punishment for his own good. The second defense was that his natural endowment and ability were far greater than those of his teacher, and that if he failed it was because of his teacher's failings. This defense was probably strengthened and perhaps encouraged openly by his mother, who had bound up so much of herself in her son's success. But although Guibert could use his sense of his teacher's incompetence as a balm for his outrage, his mother held him to the path of virtue, hard work, and success. Distressed by the beatings her son received and torn by the feeling (surely unrealistic) that his body might suffer less if he trained as a knight rather than a clerk, she still rejoiced with his teacher when her little son declared, "If I had to die on the spot, I would not give up studying my lessons and becoming a clerk" (p. 50). The positive result of this experience for Guibert was that he carried over to adult life humane and sensitive ideas about the education of children.

When Guibert was about twelve years old, his mother withdrew from the world and retired to a little house she had built near the abbey of Saint-Germer of Fly, some thirty miles from Clermont, and shortly thereafter his tutor became a monk at the abbey, where he eventually rose to the position of prior. Guibert, now possessing what he called "a perverted liberty," began "without any self-control to abuse my power, to mock at churches, to detest school, to try to gain the company of my lay cousins devoted to knightly pursuits." Free for the first time in his life to amuse himself as he pleased, this boy on the edge of puberty began to wear his clerical clothes "on wanton pursuits which my age did not permit, to emulate older boys in their juvenile rowdiness, to behave without responsibility or discretion." But significantly the culmination of his list of misdeeds was that most passive form of pleasure, excessive sleep, in which he indulged so thoroughly "that my body began to degenerate" (p. 77).

His mother heard with distress of Guibert's behavior and urged the abbot of Saint-Germer to receive her son into the monastery for training. As soon as Guibert entered the church of Saint-Germer, he conceived a longing for the monastic life which never grew cold. He told his mother of his desire, but at this point both she and his tutor, thinking him not yet ready for permanent vows, opposed his wishes. Finally, after delaying from late spring till Christmas, Guibert defied the immediate preference of his mother and tutor to begin at once the life for which they had prepared him.

In the monastery, control by his mother and master was replaced by that of the abbot and the community as a whole. If Guibert had not learned self-discipline and how to internalize his aggressive feelings before, he had every inducement to do so now. The Benedictine Rule (chs. 24 and 25) provides that if any of the brethren commits a slight fault, he is to be excluded from the common meal and the oratory, and if his offense is more serious, none of his fellows is to associate with him or speak to him till he is repentant. This was the rule of discipline with which Guibert was to live from the age of thirteen until his death.

As a young monk, Guibert plunged into his studies. Many a night he read under a blanket or made compositions when he was supposed to be asleep. His motive, he said, was "chiefly to win praise, that greater honor in this present world might be mine" (p. 78). In his fantasies he daydreamed of power and success. Other monks were hostile to him, an emotion which he attributed to jealousy. Guibert denied to himself and to God that he hated his opponents, who declared that "I was too proud of my little learning" (p. 84), though he felt that they hated him. Their envy did not provoke open resentment, but sullenness *(acedia)*, and he sought to resolve his problem by withdrawal, hoping "with the aid of my relatives to be able to transfer to some other monastery" (p. 83).

In his literary studies, Guibert was at first caught up in religious works "and thought my reading vain if I found in it no matter for meditation, nothing leading to repentance" (p. 79). But as he grew older he set aside the divine pages for "worthless vanities" and read Ovid and the *Bucolics* of Virgil. He even wrote love poems in secret, often passing them off as another's work but taking great pleasure in the praise they received, and "caught by the unrestrained stirring of my flesh through thinking on these things and the like" (p. 87). His old tutor censured him severely, however, and the Lord punished him, as he felt, with affliction of the soul and bodily infirmity. Finally, "the folly of useless learning withered away" (p. 88). The rich vocabularly and copious classical allusions of his later writings are a monument, however, to how much Guibert learned from his studies.

As a teen-age writer, Guibert managed to direct much of his energy into a treatise on virginity, quoting Ovid and Terence in the most moral fashion and noting the protection provided by the monastic vocation. In this treatise he revealed his bent for rational criticism by attacking the assertion of Eusebius of Caesarea that St. Paul had been married and by rejecting the alleged letter of Jesus to Abgar which Eusebius included in his *Ecclesiastical History*.[22] He could not subject to rational control the terrors of his dreams, however, and in his sleep he was visited by "visions of dead men, chiefly those whom I had seen or heard of as slain by swords or some such death" (p. 79). These dreams were so terrifying that the watchful protection of his master was needed to keep him quietly in bed and to prevent him from losing his wits. That Guibert looked upon his own sexuality with loathing can be seen throughout his writing; in addition, it is possible that an inclination toward homosexuality, violently suppressed on the conscious level, added to his terrors at this time.

Guibert dealt with his twin problems of ambition and carnal itch, which he himself saw as closely associated (p. 82), in the most positive way open to him: he applied himself assiduously to the hard work of study. Encouraged and taught by St. Anselm, who frequently visited Saint-Germer while he was at the abbey of Bec, Guibert eventually began to think of writing sermons and scriptural commentary himself. Knowing, as he said, that Abbot Garnier would be annoyed by his efforts at writing, Guibert begged for his permission, managing to suggest that he had only a brief work in mind. He then started on the ambitious project of a commentary on all of Genesis, beginning of course with the Hexameron. When Garnier found that the young monk, then short of twenty, was commenting on the story of Creation, a subject traditionally reserved for mature scholars, he ordered him to stop. But Guibert continued to work in secret, and when Garnier retired about 1084, he quickly

[22]Ed. Migne, cols. 579-608. For the criticism of Eusebius, see col. 587.

brought the book to completion and began other writing (p. 91).

For the next twenty years, Guibert remained a simple monk at Saint-Germer. His relatives began to seek a higher position for him, hoping, he says, to acquire an abbacy or other post through simony. Guibert's account is that although he was driven by ambition, he did not wish to reveal his "nakedness" by mounting to office on the steps of simony (p. 97). Another limitation is that probably his family could not afford to pay very much. Whatever the reasons, their negotiations produced nothing. And then, when he had finally resigned himself to a humble life, there came the offer of the abbacy of Nogent. The renown of his writing, and not simony, had brought him the post, Guibert reports proudly. By his own efforts he had written himself out of obscurity.

In 1104, at about forty, Guibert left Saint-Germer, and in fact, for the first time in his life, left his mother, who was vexed at his appointment and reminded him that he was not well-trained in legal matters. Nogent was a small abbey, founded in 1059 with an endowment Guibert called sufficient for six monks, and it appears always to have been rather poor. But it provided him with an abbacy, and Guibert made the most of it. Freed from immediate authority, he wrote to his heart's content: his history of the crusade (c. 1108), his memoirs (1115), Biblical commentaries, a tract praising the Virgin and recording some of her miracles, and the treatise on relics (c. 1125). In his twenty years as abbot, we see him involved in ecclesiastical affairs, attending the court of the bishop of Laon and larger councils, and at one time traveling to Langres to see the pope. But we know very little of Guibert's thoughts about life at Nogent. Although the *Memoirs* are quite frank about Saint-Germer, Guibert is very reticent about his position as abbot at Nogent and says nothing about any individual monk. Clearly he thought it neither useful nor edifying for his monks to know too much about their abbot or his feelings toward them. This restraint is illustrated by his brief reference to a crisis at Nogent which became so serious that Guibert retired for a while to his old monastery of Saint-Germer, which still drew him even though his mother had been dead for two years. After his eventual return to Nogent, Guibert referred to this flight as "ignominious," and rather than explaining himself he avoided giving any details about the event (p. 133). In order to fill out his section on Nogent, he reverted to stories about life at Saint-Germer.

Characteristically Guibert avoided conflict or direct confrontation by retreat or dissimulation. He was aware of this trait, and illustrated it himself in his treatise on relics. As he told the tale, he was once present at a harangue where a relicmonger (probably from the cathedral of Laon) was hawking his wares. "I have here in this little box a piece of the bread which Our Lord chewed with his own teeth. And if you don't believe me," he said, pointing at Guibert, "here is a distinguished man whose vast learning you all know. He will confirm what I say, if there is any need." Guibert blushed and kept silent, he tells us, frightened by the presence of those supporting the speaker, whom he says he ought to have denounced on the spot. His defense to himself was to repeat a jingle based on Boethius:

> *Jure insanus judicarer,*
> *Si contra insanos altercarer.*
> (If against the mad I strain,
> I'd be rightly thought insane.)[23]

In his writing, however, Guibert remained a critic to the end. But although his common sense and his dislike of ignorance and superstition can be seen throughout his work, Guibert's use of his keen mind did not lead him to embrace the new rationalism of the early twelfth century. In his commentary on Hosea, dictated when he could no longer make use of his own hands or eyes, he denounced those "who presume to discuss and examine the dogmas of the church on which they had once been nourished, treating like something new matters defined by God and the Fathers. . . . We see this today with certain grammarians, who blindly seek to shine in commenting not only on Holy Scripture but even on any given heavenly mystery."[24] Guibert may well have known Abelard at Laon. Here we have the judgment of the older generation of moral commentators on the new scholastics.

There is, in fact, a consistent conservatism in Guibert's religious

[23]Ed. Migne, col. 621. The prose text of Boethius from which the jingle comes is the Fifth Theological Tractate, ed. H. F. Stewart and E. K. Rand, Loeb Library (London, 1918), p. 74.
[24]Ed. Migne, cols. 377-378.

writing. His tropological commentaries were in the tradition of Gregory the Great, and he could barely bring himself to differ with that saint. When he differed with his contemporaries, as often happened, it was not to rationalize religion but to purify it, to rid the Church of false relics and superstition. In part, he seems simply to have been expressing his distaste for the veneration of bones, teeth, hair, and bits of skin. But his turning from the physical world led to a mystical apprehension of the spiritual. The conflict of flesh and spirit runs through his works; it is, in fact, the interpretation he gave to the first verse of Genesis and he carried the theme through his final work. The fourth book of his treatise on relics, composed shortly before his death in the mid-1120's, contains a treatment of visions and the afterlife so finely done that Father Henri de Lubac has compared his view of "transcendental reality" to that of Rudolf Bultmann.[25]

It is rare indeed for a medievalist studying an individual to have so much material on his childhood and his fantasies, reported in his subject's own words. How to use such evidence is a problem, for specialists are far from agreement in explaining the development of personality in living individuals, the application of modern concepts to past cultures is a delicate procedure at best, and "psycho-historians" have yet to develop a large enough body of evidence to permit satisfactory control, comparison, and generalization. The reader should be aware that the following study of Guibert's personality is not a scientific psychological case study. Yet historians and biographers have long agreed with Wordsworth that the child is father of the man. To exclude childhood influences from our understanding of Guibert would be to fail to see him as a whole man.

In a number of ways, Guibert's early life was not typical of that of boys of his class. He was, first of all, an oblate, vowed to the service of God from his birth, and from the age of thirteen on he was subject to the Benedictine Rule in a well-disciplined monastery. Early monastic training must surely have tended to create a "mo-

[25]*Exégèse médiévale*, II, 2 (Paris, 1964), p. 150. On the conservative character of Guibert's moral commentaries, see Beryl Smalley, "William of Middleton and Guibert de Nogent," *Recherches de théologie ancienne et médiévale*, XVI (1949), 281-291.

nastic personality," in which the discipline of the community eventually became self-discipline and monastic values were internalized. Nobles, members of the secular clergy, and those who came late to the monastic profession did not have this training. When Guibert reports the raging violence of the nobility, the hot temper and loose tongue of Bishop Gaudry of Laon, the offenses of monks who came to Saint-Germer late in life, he was looking at people who had a youth radically different from his own.

Oblates commonly grew up in their monasteries, but Guibert spent his first twelve years in the military community of the *oppidum* of Clermont. Boys of the military caste learned early the values of their group: honor, pugnacity, personal loyalty to leader, blood brother, and family, and young nobles spent their "youth" in gay and violent exploits which prepared them for the hard life of camp and castle ahead.[26] Guibert observed this world of the minor nobility, and he learned ambition, a sense of honor, respect for noble status and family ties. He admits to ambition himself, his history of the crusade condemns those knights who did not live up to the military code, and he takes clear pride in the connections his family had with the higher nobility. How thoroughly Guibert accepted the concept of family solidarity is shown by his condemnation of those who are "too eager to secure the advancement of others not only of their own family, which is bad enough, but of those unrelated to them, which is worse" (p. 53). But Guibert could never be a part of the rough world of honor and physical achievement. He was not raised with his brothers and cousins, even though an older cousin tried to take over his rearing. His mother and teacher saw to it that he was always the boy on the sidelines, dressed in his clerical garb. His mother even declared that his teacher should have no other students in his class. His father had been a man of violence and lechery, and his mother was determined that her last child should grow up to a different future. Only through the vivid and highly imaginative writing of his crusading

[26]See Georges Duby, "Dans la France du Nord-Ouest. Au XIIe siècle: les 'jeunes' dans la société aristocratique," *Annales, Economies- Sociétés-Civilisations*, XIX (1964), 835-846, trans. by Frederic L. Cheyette as "The 'Youth' in Twelfth-Century Aristocratic Society," in *Lordship and Community in Medieval Europe* (New York, 1968), pp. 198-209.

history and his *Memoirs* could Guibert express his fascination with slaughter and sexuality.

Guibert's descriptions of noble life and his comments on it reveal the conflict between the values of the male nobility and those he learned from his mother. Men lived in a world of violence, ostentation, sexuality, and irreligion. As a noble, Guibert's mother shared some of the values of her class; Guibert stresses her beauty and refers to her taste for good food and fine clothes, even though she eventually wore a hair shirt under her outer garments. But she differed from the masculine code in her respect for religion and sexual purity. This conflict between masculine and feminine values may have been as common in the middle ages as it is today in southern Italy, an area which in many ways seems peculiarly medieval.[27] What is special about Guibert's boyhood is that he had no father as a model of masculine independence; if he had lived, Guibert says, his father would have broken his vow and have trained him for military rather than monastic life. His closest male influence was his teacher, an asexual figure who was dependent on his mother and who shared her religious values. Guibert was neither encouraged to compete with other boys nor permitted to enjoy their friendship. Without a father to approve violations of his mother's moral code and without playmates to dare him to break rules or admire him for getting away with something, Guibert grew up with little sense that the measure of proper behavior was the approval of his peers or other men; instead he made the values he learned from his mother and tutor, and eventually from his monastic community, a part of himself.

In short, Guibert differed from most members of the noble class, and probably from a great many churchmen, by being more influenced by the internal effect of a sense of guilt than by the external effect of shame. He himself expressed the difference between two ways of life, the one based on a "conflict between body and spirit," a "straining after God," the other determined by "outward honor" and the desire to avoid disgrace. In his mother's

[27]Medievalists will find very suggestive parallels in Anne Parsons, "Is the Oedipus Complex Universal? The Jones-Malinowski Debate Revisited and a South Italian 'Nuclear Complex,'" *The Psychoanalytic Study of Society*, ed. Warner Muensterberger and Sidney Axelrad, III (1964), 278-326.

youth, he says, her desire was to preserve her worldly honor, and only later in her life did she surrender her desires into the keeping of God (p. 67).[28]

One measure of the tension between the old Germanic society and the Christian religion is the conflict between behavior based on the group sanctions of honor and shame and that determined by internalized personal and religious values which may conflict with those of "society." Much of the course of medieval history can be seen in the growing influence of monastic and religious reformers who had learned self-control, measured their actions against internal standards rather than group approval, and feared their own sense of guilt more than public censure. In our intimate view of Guibert of Nogent, we can see more deeply than usual into one of the men who supported the Gregorian reform movement.

Guibert was a reformer at heart; he writes as one who wished to reform and purify, and yet he differs greatly from those strong men—the Hildebrands and Anselms of one generation, the Bernards of another—who were actively engaged in changing the church and the world. Guibert was a weaker and less effective man that he wished to be. He shrank from conflict and met challenges by retreat; when forced into difficult situations, he dissimulated to avoid trouble. We have to understand not only his differences with society but his personal weakness.

Guibert did not grow up with the experience of full and healthy parental love. His mother had overwhelming importance to him, and he writes movingly of her and his regard for her. And yet, when one looks carefully at what he says about her, one sees an understratum of bitterness and unhappiness. He stresses her beauty and her virtue rather than her love. She taught him his prayers, he points out, when she had leisure from her household cares (p. 68). She spoke continually of his father (p. 72). Most notably, when Guibert was about twelve she deserted him to go to Saint-Germer, though "she knew that I should be utterly an orphan with no one at all on whom to depend. . . . I often suffered from the

[28]George F. Jones stresses the concepts of honor and shame in *The Ethos of the Song of Roland* (Baltimore, 1963). For parallels see Jean G. Péristiany, ed., *Honour and Shame: The Values of Mediterranean Society* (Chicago, 1966).

loss of that careful provision for the helplessness of tender years that only a woman can provide. . . . She knew for certain that she was a cruel and unnatural mother" (p. 74). Guibert can explain her behavior only by saying that God hardened her heart. Her austerity, her religious discipline, her very virtue, and her unending criticism of him made Guibert believe that he could not live up to her standards, that she would have died of mortification if she could look into his heart. And yet he had to trust in her to intercede for him in heaven. The reader may well be struck with the similarity of Guibert's feelings toward his mother and those toward the Virgin; at one point he goes so far as to tell the Virgin that if he is damned he will lay the blame on her (p. 44).

The death of his father during his infancy doubtless had a powerful effect on Guibert's early development. He says directly that it was fortunate that his father died, and we have no reason to doubt that this was an honest statement of his feelings. Little children find it hard to distinguish between their fantasies and their ability to affect reality. Is it not likely that on some deep level Guibert felt that he himself was responsible for his father's death? If so, that feeling can only have added to his sense of guilt and unworthiness, as well as to his sense that the dead must be cared for and their remains well treated.

After he was six, Guibert's teacher took the place of a father in his life. Perceptively, Guibert saw that his mother and his substitute father were competing to see which he preferred. It was then his mother who gave him rich clothes, his teacher who urged austerity. In these years of pre-adolescence, he was, he says, deeply in love with his teacher; he remembers that in choosing to become a clerk he felt he was following his teacher and opposing his mother. And yet what he says about his teacher contains much openly expressed bitterness. In the first place, he was a harsh, brutal, capricious man who flogged Guibert when he did not deserve it. And secondly, as a man of learning he was incompetent, far less able than Guibert himself. From all he says, it is clear the Guibert did not respect the only male model close to him. Perhaps this lack of respect was compounded by the fact, mentioned before, that his teacher was his mother's employee and servant, a dependent from a lower social class. Guibert's only models of male dominance and self-assurance were his knightly relatives, and the morality of the nobility was consistently disparaged by both his mother and his teacher.

Guibert loved his mother and was dependent on her, and he tells us that he was driven by some "inner compulsion" to love his teacher. But he did not have the satisfaction of knowing that his love was returned in full measure; instead, he seems to have felt that he could never be good enough to meet parental standards. In the end, he seems to have turned his love inward upon himself, to have developed what Freud called narcissism. In spite of his professions of sin and weakness (which he does not detail specifically in contrition), the reader will be struck throughout this book by Guibert's high regard for himself This self-satisfaction is coupled with his continual criticism of others. With the exception of his mother and a few exemplary monks and saints, no one else in the book comes off well.

Compelled as a boy to be rational, self-controlled, and sexually pure, Guibert had trouble dealing with the hostile, aggressive, lustful side of his nature. Again, he seems to have turned these feelings inward. His own internal certification of virtue was constantly threatened by his sense of guilt. His dreams and fantasies reveal his terrors, and we see again and again his irrational fear of punishment, death, and mutilation.

Guibert's fear of mutilation requires special attention because it raises the question of whether his relationship to his mother and his fears together fit the Freudian model of a castration complex. While the evidence available is insufficient to warrant any unqualified application of psychoanalytic theory to the culture of medieval Europe, the concurrence of circumstances in this particular case is striking. Guibert's mother was a domineering person with puritanical ideas about sex; it seems reasonable to consider that she was responsible for her husband's impotence during the early years of her marriage. It was also from her, we may presume, that Guibert learned his ideas of sexual purity and of the shamefulness of involuntary sexual excitement. Is it not likely that Guibert grew up with a deep-seated fear that the doctrine that "it is expedient for thee that one of thy members should perish, rather than that thy whole body go into hell" would be applied to him literally? We do know that he dreamed of those who had died by the sword (p. 79). He was distressed by the rite of circumcision,[29] and he chronicled stories of Thomas of Marle tearing the male organs off his victims, which may well have been as fantastic as his tale that Thomas pierced the windpipes of his prisoners to make them pull carts (pp. 185, 201). A particularly striking case of his turn of mind is the way he retold the tale of the man who killed himself on the way to Compostela. In the original poem by Guaiferius of Salerno, the pilgrim simply slit his throat; but as Guibert told the story the licentious man was first induced by the Devil to cut off his offending organ (pp. 218-220).

In the nineteenth century, Abel Lefranc looked at Guibert's rationality and concluded that he was "practically a modern man." In contrast, perhaps we can conclude that Guibert was a medieval man shaped by certain aspects of medieval culture, but that his irrational or unconscious nature was also influenced by the circumstances of his childhood, youth, and immediate family in ways remarkably similar to those observed by psychologists today.

This view of Guibert's personality provides a new perspective on those aspects of his work which have seemed unusual. Perhaps now we have a fuller understanding of why this inward-turning man wrote about himself. Writing became for him both a retreat and a form of defiance. As he said in the *Gesta Dei*, "In all the things I have written and continue to write, I have banished all else from my mind, thinking only of my own advantage and caring not at all to please others."[30] Like Augustine's *Confessions*, his *Memoirs* begin as a valiant attempt at introspection. Augustine was far more successful, however, for his confidence in grace permitted him to look critically at himself without recoiling in horror. Guibert shows much less insight, and may have found it possible to write what he did only because Augustine had done it first. I do not mean that he wrote with the *Confessions* open in front of him or relied on Augustine slavishly, as Einhard did on Suetonius. But he found little in himself which Augustine had not pointed out, and without the support of his guide he could not go on. Georg Misch has called

[29]In *Gesta Dei*, I, 3, p. 127, he points out that Mohammed ordained the rite of circumcision. See the quotations given below, pp. 29-30.
[30]V, Preface, p. 185.

Guibert "a mighty storyteller before the Lord."[31] But he was not mighty in self-perception or the ability or concern to write to help others. There is a whining, defiant, and yet self-satisfied tone to much of what Guibert says of himself. Augustine went on from the story of his life to present a testimony of faith; Guibert finished out his book with ancedotes and history.

Secondly, let us consider Guibert's alleged skepticism or rationalism or scientific method. The reader will soon become aware that there is much credulous or superstitious material in his writing, and if the spectacle of a medieval monk attacking relics had not seemed so impressive to critics of medieval religion, much less would have been said about his critical intelligence and historical method. In fact, Guibert was only selectively critical and was willing to distort history when it suited his purposes. For instance, he seems to have made up out of some sort of inscription a long, detailed story of how King Quilius of England brought back to Nogent from Palestine a box of holy objects and clothing of the saints but—as we would expect from our author and no other source—absolutely no corporeal relics (p. 124). The relics of Nogent he supports; the relics of Saint-Médard he attacks. In the *Gesta Dei,* he challenges Fulcher of Chartres with a rational explanation of some of the miracles Fulcher reports; he also challenges Fulcher by accepting the authenticity of the Holy Lance of Antioch, which Fulcher questioned. What is consistent about Guibert is his quickness to disagree—in writing, not in person—with the opinions of other people. The hallmark of modern critical method is that one applies the same rigorous tests to one's own hypotheses as to those of others. Guibert shared the common human failing of accepting what he liked and finding reasons for discarding what he did not like.

Moreover, his reasons for distrusting relics are sometimes neither particularly modern nor convincing on their own terms. One theoretical argument is in effect a syllogism: the hope of mortals for resurrection depends on the example of the Saviour; if any part of His body remained on earth, the Lord's resurrection would be incomplete; therefore the alleged milk tooth of Jesus preserved at Saint-Médard and other such relics cannot be genuine.[32] His-

[31]*Geschichte der Autobiographie,* p. 117.
[32]Ed. Migne, cols. 650-655.

torical arguments are brought in support, such as the assertion that His contemporaries would not have thought to preserve any relics of the young Jesus, since at the time He did not seem out of the ordinary.[33] To take that position, Guibert has to brush aside the argument of the opposition that a birth accompanied by a star, three Magi, and a chorus of angels was an unusual one, and that Mary treasured these things in her heart.

The earlier discussion of Guibert's personality suggests that behind the reasons he gives we should look for the emotional bases of Guibert's dislike of corporeal relics. Marc Bloch suggested rivalry with Saint-Médard,[34] and that may well have been a factor, but there were probably deeper, more influential forces at work. In the first place, Guibert was repelled by the idea of dismembering the human body. "All the evil of contention [over relics]," he says, "comes from not permitting the saints to have the quiet of their proper and immutable burial."[35] Fearful of death and of the power of the dead to affect the living, he understandably urged that the dead be left in peace. A second reason for his distaste may be associated with a particular relic of the Saviour's body which Guibert found offensive. In attacking directly and in detail the milk tooth at Soissons, Guibert was indirectly attacking the veneration of the Holy Prepuce, a relic treasured at Saint John the Lateran at Rome and at the abbey of Charroux near Poitiers, and perhaps at several other churches.[36] After referring to the alleged tooth possessed by his neighbors, Guibert adds: "There are some who claim to have the umbilical cord which is cut off from the newborn, others claim to have the prepuce of the circumcision of the Lord Himself, concerning which the great Origen wrote, 'Avoid those who do not blush to write books about the circumcision of the Lord.'"[37] He then addressed himself to a detailed attack on the tooth, concluding: "What we have said about the tooth applies just as well to the

[33]*Ibid.*, col. 659.

[34]*Rois thaumaturges*, p. 29. Note, however, that the abbot of Saint-Médard at the time was the personal friend to whom Guibert had dedicated a volume of his commentaries; see below, p. 238.

[35]*Gesta Dei*, I, 5, p. 132.

[36]References to this relic are gathered in Henri Denifle, *La désolation des églises en Francc* (Paris, 1897-99), I, 167.

[37]Ed. Migne, col. 629. The quotation (?) from Origen is unidentified.

umbilical cord and the other things. Clearly what is said about one covers the rest."[38] Given Guibert's fear of sexual mutilation, he may well have had a deep motivation—far removed from skepticism—to write a treatise against all the relics of Christ's body, including one he could barely mention.

This comment leads to another of Guibert's characteristic attitudes, his denunciation of the Moslems, Jews, heretics, and others for horrible sexual practices. The question is not whether Guibert made these stories up out of whole cloth, which is unlikely, or passed on, perhaps with embellishments, stories he had heard, but why he promoted these defamations so enthusiastically. It is hard to avoid finding the answer in the theory of projection; that is, of seeing in an enemy those things one most fears and hates in oneself. By an act of will, Guibert had mastered conscious sexual activity, but he had not been able to come to terms with the ferment of desire within him, and so he transferred it to those about him. No doubt many nobles of Picardy were as lustful as Guibert paints them, but he is a poor witness to the objective world. When we try to use him as a window onto medieval life, we look through the eyes of a disturbed man.

And what of the final unusual characteristic of this man, his patriotism? Let us look more closely at his approach to authority. Guibert demanded a highly structured world, one with a strong authoritarian chain. On the other hand, his tutor was the only individual man for whom he expressed any loyalty—except in the letters of dedication of his works—and even him he calls unjust and incompetent. He disobeyed Abbot Garnier and he criticized his predecessors at Nogent, the bishops of Laon, the pope and the papal court, as well as the nobles of the region and the late King Philippe. The feudal society of his day was built upon the individual loyalty of man to man, and such a personal tie was not congenial to Guibert. But if one is to have authority without honoring individuals, one must support institutions—a strong God-given monarchy even if the king is lecherous and mercenary, a church founded upon a rock even if the pope is corrupt. And if Guibert was to have a sense of political fellowship outside the feudal court,

[38] *Ibid.*, col. 653.

patriotism was a good solution. In shrinking from personal ties and loyalty, Guibert moved toward a more modern concept of government.

The progression of his book led Guibert to describe an ever-widening scene. In the first book, he wrote of himself and his family and of the abbey of Saint-Germer; in the second, he related the history of Nogent; in the third, he told the story of what he called "the tragedy of Laon," ending with an account of events in neighboring dioceses. This third book, with its vivid and detailed history of the revolt of the commune of Laon, its discussion of heretical practices, and its record of conflicts involving great lords, bishops, and the king himself, is one of our most important medieval sources. Dramatic and well-informed, Guibert's narrative has provided primary documentation of fundamental importance for the history of northern France in the early twelfth century. Historians looking for vivid illustrations of conflict between classes in the establishment of medieval communes, or for descriptions of depraved behavior by heretics or brutal feudal lords, have only to turn to Guibert for their material ready-made.

But is that material a trustworthy representation of reality? Since Guibert makes his allegiance obvious, saying that the word "commune" is an evil name and heresy a cancer, many historians have written as if they could discount Guibert's opinions and yet accept his "factual" statements. A distinguished historian of heresy and inquisition states, for instance, that "it would be an injustice to suspect his honesty."[39] But our problems with Guibert lie at a deeper level than his integrity or sincerity; they spring from his own conception of what he was writing and from his capacity to perceive and understand the world about him.

Let us hope that the sensitive article published in 1965 by Jacques Chaurand has now laid to rest any lingering remnants of the idea that Guibert was a "scientific" historian. Chaurand shows convincingly that Guibert's conceptions were not those of the nineteenth or twentieth centuries—how could they be?—but were those of a moral commentator.[40] The same author who composed tropological

[39]Henri Maisonneuve, *Études sur les origines de l'inquisition* (2nd ed., Paris, 1960), p. 102.
[40]See above, note 8.

Biblical commentaries called his *Memoirs* "homilies" and said at one point that he was "picking out examples useful for sermons" (pp. 130, 195). His narrative was meant to edify, and to do so it had to be effectively written. Close reading of his work suggests that time after time Guibert sacrificed literal truth in order to point a moral or adorn his tale. What did it matter that at one point the *vidame* Adon is struck down from behind while on his way to battle, while elsewhere Guibert tells of his death in the thick of the fight (p. 179)? Was the actual nature of payments made by the king when he visited Laon important, so long as any payment at all could illustrate Guibert's point (p. 165)? Should Guibert have been concerned to find that his explanation of a war (which he blames on uxoriousness) conflicts with that of a historian closer to the situation (p. 149)? Questions such as these should make us wonder how many other explanations or vivid details are literary or moral embellishments. The tendency to stretch the evidence to fit the framework of one's preconceptions is common to all historians. Rather than trying to guard against them, however, Guibert was like his contemporaries in thinking that such adjustments were part of his job.

In some instances discrepancies with reality may have been introduced when Guibert consciously reshaped his evidence, but in other cases the set of his mind probably led Guibert to gross distortions in perception or understanding. For instance, misunderstanding the remark of a countryman may well have led him to the "honest" belief that Thomas of Marle pierced the windpipes of his prisoners (p. 201). The belief could be held in good faith, but it should be added that he wanted to believe the worst of Thomas. Guibert may also have sincerely believed that the heretics whom he detested condemned propagation by intercourse and yet routinely engaged in fornication in their secret meetings (p. 212). Without impugning Guibert's good faith, the reader may still conclude that he was all too ready to accept abusive reports uncritically. As a theologian, Guibert saw the structure of the world as a conflict between flesh and spirit, devils and saints. As a moralist, he found it easy to think that people he did not like personally had been caught up by the forces of evil. As a tormented and introverted man, he did not have the charity, generosity, and sympathy that are necessary for understanding the motivations and behavior of others. The accuracy of Guibert's representation of medieval life is continually flawed by his limitations.

Many medieval historians surpass Guibert of Nogent in accuracy, but few can match his vigor and detail, his passionate prejudices, the personal imprint he put on his work. Guibert brought more to his *Memoirs* than his technical skills as a seasoned author. His book is marked by his own view of himself and reality and by his compulsion to write. Like the later work of Vincent van Gogh, his shapes are distorted, his colors are "unreal," and he exhibits some of the tortures of a distressed mind. Other authors give us more realistic representations of the world without. Guibert shows us how that world affected the man within.

hic liber est be marie de Nogento si q̃s eu̅ a
ac uere discretionis magistro Nor
to. Fr. Guibertus Monachus nomi
cator opib; pspis . sui suorumq; Ga

Book I

CHAPTER 1

I confess to Thy Majesty, O God, my endless wanderings from Thy paths, and my turning back so often to the bosom of Thy Mercy, directed by Thee in spite of all. I confess the wickedness I did in childhood and in youth, wickedness that yet boils up in my mature years, and my ingrained love of crookedness, which still lives on in the sluggishness of my worn body. Whenever I call to mind my persistence in unclean things, O Lord, and how Thou didst always grant remorse for them, I am amazed at the long-suffering of Thy compassion, which is beyond all that man can conceive. If repentance and a prayerful mind cannot exist without the entrance of Thy Spirit, how dost Thou so graciously suffer them to creep into the hearts of sinners, how dost Thou grant so much favor to those who turn away from Thee, indeed, even to those who provoke Thee to wrath? Thou knowest, Almighty Father, how stubbornly we set our hearts against those who incur our anger and with how much difficulty we forgive those who have offended us often or even once, either by a look or a word.

Miniature from the copy of Guibert's commentary on Hosea, Amos, and Lamentations preserved at Nogent (Paris, Bibl. nat. ms. lat. 2502, fol. 1). Wearing a black monk's robe and labeled "Abbot Guibert," the author presents his book to Christ. The prophet Hosea holds his scroll on the right; St. Jerome appears in the upper left. Reproduced with the permission of the Bibliothèque Nationale.

But Thou art not only good but truly goodness itself, even its very source. And since Thy aid goes out to all in general, shalt Thou not be able also to succor each single being? Why not? When the world lay in ignorance of God, when it was wrapped in darkness and the shadow of death, when, as night went on its course, a universal silence prevailed, by whose merit, by whose cry could Thy Almighty Word be summoned to come forth from Thy royal seat?[1] When all mankind gave no heed to Thee, Thou couldst not even then be turned from pity on them; no wonder that Thou shouldst show Thy compassion on one single sinner, great sinner though he be! It is not for me to say that Thou art merciful more readily to individual men than to men in general, for in either case there is no halting in Thy willingness, because there is nothing more willing than Thee. Since Thou art the fountain, and since Thou owest to all what flows forth from Thee, manifestly Thou dost not withhold from any what belongs to all.

I am forever sinning, and between sins ever returning to Thee, fleeing from goodness and forsaking it. When I turn back to goodness, will goodness lose its essence and, overwhelmed by manifold offenses, will it then be different? Is it not said of Thee that Thou wilt not "in Thy anger shut up Thy mercies"?[2] The same psalmist sings that this mercy shall abide both now and forever.[3] Thou knowest that I do not sin because I see that Thou art merciful, but I do confidently avow that Thou art called merciful because Thou art at hand for all who seek Thy indulgence. I am not abusing Thy mercy whenever I am driven to sin by the necessity of sinning, but it would indeed be an impious abuse if I ever took delight in the waywardness of sin because the return to Thee after sinning is so easy. I sin, it is true, but when reason returns, I repent that I yielded to the lust of my heart and that my soul, with unwilling heaviness, bedded itself in baskets full of dung.

In the midst of these daily afflictions of a fall followed by a sort of resurrection, what was I to do? Is it not far wiser to struggle toward Thee for a time, to take breath in Thee even for a moment, than to forget all healing and to despair of Thy grace? And in

[1]Cf. Wisdom 18:14-15.
[2]Psalms 76:10.
[3]Psalms 51:10.

what does despair consist, if not in throwing oneself deliberately into the pigsty of every outrageous lust? For when the spirit no longer resists the flesh, the very substance of the unhappy soul is wasted in the profligacy of pleasure. As a man who is drowning in a tempest of waters is sucked down into the deep, so one's judgment is drawn down from the mouth of the pit to the depths of evil.

Holy God, while my wits, recovering from the drunkenness of my inner being, come back to Thee, although at other times I do not go forward, yet at least meanwhile I am not turning from knowledge of myself. How could I catch even a glimpse of Thee if my eyes were blind to see myself? If, as Jeremiah says, "I am the man that sees my poverty,"[4] it surely follows that I should shrewdly search for those things by which my lacks may be supplied. And, on the contrary, if I do not understand what is good, how shall I be able to know evil, much less to forswear it? If I know beauty, I shall never be frightened by foulness. Both matters are therefore apparent, that I should seek knowledge of myself, and, enjoying that, I should consequently not fail in self-knowledge. It is a worthy act and singularly for my soul's good that through these confessions the darkness of my understanding should be dispersed by the searching rays Thy light often casts upon it, by which, being lastingly illuminated, it may forever know itself.

CHAPTER 2

The first thing to do is to acknowledge to Thee the benefits Thou hast conferred on me, O God, that Thy servants who shall read of them may weigh exactly the cruelty of my ingratitude. For hadst Thou bestowed on me only what Thou dost allot to other men, wouldst Thou not have exceeded all that I merit? But Thou didst add many more things that redound to Thy praise and not at all to mine, and still other things about which I think I should remain silent. For if my birth, wealth, and appearance, to mention no other things (if there are any), are the gifts of Thy hand, O Lord, good men do not praise them, except when those to whom Thou hast

[4]Lamentations 3:1.

given them guard them under the rule of honor; otherwise they are regarded as utterly contemptible because they are subject to the flaw of changeableness. What have I to do with those things which only serve the interests of lust and pride with their outward show and reputation? They are of such a neutral nature that according to the quality of the mind they may be turned to good or evil, and the more changeable they are, the more suspect their inconstancy renders them. If no other reason could be found, it is sufficient to observe that no one achieves by his own efforts his parentage or good looks, and of these things in particular all that he has was a gift to him.

Human effort may play a part in the acquisition of some other things, such as wealth and skill; as Solomon testifies, "When the iron be blunt, with much labor it shall be sharpened."[1] Yet even all that is confuted by the ready answer that unless the "light which enlighteneth every man that cometh into this world"[2] be shed on him, and unless Christ shall open to him the doors of learning with the key of knowledge, there is no doubt that every teacher shall spend himself in vain on dull ears. Therefore any sensible man would be foolish to claim anything as his own except his sin.

But, leaving these matters, let us return to the subject with which we began. I said, O Good and Holy One, that I thanked Thee for Thy gifts. First and above all, I render thanks to Thee because Thou didst bestow on me a mother who was beautiful, yet chaste, modest, and steeped in the fear of the Lord. Without doubt I would have proclaimed her beauty in a worldly and foolish fashion if I had not austerely declared beauty to be but an empty show. Still, just as the obligatory fasting of the utterly poor is less praiseworthy, since they cannot choose their food, while the abstinence of rich men takes its value from their abundance, in the same way beauty has the higher title to praise of every sort the more desirable it is, so long as it hardens itself against the temptations of lust. If Sallust Crispus had not thought beauty devoid of morality worthy to be praised, he would never have said of Aurelia Orestilla, "In whom good men never found aught to praise except her beauty."[3] If he

[1]Ecclesiastes 10:10.
[2]John 1:9.
[3]*The War with Catiline,* XV, 2.

declares that her good looks alone were to be praised by the good, but that in all else she was foul, I confidently affirm that this was Sallust's meaning: it is as if he had said that she was deservedly approved for a gift of nature from God, although it appears that she was defiled by added impurities. In the same way, we praise beauty in an idol which is justly proportioned, and although, where faith is concerned, an idol is called "nothing"[4] by the Apostle, and nothing more profane could be imagined, yet it is not unreasonable to commend the true modeling of its members.[5]

Certainly however transitory may be the nature of beauty, which is liable to change through the instability of the blood, yet following the usual standard of symbolic goodness, it cannot be denied to be good. For if whatever has been eternally established by God is beautiful, then all that is temporarily fair is, as it were, the reflection of that eternal beauty. "The invisible things of God are clearly seen, being understood by the things that are made," says the Apostle.[6] Angels have always presented countenances of shining beauty when they appear to men. Hence, the wife of Manue says, "There came a man of God to me having the countenance of an angel."[7] On the contrary, according to the first Peter, devils are "reserved in a mist"[8] till the day of the great judgment; they usually appear in an extremely ugly form, except when they deceitfully "transform themselves into angels of light."[9] And not unjustly so, since they have revolted from the splendor of their noble peers.

Furthermore, we are told that the bodies of the elect ought to conform to the glory of the body of Christ,[10] so that the vileness that is contracted by accident or natural decay is amended to the pattern of the Son of God as transfigured on the Mount. If their internal models are beautiful and good, those who manifest their image, especially if they do not depart from their measure, are beautiful, and hence they are good. Augustine himself, in his book *On Christian Doctrine,* if I am not mistaken, is known to have said, "He

[4]I Corinthians 8:4.
[5]By idols, Guibert means classical statues.
[6]Romans 1:20.
[7]Judges 13:6.
[8]II Peter 2:17.
[9]II Corinthians 11:14.
[10]Philippians 3:21.

who has a beautiful body and an ugly soul is less to be mourned than if he had an ugly body, too."[11] If therefore a blemished exterior is rightly a matter for sorrow, without any doubt a thing is good which can be spoiled by combination with something bad, or improved by a quality of respectability.

Thanks to Thee, O God, that Thou didst infuse her beauty with virtue. The seriousness of her manner was such as to make evident her scorn for all vanity; the gravity of her eyes, the restraint of her speech, and the modesty of her expression gave no encouragement to light looks. Thou knowest, Almighty God, Thou didst put into her in earliest youth the fear of Thy name and into her heart rebellion against the allurements of the flesh. Take note that never or hardly ever was she to be found in the company of women who made much of themselves, and just as she kept Thy gift unto herself, so was she sparing in blame of those who were incontinent, and when sometimes a scandalous tale was circulated by strangers or those of her own household, she would turn away and take no part in it, and she was as much annoyed by such whisperings as if she had been slandered in her own person. God of Truth, Thou knowest it is not something personal, such as my love for my mother, that prompts me to say these things. The power of my words should have the more force, since the rest of my race are in truth mere animals ignorant of God, or brutal fighters and murderers, who must surely become outcast from Thee unless Thou shouldst with the greatness of Thy accustomed mercy pity them. But a better opportunity will occur in this work to speak of her. Let us now turn to my own life.

CHAPTER 3

To this woman, as I hope and believe truest to me of all whom she bore, Thou granted that this worst sinner should be born. In two senses I was her last child, for while the others have passed away with the hope of a better life, I am left with a life of utter despair.

[11]*On Christian Doctrine*, IV, 28. Guibert is quoting from memory, for he does not have the exact words. *Magis* in the Latin text has been emended to *minus* to maintain the sense of both Augustine and Guibert.

Yet, through her merit next to Jesus and His Mother and the Saints, while I still live in this evil world there remains to me the hope of that salvation which is open to all. Certainly I know, and it is wrong to disbelieve, that, as in the world she showed me greater love and brought me up in greater distinction (with a mother's special affection for her last-born), she remembers me the more now that she is in the presence of God. From her youth she was full of God's fire in Zion, since the concern she had for me in her heart did not cease whether she was asleep or awake. And now that she is dead, the wall of her flesh being broken away, I know that in Jerusalem that furnace burns with greater heat than words can express,[1] the more that, being filled there with the Spirit of God, she is not ignorant of the miseries in which I am entangled, and, blessed as she is, she bewails my wanderings when she sees my feet go astray from the path of goodnes marked out by her recurrent warnings.

O Father and Lord God, Who didst give being to me (I who am bad in such manner and measure as Thou knowest) from her so truly and really good, Thou didst also grant me hope in her merit, a hope which I should not dare to have at all if I were not for a little near Thee relieved of the fear of my sins. Likewise Thou didst bring into my wretched heart perhaps not hope so much as the shadow of hope, in that Thou didst vouchsafe to me birth, and rebirth also, on the day that is the highest of all days and best-loved by Christian people. My mother had passed almost the whole of Good Friday in excessive pain of childbirth (in what anguish, too, did she linger, when I wandered from the way and followed slippery paths!) when at last came Holy Saturday, the day before Easter.

Racked by pains long-endured, and her tortures increasing as her hour drew near, when she thought I had at last in natural course come to birth, instead I was returned within the womb. By this time my father, friends, and kinsfolk were crushed with dismal sorrowing for both of us, for while the child was hastening the death of the mother, and she her child's in denying him deliverance, all had reason for compassion. It was a day on which, with the

[1]Isaiah 31: 9, "The Lord hath said it, whose fire is in Sion, and his furnace in Jerusalem."

exception of that solemn office which is celebrated exclusively and at its special time, the regular services for the household were not taking place. And so they asked counsel in their need and fled for help to the altar of the Lady Mary,[2] and to her (the only Virgin that ever was or would be to bear a child) this vow was made, and in the place of an offering this gift laid upon the gracious Lady's altar: that should a male child be born, he should be given up to the religious life in the service of God and the Lady, and if one of the inferior sex, she should be handed over to the corresponding calling. At once a weak little being, almost an abortion, was born, and at that timely birth there was rejoicing only for my mother's deliverance, the child being such a miserable object. In that poor mite just born, there was such a pitiful meagerness that he had the corpse-like look of a premature baby; so much so that when reeds (which in that region are very slender when they come up—it being then the middle of April[3]—) were placed in my little fingers, they seemed stouter in comparison. On that very day when I was put into the baptismal font—as I was so often told as a joke in boyhood and even in youth—a certain woman tossed me from hand to hand. "Look at this thing," she said. "Do you think such a child can live, whom nature by a mistake has made almost without limbs, giving him something more like an outline than a body?"

All these things, my Creator, were signs of the state in which I seem now to live. Could truth in Thy service be found in me, O Lord? I have shown no firmness toward Thee, no constancy. If to the eye any work of mine has appeared good, many times crooked motives have made it slight. God of supreme love, I have said that Thou gavest me hope, or a faint likeness of some little hope, out of the promise of that joyous day on which I was born and reborn and offered, too, to her who is Queen of all next to God. O Lord God, do I not realize with the reason Thou hast given me that the day of birth brings nothing better than the day of death to those who live an unprofitable life? It is indeed beyond dispute that no merits can exist prior to the day we are born but can exist on the day of our death; if it should be our chance not to live in

[2]One of the altars of the church of Clermont was dedicated to the Virgin; see below, p. 51, n. 2.

[3]On the date of Guibert's birth, see pp. 229-233.

goodness, then I confess that famous days, whether for birth or death, can do us no good.

For if it is true that He made me, and not I myself,[4] and that I did not fix the day, and had no right to the choice of it, its bestowal on me by God affords me neither hope nor honor unless my life, imitating the holiness of the day, justifies its promise. Certainly my birthday would then be brightened by the joyous character of the season if the purpose of my life were controlled by virtue searching for uprightness; and the glory of a man's entry into the world would appear a favor granted to his merit if his spirit continuing in righteousness should glorify his end. Whether I be named Peter or Paul, whether Remi or Nicolas, I shall not profit, in the words of the poet, "by the name that has been derived from great Iulus"[5] unless I carefully copy the examples of those whom Providence or fortune has made my namesakes. Behold, O God, how my swelling heart puffs up again, how a feather's weight will be magnified into a matter for pride!

O Lady who rules Earth and Heaven after thy only Son, how good was the thought of those who placed me under bondage to thee! And how much better would my thoughts have been if in later years I had bent my heart to that vow's resolve! Behold, I declare that I was given to be especially thy own, nor do I deny that sacrilegiously and knowingly I took myself from thee. Did I not rob thee of myself when I preferred my stinking willfullness to thy sweet odor? But although many times by such deceit I stole myself away from thee, yet to thee, and through thee to God the Father and the only Son, I returned more fearlessly when I contemplated that offering. And when, recurring a thousand times to my sins, I pined again, then out of thy never-failing compassion my sureness was born again, and I was encouraged to hope by the gift of thy earlier mercy. But why that word "earlier"? I have so often known, and continue to know daily, the constancy of thy mercy, I have escaped so often from the prison of my fall when thou didst set me free, that on those old matters I would gladly keep utter silence when such a wealth of freedom rules. As often as the repetition of

[4]Psalms 99:3.
[5]Virgil, *Aeneid*, I, 288.

sin begets in me a cruel hardening of the heart, then my resort to thee, as by a natural instinct, softens it again; and after looking at myself, after considering my misfortunes, when I come close to fainting in despair, almost involuntarily I feel springing up in my unhappy soul a certainty of recovery in thee. It lies so close to my thought that in whatever ills I am entangled, thou canst not, if I dare to say it, be a defaulter in my need. To thee in particular shall I lay the due cause of my ruin if thou hast no regard in his perversity for him who was taken straight from the womb to thee, and if thou givest him no welcome when he turns to thee again. Since clearly the power is thine at will, and the authority of the Son is known to overflow to the mother, from whom may I rather demand salvation than from thee to whom I cry out "I am thine"[6] by right of the bondage that began at my birth? At another time how gladly will I reflect upon these things with thee! But first let us touch upon other matters.

CHAPTER 4

After birth I had scarcely learned to cherish my rattle when Thou, Gracious Lord, henceforth my Father, didst make me an orphan. For when about eight months had passed, the father of my flesh died. Great thanks are due to Thee that Thou didst allow that man to depart in a Christian state. If he had lived, he would undoubtedly have endangered the provision Thou hadst made for me. Because my young body and a certain natural quickness for one of such tender age seemed to fit me for worldly pursuits, no one doubted that when the proper time had come for beginning my education, he would have broken the vow which he had made for me. O Gracious Provider, for the well-being of us both Thou didst determine that I should not miss the beginning of instruction in Thy discipline and that he should not break his solemn promise for me.

And so with great care that widow, truly Thine, brought me up, and at last she chose the day of the festival of the Blessed Gregory[1]

[6]Psalms 118:94.
[1]March 12th.

for putting me in school. She had heard that that servant of Thine, O Lord, had been eminent for his wonderful understanding and had abounded in extraordinary wisdom. Therefore she strove with bountiful almsgiving to win the good word of Thy Confessor, that he to whom Thou hadst granted understanding might make me zealous in the pursuit of knowledge. Put to my book, I had learned the shapes of the letters, but hardly yet to join them into syllables, when my good mother, eager for my instruction, arranged to place me under a schoolmaster.

There was a little before that time, and in a measure there was still in my youth, such a scarcity of teachers that hardly any could be found in the towns, and in the cities there were very few, and those who by good chance could be discovered had but slight knowledge and could not be compared with the wandering scholars of these days. The man in whose charge my mother decided to put me had begun to learn grammar late in life, and he was the more unskilled in the art through having imbibed little of it when young. Yet he was of such character that what he lacked in letters he made up for in honesty.

Through the chaplains who conducted the divine services in her house, my mother approached this teacher, who was in charge of the education of a young cousin of mine and was closely bound to some of my relatives, at whose court he had been raised. He took into consideration the woman's earnest request and was favorably impressed by her honorable and virtuous character, but he was afraid to give offense to those kinsmen of mine and was in doubt whether to come into her house. While thus undecided, he was persuaded by the following vision:

At night when he was sleeping in his room, where I remember he conducted all the instruction in our town, the figure of a white-headed old man, of very dignified appearance, seemed to lead me in by the hand through the door of the room. Halting within hearing, while the other looked on, he pointed out his bed to me and said, "Go to him, for he will love you very much." When he dropped my hand and let me go, I ran to the man, and as I kissed him again and again on the face, he awoke and conceived such an affection for me that putting aside all hesitation, and shaking off all fear of my kinsfolk, on whom not only he but everything that belonged to him was dependent, he agreed to go to my mother and live in her house.

Now, that boy whom he had been educating so far was handsome and of good birth, but he was so eager to avoid proper studies and unsteady under all instruction, a liar and a thief, as far as his age would allow, that he never could be found in productive activity and hardly ever in school, but almost every day played truant in the vineyards. Since my mother's friendly advances were made to him at the moment when the man was tired of the boy's childish folly, and the meaning of the vision fixed still deeper in his heart what he had already desired, he gave up his companionship of the boy and left the noble family to which he was attached. He would not have done this with impunity, however, if their respect for my mother, as well as her power, had not protected him.

CHAPTER 5

Placed under him, I was taught with such purity and checked with such honesty from the vices which commonly spring up in youth that I was kept from ordinary games and never allowed to leave my master's company, or to eat anywhere else than at home, or to accept gifts from anyone without his leave; in everything I had to show self-control in word, look, and deed, so that he seemed to require of me the conduct of a monk rather than a clerk. While others of my age wandered everywhere at will and were unchecked in the indulgence of such inclinations as were natural at their age, I, hedged in with constant restraints and dressed in my clerical garb,[1] would sit and look at the troops of players like a beast awaiting sacrifice. Even on Sundays and saints' days I had to submit to the severity of school exercises. At hardly any time, and never for a whole day, was I allowed to take a holiday; in fact, in every way and at all times I was driven to study. Moreover, he devoted himself exclusively to my education, since he was allowed to have no other pupil.

He worked me hard, and anyone observing us might have thought that my little mind was being exceedingly sharpened by such

[1]Guibert here puns on *infulsa,* which in classical Latin sometimes means a woolen headdress worn by a victim about to be sacrificed.

perserverance, but the hopes of all were disappointed. He was, in fact, utterly unskilled in prose and verse composition. Meanwhile I was pelted almost every day with a hail of blows and harsh words while he was forcing me to learn what he could not teach.[2]

In this fruitless struggle I passed nearly six years with him, but got no reward worth the time it took. Yet otherwise, in all that is supposed to count for good training, he devoted himself completely to my improvement. Most faithfully and lovingly he instilled in me all that was temperate and modest and outwardly refined. But I clearly perceived that he had no consideration or restraint in the trial he put me to, urging me on without intermission and with great pain under the pretense of teaching me. By the strain of undue application, the natural powers of grown men, as well as of boys, are blunted, and the hotter the fire of their mental activity in unremitting study, the sooner is the strength of their understanding weakened and chilled by excess, and its energy turned to apathy.

It is therefore necessary to treat the mind with greater moderation while it is still burdened with its bodily covering. If there is to be silence in heaven for half an hour,[3] so that while it continues the unremitting activity of contemplation cannot exist, in the same way what I may call perserverance will not stay fresh while struggling with some problem. Hence we believe that when the mind has been fixed exclusively on one subject, we ought to give it relaxation from its intensity, so that after dealing in turn with different subjects we may with renewed energy, as after a holiday, fasten upon that one with which our minds are most engaged. In short, let wearied nature be refreshed at times by varying its work. Let us remember that God did not make the world without variety, but in day and night, spring and summer, winter and autumn, He has delighted us by temporal change. Let everyone who has the name of master see in what manner he may moderate the teaching of boys

[2]A. Mollard ("L'imitation de Quintilien dans Guibert de Nogent," *Le Moyen Age*, XLII (1934), 81-87) has argued that Guibert derived his views on education from the beginning of Quintilian's *The Education of an Orator*, and that the faults of Guibert's master are drawn to contrast with Quintilian's model teacher. Since Quintilian was rarely cited in the early twelfth century and was not named by Guibert (who usually called attention to his reading), this conjecture remains doubtful. Augustine comments bitterly on the beatings he received as a schoolboy in *Confessions*, I, 9.
[3]Apocalypse 8:1.

and youths, since such men think their students should be treated like old men who are completely serious.

Now, my teacher had a harsh love[4] for me, for he showed excessive severity in his unjust floggings, and yet the great care with which he guarded me was evident in his acts. Clearly I did not deserve to be beaten, for if he had had the skill in teaching which he professed, it is certain that I, though a boy, would have been well able to grasp anything that he taught. But because he stated his thoughts poorly and what he strove to express was not at all clear to him, his talk rolled ineffectively on and on in a banal but by no means obvious circle,[5] which could not be brought to any conclusion, much less understood. He was so uninstructed that he retained incorrectly, as I have said before, what he had once learned badly late in life, and if he let anything slip out (incautiously, as it were), he maintained and defended it with blows, regarding all his own opinions as firmly established. I think he certainly should have avoided such folly, for indeed, a learned man says, "before one's nature has absorbed knowledge, it is less praiseworthy to say what you know than to keep silent about what you do not know."[6]

While he took cruel vengeance on me for not knowing what he did not know himself, he ought certainly to have considered that it was very wrong to demand from a weak little mind what he had not put into it. For as the words of madmen can be understood by the sane with difficulty or not at all, so the talk of those who are ignorant but say that they know something and pass it on to others will be the more darkened by their own explanations. You will find nothing more difficult than trying to discourse on what you do not understand, so that your subject is obscure to the speaker and even more so to the listener, making both look like blockheads. I say this, O my God, not to put a stigma on such a friend, but for every reader to understand that we should not attempt to teach as a certainty every assertion we make, and that we should not involve others in the mists of our own conjectures.

[4]*Saevus amor* is a phrase used by Virgil, *Bucolics,* VIII, 47, and Ovid, *The Art of Love,* I, 17-18.
[5]Horace, *Art of Poetry*, 132.
[6]Sidonius Apollinaris, *Letters,* VII, 9, 5. Guibert cites Sidonius by name in *Gesta Dei,* II, 2, 136-137.

It has been my purpose here, in consideration of the poorness of my subject to give it some flavor by reasoning about things, so that if the one deserves to be reckoned of little value, the other may sometimes be regarded as worth while.

CHAPTER 6

Although he crushed me by such severity yet in other ways he made it quite plain that he loved me as well as he did himself. With such watchful care did he devote himself to me, with such foresight did he secure my welfare against the spite of others and teach me on what authority I should beware of the dissolute manners of some who paid court to me, and so long did he argue with my mother about the elaborate richness of my dress, that he was thought to guard me as a parent, not as a master, and not my body alone but my soul as well. As for me, considering the dull sensibility of my age and my littleness, I conceived much love for him in response, in spite of the many weals with which he furrowed my tender skin, so that not through fear, as is common in those of my age, but through a sort of love deeply implanted in my heart, I obeyed him in utter forgetfulness of his severity. Indeed, when my master and my mother saw me paying due respect to both alike, they tried by frequent tests to see whether I would dare to prefer one or the other.

At last, without any intention on the part of either, an opportunity occurred for a test which left no room for doubt. Once I had been beaten in school—the school being no other than the dining hall of our house, for he had given up the charge of others to take me alone, my mother having wisely required him to do this for a higher wage and a better position. When my studies, such as they were, had come to an end about the time of vespers, I went to my mother's knee after a more severe beating than I had deserved. And when, as often happened, she began to ask me repeatedly whether I had been whipped that day, I, not to appear a telltale, entirely denied it. Then against my will she threw off my inner garment (which is called a shirt or *chemise*) and saw my little arms blackened and the skin of my back everywhere puffed up with the cuts from the twigs. Grieved to the heart by the very savage punishment inflicted on my tender body, troubled, agitated, and weeping with sorrow, she said: "You shall never become a clerk, nor any more suffer so much to get an education." At that, looking at her with what reproach I could, I replied: "If I had to die on the spot, I would not give up studying my lessons and becoming a clerk." I should add that she had promised that if I wished to become a knight, when I reached the age for it she would give me the arms and equipment of knighthood.[1]

When I had declined all these offers wih a good deal of scorn, she, Thy servant, O Lord, accepted this rebuff so gladly, and was made so cheerful by my disdain of her proposal, that she repeated to my master the reply with which I had opposed her. Then both rejoiced that I had such an eager longing to fulfill my father's vow. I was eager to pursue my lessons more quickly, although I was poorly taught. Moreover, I did not shirk the church offices; indeed, when the hour sounded or there was occasion, I did not prefer even my meals to that place and time. That is how it was then: but Thou, O God, knowest how much I afterward fell away from that zeal, how reluctantly I went to divine services, hardly consenting even when driven to them with blows. Clearly, O Lord, the impulses that animated me then were not religious feelings begotten by thoughtfulness, but only a child's eagerness. But after adolescence had exhausted itself in bringing forth wickedness within me, I hastened toward the loss of all shame and that former zeal entirely faded away. Although for a brief space, my God, good resolve, or rather the semblance of good resolve, seemed to shine forth, it came to pass that it soon vanished, overshadowed by the storm clouds of my evil imagination.

CHAPTER 7

At length my mother tried by every means to get me into a church living. Now, the first opportunity for placing me was not only badly but abominably chosen. My adolescent brother, a knight and defender of the castle of Clermont (which, I should say, is

[1]Bourgin suggests that this passage means that Guibert's mother not only offered to supply the arms but to dub her son a knight.

situated between Compiègne and Beauvais), was expecting some money from the lord of that stronghold, either as largess or as a moneyfief, I do not know which.[1] And when he deferred payment, probably through want of ready money, by the advice of some of my kinsmen it was suggested to him that he should give me a canonry, called a prebend, in the church of that place (which, contrary to canon law, was subject to his authority)[2] and that he should then cease to be troubled for what he owed.

At that time the Apostolic See was making a fresh attack on married priests; this led to an outburst of rage against them by people who were so zealous about the clergy that they angrily demanded that married priests should either be deprived of their benefices or should cease to perform their priestly duties.[3] Thereupon a certain nephew of my father, a man conspicuous for his power and knowledge but so bestial in his debauchery that he had no respect for any woman's conjugal ties, now violently inveighed against the clergy because of this canon, as if exceptional purity of heart drove him to horror of such practices. A layman himself, he refused to be bound by a layman's laws, their very laxity making his abuse of them more shameful. The marriage net could not hold him; he never allowed himself to be entangled in its folds. Being everywhere in the worst odor through such conduct, but protected by the rank which his worldly power gave him, he was never prevented by the reproach of his own unchastity from thundering persistently against the holy clergy.

Having found a pretext by which I might profit at the expense of a priest with a benefice, he begged the lord of the castle, with whom, as one of his intimates, he had more than sufficient influence, to summon me and invest me with that canonry, on the

[1]The lord of Clermont-en-Beauvaisis was Renaud I, who fought at the battle of Mortemer in 1054 and was still alive in 1084. Guibert refers to his brother as *municeps*, an ambiguous word which probably means that he was one of the nobles of the castle.

[2]The collegiate church attached to the castle of Clermont was consecrated to the Virgin and St. Arnoul, and came to be known as Notre-Dame-du-Châtel. Although church reformers of the late eleventh century condemned lay presentation to canonries and other ecclesiastical benefices, the practice remained common. While it would have been improper for a boy not yet twelve to be given a benefice, this abuse, too, was not uncommon.

[3]Probably a reference to the disturbances which followed the program Gregory VII began in 1074 to suppress clerical marriage north of the Alps.

ground that the cleric was an absentee and utterly unsuitable for the office. For, contrary to all ecclesiastical law and right, he held the office of abbot by permission of the bishop, and, not being under rule himself, he demanded obedience to rule from those who were.[4] At this time not only was it treated as a serious offense for the members of the higher orders[5] and the canons to be married, but it was also considered a crime to purchase ecclesiastical offices involving pastoral care, such as prebends and the offices of precentor, provost, etc., not to speak of the higher dignities. Consequently, those who were empowered to transact the affairs of the church, those who favored the side of the cleric who had lost his prebend, and many of my contemporaries began to stir up a whispering campaign about simony and excommunication, which recently the cleric had talked of publicly.

Now, married priest as he was, although he would not be separated from his wife by the suspension of his office, at least he had given up celebrating mass. Because he treated the divine mysteries as of less importance than his own body, he was rightly caught in that punishment which he thought to escape by the renunciation of the Sacrifice. And so, being stripped of his canonry, because there was no longer anything to restrain him, he now began freely to celebrate mass, while keeping his wife. Then a rumor grew that at this service he was daily repeating the excommunication of my mother and her family. My mother, always fearful in religious matters, dreading the punishment of her sins and therefore the giving of offense, thereupon surrendered the prebend which had been wickedly granted, and, in the expectation of some cleric's death, bargained with the lord of the castle for another for me. Thus "we flee from weapons of iron and fall before a bow of brass,"[6] for to grant something in anticipation of another's death is nothing else than a daily incentive to murder.[7]

[4]That is, with the authorization of the bishop of Beauvais the lord of Clermont had the right of presentation and oversight over the canons of the church in his castle.

[5]Priest, deacon, and subdeacon.

[6]Job 20:24.

[7]If, as seems likely, Guibert wrote this book in 1115, he had just been reminded by the Council of Beauvais, which met in late 1114, that it was anathema to grant prebends while the incumbent was still alive. See Robert Somerville, "The Council of Beauvais, 1114," *Traditio*, XXIV (1968), 503.

O Lord my God, at that time I was wrapped up in these evil hopes and in no wise occupied with waiting for Thy gifts, which I had not yet learned to know. This woman, Thy servant, did not yet understand the hope, the certainty, she ought to have of my sustenance in Thee and had not learned what benefits had already been won for me from Thee. Since while still in the world she had for a short time thoughts that were of the world, it is no wonder that she sought to obtain for me those things which she had chosen to get for herself, believing that I, too, would desire the things of the world. Later, however after perceiving the peril of her own soul, when she burdened the many secret places of her heart with sorrow for her past life, then she thought it the worst madness to practice for others what she scorned for herself, as though she had said, "What I do not wish to be done to me, I will not do to another,"[8] and what she had ceased to seek for herself, she thought it a wicked thing to desire for someone else, if he should be injured by it. Far different is the practice of many, whom we see with a show of poverty casting away their own advantages but too eager to secure the advancement of others not only of their own family, which is bad enough, but of those unrelated to them, which is worse.

CHAPTER 8

I should like to go a little more deeply, in speaking of our own times, into the condition of religious life and the conversions to it that I have seen; and hence it seems fitting to take up these instances and certain others as instructive examples of turning to the good. We have copious written evidence of the prevalence of the monastic way of life in ancient times. To say nothing of foreign parts, it is known that under certain kings of France the rules of this institution were practiced in various places with different founders, and in some of them there gathered together such an enormous number of men living a pious life that we wonder how the narrow accommodation of these places could hold such crowds. Among these, some were certainly harmed to a certain

[8]Cf. Tobias 11:12. This negative form of the Golden Rule is that used in the Benedictine Rule, ch. 4 and elsewhere.

degree by their power; some monasteries, in which the zeal of the brotherhood fell away, often grew immense in a notable fashion, as at one time did Luxeuil in Gaul, and some places, too, in Neustria, which is now called Normandy. But because, as the poet truly says, "the highest are not permitted to stand for long,"[1] and, as is still more true, when the world slips into the bonds of sin, the love of the holy way of life grows cold,[2] so material prosperity was also, after a time, lost by certain churches. Consequently, when manual labor itself was held to be base, there were few monastic conversions.

Thus in my youth in the oldest monasteries numbers had thinned, although they had an abundance of wealth given in ancient times and they were satisfied with small congregations, in which very few could be found who had rejected the world through scorn of sin; the churches were rather in the hands of those who had been placed in them by the piety of their kinsmen early in life. The less these monks were afraid of their own sins (for they imagined they had committed none), the more they lived a life of slackened zeal within the walls of their monasteries. Given administrative responsibilities and outside duties in accordance with the needs or wishes of their abbots, they were themselves eager enough to accept them, but they were inexperienced in outside freedom from restraint and had easy opportunities for wasting church funds, which were dispensed as the expenses of business or as free gifts. And as among them there was then little concern for religion, because of its rarity even fewer became monks.

CHAPTER 9

While this was the state of things and hardly anyone of any consequence joined them, a certain count of the castle of Breteuil, which is situated on the border between the districts of Amiens and Beauvais, came forth to arouse enthusiasm in many others. He was in the prime of life, a man of most pleasing refinement, noteworthy for the nobility of his family and the power it exercised

[1]Lucan, *Pharsalia,* I, 70–71.
[2]Cf. Matthew 24:12.

in other towns as well as its own, because of the remarkable splendor for which it was conspicuous, and widely renowned for its riches. Set for some time on a pinnacle of pride, at length the man came to his senses and turned to reflect on the wretchedness of the life which he had begun to live in the world. Perceiving the miserable condition of his soul and that he was doing nothing else in the world but destroying and being destroyed, polluting and being polluted, he continually discussed with some of his companions to whom he imparted his ardent desires what manner of life he should take up. This man's name was Evrard and he was well-known everywhere as one of the foremost men of France.[1]

At last he carried out into actual practice the convictions of his long-continued meditations. Without telling those he left behind, but in company with others whom he had induced by his secret persuasions to form a brotherhood and adopt a religious life, he fled to foreign parts to live where his name was utterly unknown. While he was pursuing a free life, supporting himself by burning charcoal and hawking it with his friends through the country and the towns, he imagined he had won the greatest riches, and considered them "all the glories of the king's daughter within."[2] Now I will add another exemplary case, the one which he imitated.

Thibaut, today universally called a saint, so that now many churches dedicated to his name celebrate him in many places, was in earlier days a young noble.[3] In the midst of his military training, conceiving a distaste for arms, he fled barefooted from his friends to take up the occupation mentioned above,[4] in this way pursuing for some time a life of indigence to which he was unaccustomed. Inspired by his example, I say, Evrard had resolved to support himself in the same humble occupation.

But there are no good things that do not at times give occasion

[1]Evrard of Breteuil, viscount of Chartres, gave up his worldly life in 1073 and, after living abroad for a time, entered the great Benedictine abbey of Marmoutier near Tours. He died sometime after 1095. On him see Adolphe de Dion, "Le Puiset aux XIe et XIIe siècles," *Mémoires de la Société Archéologique d'Eure-et-Loir,* IX (1889), 12-13, 19.

[2]Psalms 44:14.

[3]St. Thibaut, born in Provins in Champagne, entered the religious life in 1044 and died at Vicenza in Italy in 1066.

[4]That is, charcoal burning. In the nineteenth century he was considered the founder of the Carbonari.

to some wickedness. One day when he was in a village engaged in some business or other, there suddenly stood before him a man in a scarlet cloak and silk pants with puttees, damnably cut away, with hair effeminately parted in front and sweeping the tops of his shoulders, looking more like a lover than a traveler. When Evrard in his simplicity asked him who he was, the other man raised his eyebrows with a sidelong look in a bold fashion and refrained from speaking. Evrard, naturally more curious at his hesitation to speak, pressed him for a reply, and in the end the man, as if overcome by his persistence, burst out. "I am," he said, "though I must ask you not to mention it to anyone, Evrard of Breteuil, formerly count, who, as you know, was once a rich man in France, but, going into exile, I am now voluntarily doing penance for my sins." So spoke this remarkable man and amazed his questioner at this sudden assumption of the personality that he claimed for his own. Staring in disbelief at the impudence of so incredible a rascal, and scorning all further talk with his own shadow, as one might call him, he told the tale to his friends, saying, "My friends, you should know that this scheme of life may be profitable for us, but to very many others it is fatal, because from what you have heard from the mouth of this man, you may imagine what happens in many other cases. If we wish wholly to please God, we ought to avoid what is a stumbling block to others and even offers an opportunity for false pretense. Let us therefore go to some permanent abode, where, abandoning the name of exile which we endure for God's sake, we may deprive anyone of the temptation to impersonate us." After this declaration they changed their plans and set out for Marmoutier, where they took the habit of the holy order and served God continually.

We have been told that this man, while in the world, was in his love for fine clothing unsurpassed by those richer than himself, and he was of such tempestuous character that it was no easy matter for anyone even to accost him. But afterward, when he had become a monk, we have seen him show such contempt for his person that the meanness of his apparel, the humility of his looks, and the emaciation of his limbs would have proclaimed him not a count but a rough peasant. And when he was sent through cities and towns on his abbot's business, he could never be induced of his own accord to endure even once to set foot in the castles which he had relinquished. The account I have related above he told me himself, since he held me in high esteem when I was but a youth, and acknowledged me as his kinsman, so that he gave me very special tokens of his love and respect.

He had a very courtly habit of getting anyone whom he knew to be an eminent scholar to write something in prose or verse for his amusement in a little book which he often carried about with him for the purpose, so that while collecting the maxims of those who were famous in these studies, he might weigh the meaning of their maxims. And although he had no capacity for such things himself, yet those to whom he showed his notes would soon give him a clear understanding of who had expressed himself most precisely in his meaning or his verse. Enough now has been said of this man, formerly a noble but now far nobler for the good end he made. Among the men I have known, I should say he was the most outstanding in the brilliant example of his conversion.

CHAPTER 10

God, who converted Paul through Stephen's prayer, spread the example of conversion with even happier and wider results than in the previous instance through another, more powerful person, for Simon, the son of Count Raoul, enriched the religious life of our time by the renown of a sudden conversion.[1] Many who survived him and have remembered his deeds can testify to the great fame of Raoul's power throughout France, which cities he attacked, and how many towns he took and held with remarkable skill. How great he was could also be gathered from the single fact that he married the mother of King Philippe after the death of her husband.[2]

[1]Simon, count of Valois, succeeded his father, Raoul III, in 1074. He entered the monastery of Saint-Oyen (also known as Saint-Claude) in the Jura mountains in 1077, and died at Rome in 1082. On the fortunes of this remarkable family, see Pierre Feuchère, "Une tentative manquée de concentration territoriale entre Somme et Seine: La principauté d'Amiens-Valois au XIe siècle," *Le Moyen Age*, LX (1954), 1-37.

[2]Anne of Russia, widow of King Henri I of France.

Now, the young Simon, on the death of his father, succeeded him as count, but for a short time only. The story goes that the following was the cause of his quick conversion. His father's remains had been buried in a certain town which had become his by usurpation rather than by inheritance. The son, fearing this might injure his father's soul, proposed to transfer the body to a town which was his by right.[3] When he was disinterred before being taken away and was seen naked by his son, Simon, looking on the wasted body of him who had been his powerful and daring father, fell to meditation on his wretched state. And then he began to despise all the loftiness and the glory that smiled upon him. After conceiving this desire, at last with fiery eagerness he gave birth to it, and, flying from his country and his friends, he passed over the borders of France into Burgundy to Saint-Oyen in the district of Jura.

I have been told that he had been betrothed to a young girl of high rank.[4] Hearing that her beloved had renounced herself and the world and not enduring to be considered inferior to him, she joined the virginal ranks of those who serve God and determined to remain a virgin herself.

Some time after he had become a monk, he returned to France. The purity of his preaching and the humility of spirit evident in his looks inspired so many men and women of such prominence that dense crowds of both sexes gathered to escort him on his way, and everywhere numbers were incited by the example of his fame to a similar resolve. Indeed, a great swarm of men of knightly rank was won over by this man's zeal.

CHAPTER 11

It was indeed appropriate that one of the learned should also draw after him a crowd of men to the holy order with the same desire. Not long ago, there was a man named Bruno in the city of Reims who was learned in the liberal arts and the director of

[3]The body was transferred from Montdidier to Crépy-en-Valois in 1077.
[4]Judith, daughter of the count of Auvergne, who entered the nunnery of La Chaise-Dieu.

higher studies; he is supposed to have conceived his first impulse for a new life from the following occasion.[1] After the death of the renowned Archbishop Gervais, a man named Manasses thrust himself by simony into the rule of that city.[2] He was of noble birth, but he totally lacked that tranquillity of temper which is most becoming to a gentleman; he had conceived such pride from the novelty of his position that he seemed to be imitating the royal majesties of foreign nations, and even the savageness of those rulers. "Of foreign nations," I said, because in the French kings there has always been seen a strong tendency to moderation, so that although they may not have known that saying of Solomon, yet they carried it out in practice. "They have made thee a prince," he says. "Be not lifted up: be among them as one of them."[3] As Manasses paid a great deal of attention to the military class and neglected the clergy, he is reported to have said on one occasion, "The archbishopric of Reims would be a good thing if one did not have to sing mass for it."

When all good men were horrified at the great wickedness and senseless conduct of the archbishop, Bruno, the most respected man at that time in the churches of Gaul, and certain other noble clerks of Reims left the city through hatred of this notorious man. Afterward, when Manasses was more than once anathematized by Hugues of Die, the archbishop of Lyon and legate of the Apostolic See,[4] a man celebrated for the quality of his justice, and when with his band of soldiers Manasses endeavored to squander the treasures of the church, the nobles, clergy, and citizens drove him from the see which he had so evilly occupied. Sent into perpetual exile, he joined the Emperor Henry (at that time excommunicated), and, being himself excommunicated, he

[1]St. Bruno was born at Cologne about 1030; in 1076, he was chancellor of the cathedral of Reims, of which he was also a canon and schoolmaster. On his life see Bernard Bligny in the *New Catholic Encyclopedia* (New York, 1967), II, 836-837.

[2]Gervais died in July, 1067, and Manasses apparently was not consecrated until early in 1070. See below, p. 147, n. 3.

[3]Ecclesiastes 32:1. The introductory clause is a paraphrase.

[4]Hugues of Die, bishop of Die in 1073, became archbishop of Lyon in 1082. In 1077, he excommunicated Manasses, who was reinstated by Gregory VII in 1078. In 1080, Hugues presided over the Council of Lyon, which declared Manasses deposed. After this the people of Reims drove him from the city.

wandered about here and there, and in the end died without communion.[5]

An event which most certainly is worthy of being made public is something which befell the city under Manasses' wicked rule. Among the treasures of the church which he had shared out with the soldiers who had been the tools of his tyranny was a golden chalice of considerable value for two reasons: because it was of great size, and because tiny portions of the gold offered by the Magi to the Lord had supposedly been melted in it. After the chalice had been cut up into little pieces, when he was distributing it among those to whom he had given it, no one was inclined to touch so sacred an object. At last a wicked knight, as bad as the giver, dared to grasp it and lift it in shameless contempt of the majesty of the sacrament. Thereupon turning mad, he never spent the proceeds of his untoward presumption, but forthwith paid the penalty of his rash greed.

After Bruno had left the city, he decided to renounce the world, too, and, shrinking from the observation of his friends, he went on to the region of Grenoble. There, on a high and dreadful cliff, approached by a rough and rarely used path, under which there is a deep gorge in a precipitous valley, he chose to dwell and established the customs by which his followers live to this day.[6]

The church there is not far from the foot of the mountain, in a little fold of its sloping side, and in it are thirteen monks who have a cloister quite suitable for common use but who do not live together in cloister fashion like other monks. They all have their own separate cells around the cloister, in which they work, sleep, and eat. On Sunday the cellarer supplies their food, that is, bread and vegetables; the latter, which is all they eat with their bread, is cooked by each in his cell. They have water for both drinking and other purposes from a conduit, which goes around all their cells and flows into each through interior holes in the walls. They have fish and cheese on Sundays and the chief festivals; the fish, I should add, are not bought but are the gift of some good people.

[5]In 1081, Manasses was at Rome with Henry IV, who was excommunicated by Gregory VII in 1076 and 1080.

[6]Bruno, who had been forced out of Reims by Manasses, chose not to return to the city after the archbishop's fall, but in 1084 founded a monastery at La Chartreuse, the mother house of the Carthusian order.

They take gold, silver, or ornaments for their church from no one, and have nothing there but a silver chalice. Moreover, they do not go into the church at the usual hours, as we do, but at other times. If I am not mistaken, they hear mass on Sundays and the usual holy days. They hardly ever speak in any place, for when it is necessary to ask for anything, they do so by signs. Their wine, when they drink it, is so diluted that it has no strength and scarcely any taste, being very little better than ordinary water. They wear hair shirts next to the skin and few other clothes. They are governed by a prior; the bishop of Grenoble, a very religious man, acts in place of an abbot or director.[7] Although they subject themselves to complete poverty, they are accumulating a very rich library.[8] The less their store of wordly goods, the more they toil laboriously for that food which does not perish, but endures forever.[9]

Let me show how carefully they guard their poverty. This very year the count of Nevers, a most pious and powerful man, paid a visit, prompted by his devoutness and their spreading reputation, in which he earnestly warned them against wordly greed. Returning home, he remembered the poverty which he had observed but forgot his own admonitions and sent them some silver vessels; that is, cups and salvers of great value. But he found them by no means forgetful of what he had said. As soon as he had made his intentions known to them, they gave him back his own words exactly repeated. "We have chosen," they said, "to keep no money given to us from outside, either for our expenses or for furnishing our church. And if it is spent on neither of these objects, to what end should we accept it?" And so, ashamed of his offering, which gave the lie to his advice, the count pretended not to see their rebuff and sent instead a large quantity of hides and parchment, which he knew they would certainly need.[10]

[7]St. Hugues of Grenoble, bishop from 1080 till his death in 1132, aided Bruno in the foundation of La Chartreuse.

[8]The Carthusians built up their library by borrowing manuscripts and copying them; see *The Letters of Peter the Venerable*, ed. Giles Constable (Cambridge, Mass., 1967), I, 45-47, and II, 112.

[9]John 6:27.

[10]Guillaume II of Nevers maintained his attachment to La Chartreuse and became a monk there in 1147, a year before his death. This sentence helps to date the composition of Book I of the *Monodiae* to the year 1115 or before, for Guillaume was held prisoner by Thibaut of Blois-Champagne from the fall of 1115 till late in 1119; see René de Lespinasse, *Le Nivernais et les*

In that place, which is called La Chartreuse, the soil is very little cultivated by them for grain. With the fleeces of their sheep, however, which they raise in great numbers, they are accustomed to buy the produce they need. Moreover, at the foot of that mountain there are dwellings sheltering faithful laymen, more than twenty in number, who live under their careful rule. These monks are so filled with zeal for the life of meditation which they have adopted that they never give it up or grow lukewarm, however long their arduous mode of living may last.

Leaving this place on some occasion or other, this wonderful Bruno, after impressing on them by word and deed the principles of which we have spoken, departed either to Apulia or Calabria, and there instituted a similar manner of living.[11] After he was established there in great humility and was in every way setting an example of piety that shone all round, he was sought out by the Apostolic See for the honor of a bishopric, but, when chosen for it, he fled. Fearing the world and the loss of that enjoyment of God he had already savored, in putting from him such an honor he refused not the spiritual office but the worldly rank.

These persons, I say, sowed the first seeds of the monastic life. Forthwith flocks of adherents, men and women of all ranks, gathered to join them. What shall I say of their ages when little children of ten and eleven thought as old men and mortified their flesh beyond the endurance of such tender years? In those conversions, there were the same results as in the martyrs of olden times: a more lively faith was found in weak and tender bodies than in those who had the vigor of maturity and the power of knowledge.

Since nowhere but in the oldest monasteries was there room for many of the monks, new structures were begun everywhere, and a large income was employed for the supplies of those who flocked in from all sides. When the means did not exist for building on a large scale, they arranged for the food and shelter of the

---

comtes de Nevers (Paris, 1909-14), I, 281-282. Probably Guibert acquired his information about Carthusian life from a monk of Nogent who was the companion of Bishop Godfrey of Amiens at the time of his self-imposed exile at La Chartreuse in 1115 (see below, p. 202).

[11]In 1090, St. Bruno went to Rome at the request of Urban II, his former pupil at Reims. He refused the see of Reggio but retired to Calabria, where he died at Santa Maria della Torre near Catanzaro.

monks by twos or fours or as many as could be supported. Consequently, in manors and towns, cities and castles, and even in the very woods and fields, there suddenly appeared swarms of monks spreading in every direction and busily occupied, and places which had contained the lairs of wild beasts and the caves of robbers were suddenly devoted to the name of God and the worship of the saints.

With so many examples around them, the nobles became eager to submit to voluntary poverty, and, scorning their possessions, they stuffed the monasteries they entered with the goods they had given up, and in a pious kind of hunting they continually strove to capture others to do the same. Moreover, the noble wives of well-known men, forsaking marriage and putting from their pious hearts the love of their children, entrusted their wealth to the churches and granted ecclesiastical stipends. Those who could not wholly surrender their property supported those who had done so by frequent gifts from their own substance, surrounding churches and altars with abundant and welcome offerings and making it their aim to equal the prayers and the pious way of life which they could not follow themselves by imitating these people and by helping with their possessions—as far as they could—to make that way of life possible.

And so it came to pass that in those days the monasteries made great progress through the multitude of gifts and givers, and still more by the generosity of those who came to the monastic life and of those who aided the inmates of the churches by caring for them in every way; whereas through the growing laxity of modern times, each day there seems to be a falling away from the conditions which flourished then. For now, alas, those gifts which their parents, moved with love of such things, made to the holy places, the sons now withdraw entirely or continually demand payment for their renewal, having utterly degenerated from the good will of their sires.

CHAPTER 12

After these lengthy accounts I return to Thee, my God, to speak of the conversion of that good woman, my mother. When hardly of marriageable age, she was given to my father, a mere youth, by the provision of my grandfather, since she was of the nobility, had a very pretty face, and was naturally and most becomingly of sober mien. She had, however, conceived a fear of God's name at the very beginning of her childhood. She had learned to be terrified of sin, not from experience but from dread of some sort of blow from on high, and—as she often told me herself—this dread had so possessed her mind with the terror of sudden death that in later years she grieved because she no longer felt in her maturity the same stings of righteous fear as she had in her unformed and ignorant youth.

Now, it so happened that at the very beginning of that lawful union conjugal intercourse was made ineffective through the bewitchments of certain persons. It was said that their marriage drew upon them the envy of a stepmother, who had some nieces of great beauty and nobility and who was plotting to slip one of them into my father's bed. Meeting with no success in her designs, she is said to have used magical arts to prevent entirely the consummation of the marriage.[1] His wife's virginity thus remained intact for three years, during which he endured his great misfortune in silence; at last, driven to it by those close to him, my father was the first to reveal the facts. In all sorts of ways, his kinsmen endeavored to bring about a divorce, and by their constant pressure upon my father, who was then young and dull-witted, they tried to induce him to become a monk, although at that time there was little talk of this order. They did not do this for his soul's good, however, but with the purpose of getting possession of his property.

When their suggestion produced no effect, they began to hound the girl herself, far away as she was from her kinsfolk and harrased by the violence of strangers, into voluntary flight out of sheer exhaustion under their insults, and without waiting for divorce. She endured all this, bearing with calmness the abuse that was aimed at her, and if out of this rose any strife, she pretended ignorance of it. Besides this, certain rich men, perceiving that she was not in fact a wife, began to assail the heart of the young girl; but Thou, O Lord, the builder of inward chastity, didst inspire her with purity stronger than her nature or her youth. Thy grace it was that

[1]On the continuing medieval belief in magical "ligatures," see Henry C. Lea, *Materials Toward a History of Witchcraft* (Philadelphia, 1939), I, 162-170.

saved her from burning, though set in the midst of flames,[2] Thy doing that her weak soul was not hurt by the poison of evil talk, and that when enticements from without were added to those impulses common to our human nature, like oil poured upon the flames,[3] yet the young maiden's heart was always under her control and never won from her by any allurements. Are not such things solely Thy doing, O Lord? When she was in the heat of youth and continually engaged in wifely duties, yet for seven whole years[4] Thou didst keep her in such contenence that, in the words of a certain wise man, even "rumor dared not speak lies about her."[5]

O God, Thou knowest how hard, how almost impossible it would be for women of the present time to keep such chastity as this; whereas there was in those days such modesty that hardly ever was the good name of a married woman sullied by evil rumor. Ah! how wretchedly have modesty and honor in the state of virginity declined from that time to this our present age, and both the reality and the show of a married woman's protection fallen to ruin. Therefore coarse mirth is all that may be noted in their manners and naught but jesting heard, with sly winks and ceaseless chatter. Wantonness shows in their gait, only silliness in their behavior. So much does the extravagance of their dress depart from the old simplicity that in the enlargement of their sleeves, the tightness of their dresses, the distortion of their shoes of Cordovan leather with their curling toes, they seem to proclaim that everywhere modesty is a castaway. A lack of lovers to admire her is a woman's crown of woe, and on her crowds of thronging suitors rests her claim to nobility and courtly pride. There was at that time, I call God to witness, greater modesty in married men, who would have blushed to be seen in the company of such women, than there is now in brides. By such shameful conduct they turn men into

[2]Variations of this idea and phrase, "in igne posita non ardebat," are common in the twelfth century, appearing in the works of the Archpoet, Andreas Capellanus, and Jean of Haute-Seille. The phrase echoes Proverbs 6:27-28.
[3]A phrase Guibert used often, based on Horace, *Satires,* II, 3, 321.
[4]Since earlier in the chapter Guibert says that consummation was delayed for three years, this and the following reference to seven years may be figurative and intended to call to mind the seven-year periods Jacob served for Rachel.
[5]*The Sayings of the Seven Wise Men,* l. 5, slightly altered, in Ausonius, *Opera,* ed. Hugh G. F. White, Loeb Library (London, 1921), II, 272.

greater braggarts and lovers of the market place and the public street.

What is the end of all this, Lord God, but that no one blushes for his own levity and licentiousness, because he knows that all are tarred with the same brush, and, seeing himself in the same case as all others, why then should he be ashamed of pursuits in which he knows all others engage? But why do I say "ashamed" when such men feel shame only if someone excels them as an example of lustfulness? A man's private boastfulness about the number of his loves or his choice of a beauty whom he has seduced is no reproach to him, nor is he scorned for vaunting his love affairs before Thee. Instead, his part in furthering the general corruption meets with the approval of all. Listen to the cheers when, with the inherent looseness of unbridled passions which deserve the doom of eternal silence, he shamelessly noises abroad what ought to have been hidden in shame, what should have burdened his soul with the guilt of ruined chastity and plunged him in the depths of despair. In this and similar ways, this modern age is corrupt and corrupting,[6] distributing evil ideas to some, while the filth thereof, spreading to others, goes on increasing without end.

Holy God, scarcely any such thing was heard of in the time when Thy handmaid was behaving as she did; indeed, then shameful things were hidden under the cloak of sacred modesty and things of honor had their crown. In those seven years, O Lord, that virginity which Thou didst in wondrous fashion prolong in her was in agony under countless wrongs, as frequently they threatened to dissolve her marriage with my father and give her to another husband or to send her away to the remote houses of my distant relatives. Under such grievous treatment she suffered bitterly at times, but with Thy support, O God, she strove with wonderful self-control against the enticements of her own flesh and the inducements of others.

I do not say, gracious Lord, that she did this out of virtue, but that the virtue was Thine alone. For how could that be virtue that came of no conflict between body and spirit, no straining after God, but only from concern for outward honor and to avoid dis-

[6]Tacitus, *Germania,* XIX, 3.

grace? No doubt a sense of shame has its use, if only to resist the approach of sin, but what is useful before a sin is committed is damnable afterward. What prostrates the self with the shame of propriety, holding it back from sinful deeds, is useful at the time, since the fear of God can bring aid, giving holy seasoning to shame's lack of savor, and can make that which was profitable at the time (that is, in the world) useful not for a moment but eternally. But after a sin is committed a sense of shame which leads to vanity is the more deadly the more it obstinately resists the healing of holy confession. The desire of my mother, Thy servant, O Lord God, was to do nothing to hurt her worldly honor, yet following Thy Gregory, whom, however, she had never read or heard read, she did not maintain that desire, for afterward she surrendered all her desires into Thy sole keeping.[7] It was therefore good for her at that time to be attached to her worldly reputation.[8]

Since the bewitchment by which the bond of natural and lawful intercourse was broken lasted seven years and more, it is all too easy to believe that, just as by prestidigitation the faculty of sight may be deceived so that conjurers seem to produce something out of nothing, so to speak, and to make certain things out of others, so reproductive power and effort may be inhibited by much less art; and indeed it is now a common practice, understood even by ignorant people.[9] When that bewitchment was broken by a certain old woman, my mother submitted to the duties of a wife as faithfully as she had kept her virginity when she was assailed by so many attacks. In other ways she was truly fortunate, but she laid herself open not so much to endless misery as to mourning when she, whose goodness was ever growing, gave birth to an evil son who

[7]On Gregory the Great's teaching on the transition from the active to the contemplative life, see Cuthbert Butler, *Western Mysticism* (2nd ed., New York, 1966), pp. 173 ff.

[8]On shame and guilt, see the Introduction, pp. 23-24.

[9]Writing early in the eleventh century, Burchard of Worms proposed that priests hearing confessions might ask, "Hast thou done what some adulteresses are wont to do? When first they learn that their lovers wish to take legitimate wives, they thereupon by some trick of magic extinguish the male desire, so that they are impotent and cannot consummate their union with their legitimate wives. If thou hast done or taught others to do this, thou shouldst do penance for forty days on bread and water." See *Medieval Handbooks of Penance*, trans. John T. McNeill and Helena M. Gamer (New York. 1938), p. 340.

(in my own person) grew worse and worse. Yet Thou knowest, Almighty One, with what purity and holiness in obedience to Thee she raised me, how greatly she provided me with the care of nurses in infancy and of masters and teachers in boyhood, with no lack even of fine clothes for my little body, so that I seemed to equal the sons of kings and counts in indulgence.

And not only in my mother, O Lord, didst Thou put this love for me, but Thou didst inspire with it other, far richer persons, so that rather because of the grace Thou didst grant me than under the obligations of kinship, they lavished on me careful tending and nurture.

O God, Thou knowest what warnings, what prayers she daily poured into my ears not to listen to corrupting words from anyone. Whenever she had leisure from household cares, she taught me how and for what I ought to pray to Thee. Thou alone knowest with what pains she labored so that the sound beginning of a happy and honorable childhood which Thou hadst granted might not be ruined by an unsound heart. Thou didst make it her desire that I should without ceasing burn with zeal for Thee, that above all Thou might add to my outward comeliness inner goodness and wisdom. Gracious God, Gracious Lord, if she had known in advance under what heaps of filth I should blot out the fair surface of Thy gifts, bestowed by Thee at her prayer, what would she have said? What would she have done? How hopeless the lamentations she would have uttered! How much anguish she would have suffered! Thanks to Thee, sweet and temperate Creator, "Who hath made our hearts."[10] If, indeed, her vision had pierced the secret places of my heart, unworthy of her pure gaze, I wonder if she would not there and then have died.

CHAPTER 13

After introducing these comments by way of anticipation, let us return to what we left farther back. I have learned that this woman had such a fear of God's name, even while she was serving the world, that in her obedience to the church, in almsgiving, in her offerings for masses, her conduct was such as to win respect from

[10] Psalms 32:15.

all. Full belief in my story will, I know, be made difficult by a natural suspicion that the partiality of a son has exaggerated her virtues. If to praise one's mother be thought a cautious, disingenuous way of glorifying oneself, I dare to call Thee to witness, O God, Who knowest her soul, in which Thou didst dwell, that I have truthfully asserted her surpassing merit. And indeed, since it is clearer than daylight that my life has strayed from the paths of the good and that my pursuits have always been an affront to any sensible person, of what avail will the reputation of my mother or father or ancestors be to me when all their grandeur will be squeezed out of their wretched offspring? I, who through lack of will and deed fail to make their behavior live again, am riding posthaste to infamy if I claim their praise for myself.

While she was still a young married woman, something happened which gave no slight impulse to the amendment of her life. The French in the time of King Henri were fighting with great bitterness against the Normans and their Count William, who afterward conquered England and Scotland, and in that clash of the two nations it was my father's fate to be taken prisoner.[1] It was the custom of this count never to hold prisoners for ransom, but to condemn them to captivity for life.[2] When the news was brought to his wife (I put aside the name of mother, for I was not yet born, nor was I for a long time after),[3] she was struck down half dead with wretched sorrow; she abstained from food and drink, and sleep was still more difficult through her despairing anxiety, the cause of this being not the amount of his ransom but the impossibility of his release.

In the dead of that night, as she lay in her bed full of deep anxiety, since it is the habit of the Devil to invade souls weakened

[1]Probably at the battle of Mortemer in 1054, at which the French forces were routed, Count Guy of Ponthieu was taken prisoner, and Count Raoul of Valois and Renaud of Clermont narrowly escaped capture. See the sources cited by David C. Douglas, *William the Conqueror* (Berkeley, 1964), pp. 67-69.
[2]Although Guibert does not spoil his story here by saying so, we know that his father was later released, for he was present at Clermont to make a vow at his son's birth; see pp. 41 and 44. Guillaume of Poitiers reports that Henri obtained the release of some of his vassals captured at Mortemer; see his *Gesta Guillelmi ducis Normannorum et regis Anglorum,* ed. Raymonde Foreville (Paris, 1952), p. 74.
[3]The issue of the date of Guibert's birth hangs on the translation of this phrase; see pp. 230-231.

with grief, suddenly, while she lay awake, the Enemy himself lay upon her and by the burden of his weight almost crushed the life out of her.[4] As she choked in the agony of her spirit and lost all use of her limbs, she was unable to make a single sound; completely silenced but with her reason free, she awaited aid from God alone. Then suddenly from the head of her bed a spirit, without doubt a good one, began to cry out in loud and kindly tones, "Holy Mary, help her." After the spirit had spoken out in this fashion for a bit, and she had fully understood what he was saying and was aware that he was thoroughly outraged, he sallied forth burning with anger. Thereupon he who lay upon her rose up, and the other met and seized him and by the strength of God overthrew him with a great crash, so that the room shook heavily with the shock of it, and the maidservants, who were fast asleep, were rudely awakened. When the Enemy had thus been driven out by divine power, the good spirit who had called upon Mary and routed the Devil turned to her whom he had rescued and said, "Take care to be a good woman." The attendants, alarmed by the sudden uproar, rose to see how their mistress was and found her half dead, with the blood drained from her face and all the strength crushed out of her body. They questioned her about the noise and heard about the causes of it from her, and they were scarcely able by their presence and talk and by the lighting of a lamp to revive her.

Those last words of her deliverer—nay, Thy words, O Lord God, through the mouth of Thy messenger—were stored up forever in the woman's memory and she stood ready to be guided to a greater love, if with God's help the opportunity should occur later. Now, after the death of my father, although the beauty of her face and form remained undimmed, and I, scarcely half a year old, gave her reason enough for anxiety, she resolved to continue in her widowhood. With what spirit she ruled herself and what an example of modesty she set may be gathered from the following event. When my father's kinsmen, eager for his fiefs and possessions, strove to take them all by excluding my mother, they fixed a day in court for advancing their claims. The day came and the barons were assembled to deliver justice. My mother withdrew into the

[4]On Guibert's belief in *incubi*, see below, p. 223.

church, away from the avaricious plotters, and was standing before the image of the crucified Lord, mindful of the prayers she owed. One of my father's kinsmen, who shared the views of the others and was sent by them, came to request her presence to hear their decision, as they were waiting for her. Whereupon she said, "I will take part in this matter only in the presence of my Lord." "Whose lord?" said he. Then, stretching out her hand toward the image of the crucified Lord, she replied, "This is my Lord, this is the advocate under whose protection I will plead." At that the man reddened and, not being very subtle, put on a wry smile to hide his evil intent and went off to tell his friends what he had heard. And they, too, were covered with confusion at such an answer, since they knew that in the face of her utter honesty they had no just grounds, and so they ceased to trouble her.

Shortly after that, one of the leading men of that place and province, my father's nephew, who was as greedy as he was powerful, addressed the woman in the following terms: "Madame," said he, "since you have sufficient youth and beauty, you ought to marry, so that your life in this world would be more pleasant, and the children of my uncle would come under my care to be brought up by me in a worthy fashion, and finally his possessions would devolve to my authority, as it is right they should."[5] She replied, however, "You know that your uncle was of very noble descent. Since God has taken him away, Hymen shall not repeat his rites over me, my lord, unless a marriage with some much greater noble shall offer itself." Now, the woman was quite crafty in speaking of marrying a greater noble, knowing that could hardly, if at all, come to pass. Consequently, since he bristled at her talk of a higher noble, she, who was wholly set against nobles and commoners alike, put an end to all expectation of a second marriage. When he set down to overweening pride her talk of a greater noble, she replied, "Certainly either a greater noble or no husband at all." Perceiving the resolution with which the lady spoke, he desisted from his designs, and never again sought anything of the kind from her.

[5]By the law of succession being applied here, if a widow remarried, her dower was held in trust by the family of her first husband to be administered for the children of that marriage.

In great fear of God and with no less love of all her kin and especially of the poor, this woman wisely ruled our household and our property. That loyalty which she had given her husband in his lifetime she kept unbroken and with double constancy to his spirit, since she did not break the ancient union of their bodies by a substitution of other flesh on his departure, and almost every day she endeavored to help him by the offering of the life-bringing Sacrifice. Friendly to all the poor in general, to some in her great pity she was generous and courtly to the full extent of her means. The sting of remembering her sins could not have been sharper if she had been given up to all kinds of wickedness and dreaded the punishment of every ill deed that is done. In plainness of living there was nothing she could do, for her delicacy and her customary sumptuous diet did not accord with frugality. In other matters her behavior was completely unexpected. I personally have both seen and made certain by touch that although on certain occasions she wore outer garments of rich material, next to her skin she was covered with the roughest haircloth. Although her delicate skin was completely unaccustomed to it, she wore this cloth throughout the day and even went to bed in it at night.

She never or hardly ever missed the night offices, while she regularly attended the assemblies of God's people in holy seasons, in such fashion that scarcely ever in her house was there rest from the singing of God's praises by her chaplains, who were always busy at their office. So constantly was her dead husband's name on her lips that her mind seemed to turn on no other subject, and in her prayers, in giving alms, even in the midst of ordinary business, she continually spoke of the man, because she could do nothing without thinking of him. For when the heart is full of love for someone, the mouth shapes his name whether one wants to or not.

CHAPTER 14

Passing over those matters in which she showed her goodness, but not her most admirable qualities, let us proceed with what is left. When I had passed about twelve years, as I was told, after my father's death, and his widow had managed her house and children while wearing a laywoman's clothes, she now made haste to bring to happy birth a resolve with which she had long been in labor. While she was still pondering this idea, discussing it with no one but that master and teacher of mine whom I discussed before, I heard a certain devil-possessed dependent of hers, who was rambling on under the Devil's influence about other matters, shouting out these words, "The priests have placed a cross in her loins." Nothing indeed could have been truer, although I did not then understand what he was intimating, for thereafter she submitted not to one but to many crosses. Soon afterward, while her intention was still unknown to anyone but the person I have mentioned, who was then a sort of steward in her house and who himself a little later followed her in her conversion by renouncing the world, she saw the following vision in a dream: she seemed to be marrying a man and celebrating her nuptials, much to the amazement and even stupefaction of her children, friends, and kinsfolk. The next day when my mother went into the country for a walk attended by the man who was my teacher and her steward, he explained what she had seen. My mother did not need to be a skilled interpreter in such matters. One look at my master's face, and without speech from him she knew that the vision pointed to the subject of their many conversations about the love of God, to Whom she longed to be united. Making haste with what she had begun and overcome by the burning zeal within her, she withdrew from the life of the town in which she lived.

At the time of this withdrawal, she stayed with the owner's permission at a certain manor belonging to the lord of Beauvais, Bishop Guy.[1] This Guy was a man of courtly manner and noble birth, in person well-fitted for the office he held. After conferring notable benefits on the church of Beauvais, such as laying the first stone of a church for regular canons dedicated to St. Quentin, he was charged before Archbishop Hugues of Lyon, the papal legate,

[1]Guy was first dean of Saint-Quentin, then archdeacon of Laon, and became bishop of Beauvais in 1063 or early 1064. Presumably he was bishop of Beauvais when he was present at Guibert's first sacrament, his baptism; see p. 232. He founded the abbey of Saint-Quentin of Beauvais in 1067. His deposition by Hugues of Die took place in 1085, and he died at Cluny about 1087. See *Gallia Christiana* (Paris, 1715-1865), IX, 708-711.

with simony and other crimes by those who owed their training and advancement to him. Because he did not appear when summoned, he was declared deposed by default, and, being at Cluny and afraid of the sentence pronounced against him, he retired into the monastery there. Since he seemed to cherish my mother and my family and loved me most of all with a special affection, as one who had received from him every sacrament of benediction except that of the priesthood, when members of my mother's household asked him to allow her to live for a while in his property adjoining the church of that place, he gladly consented. Now, this manor, named Catenoy, was about two miles distant from our town.[2]

While staying there, she resolved to retire to the monastery of Fly.[3] After my master had had a little house built for her there near the church, she then came forth from the place where she was staying. She knew that I should be utterly an orphan with no one at all on whom to depend, for great as was my wealth of kinsfolk and connections, yet there was no one to give me the loving care a little child needs at such an age; though I did not lack for the necessities of food and clothing, I often suffered from the loss of that careful provision for the helplessness of tender years that only a woman can provide. As I said, although she knew that I would be condemned to such neglect, yet Thy love and fear, O God, hardened her heart. Still, when on the way to that monastery she passed below the stronghold where I remained, the sight of the castle gave intolerable anguish to her lacerated heart, stung with the bitter remembrance of what she had left behind.[4] No wonder indeed if her limbs seemed to be torn from her body, since she knew for certain that she was a cruel and unnatural mother. Indeed, she heard this said aloud, as she had in this way cut off from her heart and left bereft of succor such a fine child,

[2]Catenoy is over four modern statute miles to the east of Clermont.

[3]Saint-Germer of Fly, where Guibert was to pass much of his life, is 32 miles to the west of Clermont. The monastery was founded by St. Germer on his estates at Fly in 661. In 906, the monks fled in panic from the Normans, taking the body of St. Germer with them to Beauvais. The monastery was restored by Bishop Drogo of Beauvais in 1036 with monks brought from the abbey of Saint-Maur-des-Fossés. See Joseph Depoin, "La vie de Saint Germer," *Congrès archéologique de France*, t. 72 (1905), pp. 392-406.

[4]The road from Catenoy to Beauvais and on to Fly would take Guibert's mother directly past the hill on which Clermont sits.

made worthy, it was asserted, by so much affection, since I was held in high regard not only by our own family but by outsiders. And Thou, good and gracious God, didst by Thy sweetness and love marvelously harden her heart, the tenderest in all the world, that it might not be tender to her own soul's harm. For tenderness would then have been her ruin, if she, neglecting her God, in her worldly care for me had put me before her own salvation. But "her love was strong as death,"[5] for the closer her love for Thee, the greater her composure in breaking from those she loved before.

Coming to the cloister, she found an old woman in the habit of a nun whom she compelled to live with her, declaring that she would submit to her discipline, as she gave the appearance of great piety. "Compelled," I say, because once she had tested the woman's character, she exerted all her powers of persuasion to get her companionship. And so she began gradually to copy the severity of the older woman, to imitate her meager diet, to choose the plainest food, to give up the soft mattress to which she had been accustomed, to sleep in contentment with only straw and a sheet. And since she still had much beauty and showed no sign of age, she purposely strove to assume the appearance of age with an old woman's wrinkles and bowed form. Her long flowing locks, which usually serve as a woman's crowning beauty, were frequently cut short with the scissors; her dress was black and unpleasant-looking, its unfashionable width adorned with countless patches; her cloak was undyed and her shoes were pierced with many a hole past mending, for there was within her One whom she tried to please with such mean apparel.

Since she had learned the beginning of good deeds from the confession of her old sins, she repeated her confessions almost daily. Consequently, her mind was forever occupied in searching out her past deeds, what she had thought or done or said as a maiden of tender years, or in her married life, or as a widow with a wider range of activities, continually examining the seat of reason and bringing what she found to the knowledge of a priest, or rather to God throught him. Then you might have seen the woman praying with such sharp sighs, pining away with such

[5]Song of Songs 8:6.

anguish of spirit that as she worshiped, there was scarcely ever a pause in the heart-rending sobs that went with her entreaties. She had learned the seven penitential psalms[6] from the old woman I mentioned before, not by sight but by ear, and day and night she turned them over in her mind, chewing them with such savor, one might say, that the sighs and groans of those sweet songs never ceased to echo in Thy ears, O Lord. But whenever assemblies of people from outside disturbed her beloved solitude—for all who were acquainted with her, especially men and women of noble rank, took pleasure in conversing with her because of her wondrous wit and forbearance—on their departure, every untrue, idle, or thoughtless word she had uttered during their talk begat in her soul indescribable anguish until she reached the familiar waters of penitence or confession.

Whatever the zeal and anxiety she showed in such matters, she could win for her soul no confidence, no composure to stay her unceasing lamentations, her earnest and tearful questionings whether she could ever earn pardon for her offenses. Thou knowest, O Lord, the extent of her sins, and I have some knowledge of it. How small was their whole sum compared with those of others who neither sorrow nor sigh! Thou knowest, O Lord, how well I was able to assess the condition of her thoughts, because I never saw her heart grow cold in the fear of punishment and in her love for Thee.

CHAPTER 15

Why go on? While she was divorcing herself from the world in the manner I have described, I was left without a mother, teacher, and master. For he who after my mother had so faithfully trained and taught me, fired by my mother's example, love, and counsel, himself entered the monastery of Fly. Possessing a perverted liberty, I began without any self-control to abuse my power, to mock at churches, to detest school, to try to gain the company of my young lay cousins devoted to knightly pursuits by cursing the appearance of a clerk, to promise remission of sins, and to indulge

[6]Psalms 6, 31, 37, 50, 101, 129, 142.

in sleep, in which formerly I was allowed little relaxation, so that by unaccustomed excess of it my body began to degenerate. Meanwhile my mother heard the agitating news of my doings and was struck half dead by what she heard, surmising my immediate ruin. For the fine clothing which I had for the church processions, provided by her in the hope that I might be the more eager for the clerk's life, I wore everywhere on wanton pursuits which my age did not permit; I emulated older boys in their juvenile rowdiness, and I was completely bereft of responsibility and discretion.

The more restrained and chastened I had been before, the worse my looseness, or even madness, now became. Unable to endure what she heard, my mother therefore went to the abbot and begged him and the brotherhood that my master might be allowed to resume my training.[1] The abbot, brought up by my grandfather and under obligation for benefits received at his court, was amenable; he gave me a ready welcome and followed up his kind reception with still kinder treatment thereafter. I call Thee to witness, Holy God and my Provider, that from the moment I entered the monastery church and saw the monks sitting there, at that sight I was seized by a longing for the monk's life which never grew cold, and my spirit had no rest until its desire was fulfilled. Since I lived with them in the same cloister and observed their whole existence and condition, as the flame increases when fanned by the wind, so by contemplation of them my soul, yearning continually to be like them, could not but be on fire. Lastly, with redoubled entreaties the abbot of the place daily urged me to become a monk there, and although I passionately desired to do so, my tongue could not be loosened by any of the demands of those who desired me to make such a promise. Although now that I have grown older it would be very hard for me to keep silent with such a full heart, as a boy I was able to maintain that silence without much difficulty.

After some time I brought up the matter with my mother, and she, fearing the instability of boyhood, rejected my proposal with a great many arguments, which made me very sorry that I had

[1]The abbot of Saint-Germer at this time was Garnier, who took office in 1058.

revealed my intention. When I also told my master, he opposed it still more. Deeply annoyed at the opposition of both, I determined to turn my mind elsewhere; and so I began to act as if I had never had such a desire. After putting the matter off from the week of Pentecost until Christmas, and being both eager and anxious to bring the matter to an end, I was unable to bear Thy incitement within me, O Lord, and threw off my respect for my mother and my fear of my master. I went to the abbot, who greatly desired this to happen but had failed to draw any promise from me, and cast myself at his feet, tearfully imploring him, using these very words, to receive a sinner.[2] He gladly granted my prayer and provided the necessary habit as soon as he could—that is, on the next day—and invested me with it while my mother watched in tears from afar, and he ordered that alms should be offered on that day.

Meanwhile my former master, who was unable to teach me any longer because of the stricter rule, at least took care to urge me to subject to close interrogation those holy books which I was reading, to reflect upon those discourses less known by more learned men, and to compose short pieces of prose and verse, warning me to apply myself the more closely because less care was being expended by others on my instruction. O Lord, True Light, I well remember the inestimable bounty Thou didst then bestow on me. For as soon as I had taken Thy habit at Thy invitation, a cloud seemed to be removed from the face of my understanding and I soon began to find my way through those things in which earlier I had wandered blindly and in error. Besides, I was suddenly inspired with such a love of learning that I yearned for it above all else and thought the day was lost on which I did not engage in some such work. How often they thought I was asleep and resting my little body under the coverlet when my mind was really concentrated on composition, or I was reading under a blanket, fearful of the rebuke of the others.

And Thou, Holy Jesus, didst know with what motive I did this, chiefly to win glory and so that greater honor in this present

[2]According to the Benedictine Rule (ch. 58), a novice seeking admission to a monastery should publicly recite the verse which begins "Receive me, O Lord, according to Thy word, and I shall live" (Psalms 118:116).

world might be mine. My friends were clearly my enemies, for although they gave me good advice, yet they often plied me with talk of fame and literary distinction and, through these things, the winning of high status and wealth. They put into my shortsighted mind hopes worse than the egg of asps,[3] and since I believed that all their promises would quickly come to pass, they deceived me with the vainest expectations. What they said might come to pass in the fullness of age, I thought I would surely attain in adolescence or early manhood. They proclaimed my learning (which by Thy gift was daily increasing) and good birth according to worldly standards and good looks, but they did not remember that by such steps a man "shall not go up unto Thy altar, lest his nakedness be discovered."[4] For he that "climbeth up another way, the same is a thief and a robber,"[5] which is nakedness.

But in these beginnings of mine under Thy inspiration, if it had any wisdom at all, my mind ought to have been prepared for temptation. In truth my wisdom at that time was to some degree foolishness. Although I was moved by the childish emotions of joy or anger, would that I now, O Lord, so hated my great sins as then I feared Thy judgment and hated sins that were minor or scarcely sins at all. Sensibly and with great eagerness, I imitated those whom I saw weeping bitterly for their sins, and whatever came from Thee gave delight to my sight and hearing. And I who now search the Scriptures for vocabulary and matter for display, and even store in my mind the disreputable sayings of pagan writers to make mere babbling, in those days got from them tears and matter for sorrow, and thought my reading vain if I found in it no matter for meditation, nothing leading to repentance. So, unknowingly, I acted wisely.

But that old Foe, who has learned from ages of experience how to deal with the varying conditions of heart and age, he, I say conceived new conflicts for me, according to the measure of my mind and little body. He presented to my gaze in sleep many visions of dead men, especially those whom I had seen or heard of as slain with swords or by some such death, and by such sights he so terrified

[3]Cf. Isaiah 59:5.
[4]Exodus 20:26, slightly altered.
[5]John 10:1.

my spirit when it was relaxed in sleep that but for the watchful protection of that master of mine, I could not have been kept in my bed at night, or prevented from calling out, and I would have nearly gone out of my mind. Although this trouble may seem childish and ridiculous to those who have not felt it, it is regarded as a great calamity by those who are oppressed by it, so that fear itself, which most men consider absurd, can be held in check by no reasoning or counsel. Although the sufferer himself cares not at all for what he suffers, his spirit, when once for a brief moment it is plunged in sleep, has no power to shake off the horrid sights; indeed, the mind, deeply disturbed by its terrors, dreads the return of sleep itself. To this emotion, crowds or solitude are the same, since the company of others is no defense against such fear, and dwelling alone either leaves it as bad as before or makes it worse.

My condition, Lord God, was then far different from my present state. Then I clearly had great respect for Thy law and unbounded loathing for all sin, and I eagerly drank in all that could be said or heard or known from Thee. I know, Heavenly Father, that by such childish application the Devil was savagely enraged, although later he was appeased by the surrender of all my pious fervor. One night, in winter, I believe, kept awake by my wretched anxiety, I was lying in my bed, thinking I was safer with a lamp close by that gave a bright light, when suddenly and apparently close above my head there arose the tumult of many voices, although it was the dead of night. One voice uttered no words, but only a howl of distress. Shaken by these nightmarish events, I lost my senses and seemed to see a certain dead man who, someone cried out, had been killed at the baths. Struck with the terror of the phantasy, I leaped screaming from my bed, and, looking around as I leaped, I saw the lamp extinguished and through the shadows of a high cloud of darkness I saw standing near me a demon in his own shape. At that horrible sight I should have gone almost mad, had not my master, who very frequently stayed on guard to control my terrors, adroitly soothed my perturbed and terror-struck wits.

Even in the tender years of childhood, I was aware that the desire for a good endeavor which burned in my heart enraged the Devil in no small measure to stir up wickedness in me. Gracious

God, what victories, what crowns for victories I would deserve today if I had stood fast to the end in that struggle! I have concluded from many tales I have heard that devils are most fiercely embittered against recent converts or those who continually aspire to this manner of life. I remember that in the time of Bishop Guy of Beauvais, whom I mentioned before, there was a certain young knight in his household whom the bishop cared more for than almost all his retainers. This man, repenting with horror of his vices, resolved at all costs to fly from contact with the world. While torn with anxious thoughts about this return to a pristine state, he was sleeping one night in the bishop's chamber along with the bishop and a God-fearing man named Ivo, a native of Saint-Quentin, I think, who was very famous for his writing and distinguished for his almost more famous eloquence, and who was a monk of Cluny who filled the office of prior there for a long time under Abbot Hugues of blessed memory.[6] Some other men who were equally outstanding in the holy life were there as well. One of the chief nobles from a neighboring town, a very courtly and discreet man, kept watch while the rest slept in the dead of the night. As his thoughts wandered at will and his eyes roved hither and thither, suddenly the figure of a chief devil with a small head and a hunched back appeared advancing toward the man, and, looking at each of the beds in turn, he proceeded to walk slowly around the room. When the great Deceiver came to the mattress of the young man whom I mentioned as being most beloved by the bishop, he halted and, turning his gaze on the sleeper, said: "This man troubles me most bitterly and worst of all those who sleep here." After saying that, he headed for the door of the latrine and went in. The man who was looking on, while paying attention to all this, was oppressed with a burden which made speech or movement impossible. But when the Adversary went out, both faculties returned to him, and in the morning, on relating his vision to the wiser men and inquiring with them into the condition and disposition of the young man, he found that his heart was earnestly set on entering a holier life. If there is more joy in heaven over one sinner that is converted than over ninety just men who need not

[6]On Ivo, prior of Cluny from 1087 to 1093 or 1094, see *Histoire littéraire de France* (Paris, 1733-), IX, 513-515.

penance,[7] then without doubt we may fully believe that the enemies of the human race are vexed with the most bitter hatred at the rescue of those who change for the better. And just as I, after a good beginning, have clearly followed a pestilent course, so he, after accepting the Devil's testimony, henceforward gradually fell away and grew cold, returning to his worldly interests. Still, one may believe how painfully that sudden stirring of our good intentions must sting the hearts of devils. And no wonder that the Devil is grieved by the sudden and transient emotions of any penitent, since even the shallow self-abasement of that wicked king Ahab brought him to the attention of God before that of men. Hence the Lord said to Elias, if I am not mistaken, "Hast thou not seen Ahab humbled before me? Therefore, because he has humbled himself for my sake, I will not bring the evil in his days."[8]

CHAPTER 16

With the gradual growth of my young body, as the life of this world began to stir my itching heart with fleshly longings and lusts to suit my stature, my mind repeatedly fell to remembering and dwelling on what and how great I might have been in the world, in which my imaginings often traveled beyond the truth. These thoughts, Gracious God Who cares for all, Thou didst reveal to Thy servant, my mother. Whatever the state, healthy or diseased, to which my unstable heart changed, an image of it came to her in a vision by Thy will, O God. But since dreams are said to follow many cares,[1] and that is indeed true, yet her cares were not aroused by the heat of greed, but were created by a real eagerness for inward holiness. Soon after the troubling vision was impressed on her most pious mind, as she was very subtle and clear-sighted in the interpretation of such matters, when she had perceived what trouble was betokened by her dream, she soon summoned me and in private questioned me about my activities, what I was doing, and

[7]Luke 15:7, slightly altered.
[8]III Kings 21:29.
[1]Ecclesiastes 5:2.

how I was behaving. Since I was in such submission to her that my will was one with hers, I readily confessed all those things in which my mind seemed to grow slack, following the content of the dreams which I had heard, and after she had warned me to improve, with true affection I at once promised to do so.

O my God, she often spoke to me in enigmas concerning that state in which I now suffer, and what she believed I had done or should do in that state in which I was then, so that every day I now experience in the secret places of my heart the truth of her statements and contemplate their fulfillment. Since my master was also moved by an incessant and heartfelt solicitude, enlightened by Thee, he saw through many kinds of figures[2] what was happening at the time and what might come to pass in the future. By God's gift, both foretold adversity and success, on the one hand terrifying me, on the other comforting me, so that whether I would or not, I abstained from hidden wickedness, because by Thy wonder-working so much was revealed to those who loved me, and sometimes I rejoiced in the promise of a better hope.

At a time when I was swayed by a spirit of sullenness because of the envy which I suffered from my superiors and equals, I hoped with the aid of my relatives to be able to transfer to some other monastery. Some of our brotherhood, seeing me once far below them both in age and learning, in ability and understanding, and afterward perceiving that I equalled them, or, if I may say so, altogether surpassed them—since He Who is the key to all knowledge had by His gift alone stimulated in me a hunger for learning—raged against me with such burning and evil wrath that, wearied with everlasting disputes and quarrels, I often regretted I had ever seen or known letters. They so greatly disturbed my work and, when an occasion arose over some matter of learning, so often started disputes with their constant questions that they seemed to have as their sole object to make me change my resolve and to impede my talents. But as when oil is poured on a fire a livelier flame creeps forth from what was supposed to put it out, the more my ingenuity was overtaxed in such labors, the better it became, like an oven rendered stronger by its own heat. The ques-

[2]Cf. Numbers 12:8.

tions by which they thought to crush me gave great keenness to my intelligence, and the difficulty of their objections, which required much pondering to find answers and the turning over of many books, brought about a strengthening of my wits and ability in debate. Although I was thus bitterly hated by them, yet Thou knowest, O Lord, how little, if at all, I hated them, and when they could not put any stigma upon me, as they wished, in disparagement they told everyone that I was too proud of my little learning.

Although from difficulties of this sort abundant good was produced, yet my spirit grew weak, languishing under the endless torture of its thoughts and surrounded by these annoyances, which affected me bitterly. With a fearful heart and failing powers of reason, I did not consider what profit there was in hardship, but eagerly decided to seek the solution which the weakness of my flesh suggested. When I therefore proposed to leave the place, not so much with the kindly permission of my abbot as at the suggestion and demand of my kinsfolk, my mother gave her assent, too, believing that I was doing this from pious motives, for the place to which I wished to retire was considered very holy. Then the following vision appeared to her to witness to the good and evil in me.

She thought she was in the church of that monastery; that is, of Saint-Germer of Fly. When she looked at the church more closely, she saw it was forsaken in a most lonely fashion; the monks, too, were not only ragged and covered with cassocks huge beyond belief, but all alike were shortened to a cubit in height like those commonly called dwarfs. But since "where your treasure is, there is your heart, and where your gaze is turned, there is your love,"[3] she fixed a long look on me, and saw that I stood no higher than the rest and was covered with no better apparel. While she was mourning my plight and that of such a church, suddenly a woman of beauty and majesty beyond measure advanced through the midst of the church right up to the altar, followed by one like a young girl whose appearance was in its deference appropriate to her whom she followed. Being very curious to know who the lady

[3]"Ubi thesaurus, ibi cor, et ubi contuitus, ibi amor," apparently a proverbial saying based on Luke 12:34.

was, my mother was told that she was the Lady of Chartres. At once she interpreted this to mean the Blessed Mother of God, whose name and relics at Chartres are venerated throughout almost all the Latin world.[4] Going up to the altar, the lady knelt in prayer and the noble attendant who in the vision was following her did the same behind her. Then, rising and stretching out her hand with the appearance of great reproof, she said, "I founded this church. Why should I permit it to be deserted?" Then this standard-bearer of piety turned her tranquil gaze on me and, pointing with her shining hand, said, "I brought him here and made him a monk. By no means will I permit him to be taken away." After this the attendant repeated these same words in like fashion. No sooner had that powerful one spoken than in a moment all that ruin and waste was changed and appeared as it had before, and the dwarf stature both of the rest and of myself, too, was amended and made normal by the power that attended her command. When my prudent mother had given me an orderly narrative of this dream, I received such a story with much remorse and tears, and, influenced by the meaning of so desirable a dream, I so restrained my indulgence in thoughts of wandering that I was never again drawn by a desire for another monastery.

O Lady, Mother of Heaven, this and other things like it gave me the opportunity to return to you, rising above the horror of my sins and the countless apostasies by which I rebelled from your love and service, while my heart prophesies that the wide bosom of Thy mercies cannot be closed against me even by mountains of my ill deeds. I shall always remember, too, Lady of Heaven, that when, as a boy, I was eager to put on this habit, one night in a vision I was in the church dedicated to you and I thought I was carried from it by two devils. And when they had taken me to the roof of the church, they fled away and let me go uninjured within the walls of that church. I often recall these things when I consider my incorrigibility, and the more often I

[4]The chief relic of Chartres was the "tunic" or "shirt" the Virgin was said to have worn at the Nativity (cf. below, p. 124). Given to the church by Charles the Bald about 876, the fabric was about 1000 enclosed in a reliquary which was opened in 1712. The relic then proved to be a long piece of raw silk; its remains are now known as a "veil." See *Dictionnaire d'histoire et de géographie ecclésiastique* (Paris, 1912-), XII, 550.

repeat those sins, or rather add to them sins which get worse and worse, I turn back to you, most holy one, as a refugee from the peril of despair, abusing my little hope or faith.

Although I am forever sinning, compelled by my weakness and not through the willfulness of pride, yet I in no wise lose the hope of amendment. Clearly "a just man falls seven times and rises again."[5] If the number seven here stands for an entirety,[6] as it usually does, then no matter how many ways a man falls by sin and although his flesh is weak, if he resolves to rise again to righteousness, if he shows the grief of a penitent, he does not at all lose the name of a just man. Why would we cry aloud to God to deliver us from our necessities[7] if the corruption of our nature did not condemn us, whether we will or no, to the servitude of sin? "I see it," the Apostle says, "leading me captive in the law of sin, that is in my members; for I do not that good which I will; but the evil which I hate, that I do."[8]

There is a depth of certain evils which a wicked man despises when he enters.[9] Moreover, concerning certain other depths a cry is made to God,[10] and the petitioner does not doubt that his voice is heard. There is a scorn of despair begotten by excess of sinning, which can be of this depth, where "there is no sure standing,"[11] in which misery does not stand.[12] There is lastly the depth out of which Jeremiah was drawn by a rope of rags,[13] and although that be deep, yet farther on it has a bottom; for despite the loosening of the understanding through much sinning, yet reason gives some little check, so that it is not swallowed up in the bottomless gulf without any knowledge of all its iniquity.

[5]Proverbs 24:16.
[6]*The City of God* (XI, 31) gives this meaning for the number seven wiith reference to this same passage from Proverbs; significantly, Augustine says the passage does not refer to sins but to afflictions.
[7]Cf. Psalms 24:17.
[8]Romans 7:23 and 19, slightly altered. On Guibert's use of this passage with reference to modesty, see the Introduction, pp. 13-14.
[9]Proverbs 18:3.
[10]A reference to Psalm 129, *De profundis,* which began the burial service and, as part of the office for the dead, was sung daily in the monastic liturgy.
[11]Psalms 68:3.
[12]Cf. Psalms 139:11.
[13]Jeremiah 38:11-13.

CHAPTER 17

After steeping my mind unduly in the study of versemaking, with the result that I put aside for such ridiculous vanities the matters of universal importance in the divine pages, I was so far guided by my folly as to give first place to Ovid and the pastoral poets and to aim at a lover's urbanity in distributions of types and in a series of letters.[1] Forgetting proper severity and abandoning the modesty of a monk's calling, my mind was led away by these enticements of a poisonous license, and I considered only if I could render the conversation of the courts in the words of some poet, with no thought of how much the toil which I loved might hurt the aims of our holy profession. By love of it I was doubly taken captive, being snared both by the wantonness of the sweet words I took from the poets and by those which I poured forth myself, and I was caught by the unrestrained stirring of my flesh through thinking on these things and the like. Since my unstable mind, unaccustomed now to discipline, was grinding out these things, no sound could come from my lips but that which my thought prompted.

Hence it came to pass that, from the boiling over of the madness within me, I was carried along to words which were a bit obscene and composed some sort of little compositions, irresponsible and indiscreet, in fact bereft of all decency. When this came to the attention of the master I have mentioned, he took it very bitterly, and while he was provoked by his distaste, he fell asleep. As he slept, there appeared to him the following vision: an old man with beautiful white hair—in fact that very man, I dare say, who had brought me to him at the beginning and had promised his love for me in the future—appeared to him and said with great severity, "I wish you to give account to me for the writings that have been composed; however, the hand which wrote them is not his who wrote."[2] When my master had related this to me, he and

[1]The phrase "in distributionibus specierum" may refer to the practice of writing schoolboy verses describing the beauties of the parts of the human body.
[2]Guibert related this incident in almost the same words in the introductory letter to his tract on the Incarnation (ed. Migne, col. 490). His earlier reference to the old man who appeared to his teacher in a dream is on p. 45.

I gave much the same interpretation to the dream. We mourned and were joyful in Thy hope, on the one hand seeing Thy displeasure in that fatherly rebuke, and on the other thinking from the meaning of the vision that confidence in some amendment of my frivolity was to come. For when the hand that wrote the letters was said not to be his who write them, without doubt it meant that the hand would not continue in such shameful activity. It was mine and is not, as it is written, "Turn the wicked and they shall not be,"[3] and that which was mine in the practice of vice, when applied to the pursuit of virtue, lost all the efficacy of that utterly worthless ownership.

And yet Thou knowest, O Lord, and I confess, that at that time my life was chastened neither by fear of Thee, nor by shame, nor by respect for that holy vision. I put no check on that irreverence I had within me, and did not refrain from the vain jests of frivolous writers. I hammered out these verses in secret and dared to show them to no one, or at least only to a few like myself, but I often recited those which I could, inventing an author for them. I was delighted when those which I though it inconvenient to acknowledge as mine were praised by those who shared such studies, and what did not produce the profit of any praise for their author still left him to enjoy the profit, or rather the shamefulness, of sin. But Thou didst punish these acts, O Father, in Thy own good time. Thou didst fence in my wandering soul with rising misfortune against me for such work and with great adversity, and Thou didst hold me down with bodily infirmity. Then "the sword reached even to the soul,"[4] and vexation touched my understanding.[5]

When the punishment of sin had brought understanding to my hearing,[6] then at last the folly of useless study withered away. Since I could not bear to be idle, as if by some necessity I rejected these fancies of mine, took up the spiritual life again, and turned to more appropriate exercises. All too late I began to pant for the knowledge that had repeatedly been distilled for me

[3]Proverbs 12:7.
[4]Jeremiah 4:10.
[5]Cf. Isaiah 28:19.
[6]*Ibid.*

by many good scholars: to busy myself, that is, with commentaries on the Scriptures, to study frequently the works of Gregory, in which are to be found the best keys to that art, and, according to the rules of ancient writers, to treat the words of the prophets and the Gospels in their allegorical, their moral, and finally their anagogical meaning.[7] In this work I had the special encouragement of Anselm, the abbot of Bec, afterward archbishop of Canterbury, who was born across the Alps in the region of Aosta, a man of sublime example and holiness of life.[8] While he was still prior at Bec, he admitted me to his acquaintance, and though I was a mere child of most tender age and knowledge, he readily offered to teach me to manage the inner self, how to consult the laws of reason in the government of the body. Both before he became abbot and as abbot, he was a familiar visitor at the abbey of Fly where I was, welcomed for his piety and his teaching. He bestowed on me so assiduously the benefits of his learning and with such ardor labored at this that it seemed as if I alone were the unique and special reason for his frequent visits.

His teaching was to divide the mind in a threefold or fourfold way, to treat the operations of the whole interior mystery under the headings of appetite, will, reason, and intellect. By a resolution, based on clear analyses, of what I and many others thought to be

[7]Medieval commentators found three levels of Scriptural interpretation beyond the literal. A common verse explained the terms:

Litera gesta docet; quid credas allegoria;
Moralis quid agas; quo tendas, anagogia.
(The letter teaches what we know;
Anagogy where we go;
Faith's set out by allegories;
Conduct's shaped by moral stories.)

[8]St. Anselm was born in Aosta c. 1033-34, entered the monastery of Bec in 1060, became prior in 1063, was elected abbot in 1078, and became archbishop of Canterbury in 1093. He died in 1109. See Richard W. Southern, *St. Anselm and His Biographer* (Cambridge, 1963).

[9]Augustine described the three faculties of the soul as memory, intelligence, and will. Anselm's novelty was to replace memory with reason and add appetite or desire; this allowed him to argue that the will was always free, since appetite was a separate function. Under the control of reason, will and appetite could be one. Cf. Southern, *St. Anselm*, pp. 224-225, and Anselm of Canterbury, *Truth, Freedom, and Evil*, ed. and trans. Jasper Hopkins and Herbert Richardson (New York, 1967), pp. 26-27.

one, he showed that appetite and will are not identical, although it is established by evident assertions that in the presence of reason or intellect they are practically the same.[9] He discussed with me certain chapters of the Gospels on this principle, and most clearly explained the difference between willing and being subject to appetite; it was plain, however, that he did not originate this, but got it from books at hand which did not so explicitly deal with these matters. I then began to endeavor to equal his methods in similar commentaries, so far as I could, and to search carefully with all the keenness of my mind everywhere in the Scriptures to see if anything accorded on the moral level with these thoughts.

It came to pass that when I was traveling with my former abbot to a certain monastery in our province, I suggested to him as a man of great piety that on coming to the chapter meeting he should preach a sermon there. He turned over to me what he was asked to do, exhorting and ordering me to do it in his place. Now, the birth of Mary Magdalene is celebrated on that day.[10] Taking the text of my sermon from the Book of Wisdom, I contented myself with that single word for the homily I was asked to give: "Wisdom," that is, "overcomes evil; she reaches therefore from end to end mightily, and orders all things sweetly."[11] When I had explained this with such oratory as I could, and had pleased my audience with the suitability of these remarks, the prior of the church, who was no mean student of sacred literature within the limits of his understanding, in a friendly way asked me to write something which would give him the material for preparing sermons on any subject. Since I knew that my abbot, in whose presence I had said this, would be annoyed by my writings, I approached the man with caution and, acting as if I came on behalf of his friend and did not care much about it myself, I begged him to grant what I was asking for the sake of the prior, whom he professed to love. Supposing that I would write very briefly, he consented. When I had snatched his consent from his mouth, I began to work at what I had in mind.

I proposed to undertake a moral commentary on the beginning of Genesis, that is, the Six Days of Creation. To the commentary, I

[10]July 22nd.
[11]Wisdom 7:30-8:1, slightly altered.

prefixed a treatise of moderate length showing how a sermon ought to be composed.[12] I followed up this preface with a tropological[13] exposition at length of the Six Days, with poor eloquence but such as I was capable of. When my abbot saw that I was commenting on the first chapter of that sacred history, he no longer took a favorable view of the matter and warned me with great reproof to put an end to these writings.[14] I saw that such works only put thorns in his eyes, and by avoiding both his presence and that of anyone who might report it to him, I pursued my task in secret. For the composition and writing of this or my other works, I did not prepare a draft on the wax tablets, but committed them to the written page in their final form as I thought them out. In that abbot's time my studies were carried on in complete secrecy. But when he was gone, finding my opportunity when the pastoral office was vacant, at last I attacked and quickly finished my work.[15] It consisted of ten books which followed the four activities of the inner man mentioned before, and I so carried out the moral treatment in all of them that they went from beginning to end with absolutely no change in the order of the passages.[16] Whether in this little work I helped anyone, I do not know, although I have no doubt that most learned men were

[12]The commentary and the introductory treatise exist as Guibert describes them in the copy he gave to the abbey of Nogent (Paris, Bibl. nat. ms. lat. 2500). They are printed in this form by Migne, cols. 19-340. Guibert continued his commentary to the very end of Genesis.

[13]That is, an analysis on the moral level.

[14]Origen and Jerome refer to a Hebrew tradition that no one under thirty should read the beginning of Genesis, the beginning and end of Ezekiel, and the Song of Songs; see Migne, *Patrologia graeca*, t. 13, cols. 63-64 (Origen); *Patrologia latina*, t. 22, col. 547, and t. 25, col. 17 (Jerome), and t. 178, col. 731 (Abelard); and cf. the *Jewish Encyclopedia* (New York, 1901-06), IV, 338. Abbot Garnier may well have thought that Guibert was too young to comment on the Hexameron.

[15]Garnier retired from the abbacy after 26 years of rule, that is, about 1084; see Jean Baptiste de Boulogne, *Historia monasterii S. Geremari Flaviacensis* (Paris, Bibl. nat. ms. lat. 13890), pp. 357-358. The author, who was prior of Saint-Germer in the mid-seventeenth century, provided information used by d'Achery in his edition and may have had access to a better manuscript of the *Monodiae* than that now available.

[16]Guibert's commentary actually disagrees with Anselm's teaching. At the first opportunity, Guibert explained that "reason really is identical with intellect," (ed. Migne, col. 33D), and he emphasized the instability of the will, which he compared to the moon (col. 48C).

greatly pleased with it. This much is certain, that I gained no little profit from it myself, seeing that it saved me from idleness, that servant of vice.

Since then, I wrote a little book in chapters on various meanings in the Gospels and the prophets, including some things from the books of Numbers, Joshua, and Judges. I am putting off the completion of this because after finishing what I have in hand, I propose, if I am still alive and God prompts me, to engage at times in similar exercises.[17] As I did in treating Genesis, I mostly followed the tropological approach, and the allegorical in a few instances. In Genesis, I therefore gave my attention chiefly to morals, not that there was wanting matter for thought on the allegorical level, had I equally worked that out, but because in my opinion moral meanings are in these times more useful than allegories, since faith is established unchanged by God but morals are almost universally debased by the many forms of vice, and because I had neither the freedom nor the wish to enlarge my book to excessive length.

CHAPTER 18

As much as my mother esteemed my success in learning, she was greatly perturbed by her dread of the excesses of a dangerous time of life. How earnestly she begged me to follow her example! Although God had given her such great good looks, she thought little of that in her which won praise, as though she were unaware of her beauty, and she cherished her widowhood as if, unable to bear them, she had always loathed a wife's bedtime duties. Yet Thou knowest, O Lord, how much loyalty, how much love she rendered to her dead husband, how with almost daily masses, prayers, and tears, and much almsgiving, she strove without ceasing to release his soul, which she knew was fettered by his sins. By the wonderful dispensation of God, it came about that in frequent visions she saw in the clearest images what pains he

[17] By the time of his death, Guibert had written commentaries on the minor prophets, but no manuscript of a commentary on Numbers, Joshua, and Judges has been ascribed to him. The "little book in chapters" has also not been identified.

endured in his purgation. Without doubt such visions come from God; for when no perverse sense of security is falsely caused by the assumption of the beauty of light,[1] but a stimulus is given to prayer and almsgiving by the sight of suffering and punishment, and when the remedies of the divine office are clearly demanded by the dead, or rather by the angels, who care for dead Christians, it is proof enough that these things come from God, because devils never seek the salvation of any man's soul. The anxious mind of that good woman was kindled again by these signs and was inflamed by the intimation of his soul's torments to constant efforts to intercede for her former husband.

One summer night, for instance, on a Sunday after matins, after she had stretched out on her narrow bench and had begun to sink into sleep, her soul seemed to leave her body without her losing her senses. After being led, as it were, through a certain gallery, at last she issued from it and began to approach the edge of a pit. After she was brought close to it, suddenly from the depths of that abyss men with the appearance of ghosts leaped forth, their hair seemingly eaten by worms, trying to seize her with their hands and to drag her inside. From behind the frightened woman, who was terribly distressed by their attack, suddenly a voice cried out to them, saying, "Touch her not."[2] Compelled by that forbidding voice, they leaped back into the pit. Now, I forgot to say that as she passed through the gallery, as she knew she had left her mortal being, her one prayer to God was to be allowed to return to her body. After she was rescued from the dwellers in the pit and was standing by its edge, suddenly she saw that my father was there, appearing as he did when he was young. When she looked hard at him and piteously asked of him whether he was called Evrard (for that had been his name), he denied that he was.

Now, it is no wonder that a spirit should refuse to be called by the name which he had as a man, for spirit should give no reply to a spirit which is inconsistent with its spiritual nature.[3] Moreover, that spirits should recognize each other by their names is too absurd to be believed; otherwise in the next world it would

[1]That is, by the Devil.
[2]Cf. Psalms 104:15.
[3]Cf. I Corinthians 2:12-15.

be rare to know anyone except those close to us. Clearly it is not necessary for spirits to have names, since all their vision, or rather their knowledge of vision, is internal.

Although he denied that he was called by that name, and yet nonetheless she felt that it was he, she then asked him where he was staying. He indicated that the place was located not far away, and that he was detained there. She also asked how he was. Baring his arm and his side, he showed both of them so torn, so cut up with many wounds, that she felt great horror and emotional distress as she looked. The figure of a little child was also there, crying so bitterly that it troubled her greatly when she saw it. Moved by its cries, she said to him, "My lord, how can you endure the wailing of this child?" "Whether I like it or not" said he, "I endure it." Now, the crying of the child and the wounds on his arm and side have this meaning. When my father in his youth was separated from lawful intercourse with my mother through the witchcraft of certain persons, some evil counselors appealed to his youthful spirit with the vile advice to find out if he could have intercourse with other women. In youthful fashion he took their advice, and, having wickedly attempted intercourse with some loose woman unknown to me, he begat a child which at once died before baptism. The rending of his side is the breaking of his marriage vow; the cries of that distressed voice indicate the damnation of that evilly begotten child. Such, O Lord, O Inexhaustible Goodness, was Thy retribution on the soul of Thy sinner, who yet lives by faith.[4] But let us return to the orderly narrative of the vision.

When she asked him whether prayer, almsgiving, or the mass gave him any relief (for he was aware that she frequently provided these things for him), he replied that they did, adding, "But among you there lives a certain Liégearde." My mother understood that he named this woman so that she would ask her what memory of him she had. This Liégearde was very poor in spirit,[5] a woman who lived for God alone apart from the customs of the world.

Meanwhile, bringing her talk with my father to an end, my mother looked toward the pit, above which was a picture, and in the picture she saw a certain knight named Renaud, of no mean

[4]Cf. Romans 1:17.
[5]Matthew 5:3.

reputation among his countrymen. After dinner on that very day, which as I said before was a Sunday, this Renaud was treacherously killed at Beauvais by those close to him.[6] In that picture he was kneeling with his neck bent down, puffing to blow up a fire in a heap of fuel. This vision was seen in the early morning, whereas he perished at midday, doomed to descend into those flames which he had kindled by his deserts. In the same picture she saw a brother of mine who was helping, but he died long afterward. He was taking a dreadful oath by the sacrament of God's body and blood. The significance of this is precisely that by false swearing and by taking the holy name of God and His sacred mysteries in vain, he earned both his punishment and the place of his punishment.

In the course of the same vision, she also saw that old woman who, as I said, lived with her at the beginning of her conversion, a woman who clearly was always mortifying her body with crosses on the outside, but, it was said, was not enough on her guard against a hunger for vainglory. She saw this woman carried off by two coal-black spirits, her form a mere shadow. Moreover, while that old woman was alive and the two were living together, when they were talking of the state of their souls and the coming of death, they once took a mutual pledge that the one who died first should, through the grace of God, appear to the survivor and make known to her the nature of her condition, whether good or bad. They confirmed this by prayer, earnestly beseeching God that after the death of either the other should be allowed to discover by the revelation of some vision her happy or unhappy state. When the old woman was about to die, she had seen herself in a vision deprived of her body and going with others like her to a certain temple, and, as she went, she seemed to be carrying a cross on her shoulders. Coming to the temple with that company, she was compelled to stay outside, the doors being barred against her.

[6]Bourgin (*De vita sua,* p. 72, note 1) follows earlier historians in associating the killing at Beauvais with one discussed in the letters of Ivo of Chartres. Since Ivo does not indicate the name or status of the murdered man, the connection is questionable and the event cannot be used to date the composition of Guibert's book. The killing must, of course, have occurred before the death of Guibert's mother, that is, well before 1114, which is the date Luchaire proposes for the murder; see Achille Luchaire, *Louis VI le Gros: Annales de sa vie et de son règne* (Paris, 1890), pp. 88-89.

Finally, after her death she appeared to someone else in the midst of a great stench to express her gratitude for giving prayers which had saved her from decay and pain. While the old woman was dying, at the foot of the bed she saw standing a horrible devil with eyes of dreadful and monstrous size. When she adjured him by the holy sacraments to flee in confusion from her and seek nothing of her, with that frightful charge she drove him off.

My mother drew her conclusions about the cries of the infant, of whose existence she had been aware, from the exact way in which the vision agreed with the facts, when she put them together, and from the immediate prophecy of the impending slaying of the knight, whom she had seen assigned to the place of punishment below. Having no doubt about these things, she devoted herself wholly to bringing help to my father. Setting like against like, she chose to take on the raising of a little child only a few months old that had lost its parents. But since the Devil hates good intentions no less than faithful actions, the baby so harassed my mother and all her servants by the madness of its wailing and crying at night—although by day it was very good, by turns playing and sleeping—that anyone in the same little room could get scarcely any sleep. I have heard the nurses whom she hired say that night after night they could not stop shaking the child's rattle, so naughty was he, not through his own fault, but made so by the Devil within, and that a woman's craft failed entirely to drive him out. The good woman was tormented by extreme pain; amid those shrill cries no contrivance relieved her aching brow, nor could any sleep steal over her sorely tried and exhausted head, since the frenzy of the child goaded from within and by the Enemy's presence caused continual disturbance. Although she passed her sleepless nights in this way, she never appeared listless at the performance of the night offices. Since she knew that these troubles were to purge away those of her husband, which she had seen in her vision, she bore them gladly, because she rightly thought that by sharing his suffering herself she was lessening the pains of the other sufferer. Yet she never shut the child out of her house, never appeared less careful of him. Indeed, the more she perceived that the Devil was cruelly blazing against her to destroy her resolve, the more she chose to submit with equanimity to any inconvenience rising from it; and the more she happened to experience the eagerness of the Devil in the irritation of the child, the more she was assured that his evil sway over the soul of her husband was being countered.

CHAPTER 19

O Lord God, Thou didst show many other things to Thy handmaid and to that master of mine, whom Thou didst especially appoint over me. Some of these, which might be set down to my boasting if I were to write of them here, showed that good hope for which even now I wait at the feet of Thy most gracious Mother, before whom I was laid at birth; and some, sweet Jesus, shown to them when I was still but a child, I am now marvelously experiencing in my ripening age.

At last the heat of my desires burst into flame, and because Thou hadst put into my heart the tinder of a little knowledge and hadst bestowed on me a person well-fitted for worldly success with moderately good birth, both my own heart and some of my associates (who in this matter were not my friends) evilly suggested to me that it would be proper for me to advance in this world by promotion to some office. But I know, O Lord, that in Thy law Thou didst forbid us to "go up by steps to Thy altar," for Thou didst teach that in this way the nakedness of a holy leader can be revealed.[1] Those who have attained to spiritual rule through the dung of external prominence fall with greater shame on that account, because, leaving the level ground, they have tried to scale the heights of glory above their heads. In my open desire for promotion through the influence of my kinsfolk, my ears were often gratified by rumors of success in attaining such heights. Many flattered me; some wished for their own ends to test my character, in order to carry out their purpose of reporting it to those who were wickedly jealous of me; others supposed that they would please me by pretending to desire my advancement and said that my advantage would be their gain, too, and they were therefore always grasping for advantages through my rise.

[1]Exodus 20:26.

As Thou knowest, my Creator, by Thy impulse and inspiration alone I came to my senses, so that through fear of Thee I scorned to seek favors from any man or to give consent or speak with anyone who was working on my behalf to secure what is for Thee alone to give, an office in the church. And Thou knowest, Lord, that in this matter at least I desire nothing at all, nor should have desired anything, except what I may receive or should have received from Thee. My desire is that in this as in other things, it is Thou Who hast made me, and not I myself.[2] Otherwise, Israel would have rejoiced improperly in Him Who made him.[3] My God, by what opposition, by what envy was I then oppressed! Consequently, my mind was in secret turmoil at the suggestions made to it from without, at its flight, as it were, from temptation. But although that ambition was hot within me, yet its heat could not move my tongue. Although I was agitated, yet I did not speak. Thou knowest, Jesus, that once when sin tripped me up, I charged someone who was working for my advancement, but not at my prompting, to do quickly whatever he was doing. Thou knowest, I say, how vexed I was that I had said this. For however often I may have wickedly fallen, I always feared to be a buyer of doves,[4] or rather their betrayer. Clearly, although there is only one dove, there is more than one chair among them.[5] Whatever division there is in God and the church is certainly not created by He Who suffers from it. "Let them be one," He says, "as we also are one,"[6] and "There are diversities of graces, but the same spirit, dividing to everyone according as He will,"[7] and "The throne of God," not thrones, "is forever and ever,"[8] and "Of the fruit of thy womb I will set upon thy throne."[9] Therefore, those things which are one with God become several through the aims of human perversity.

[2]Cf. Psalms 99:3.
[3]Cf. Psalms 149:2.
[4]Cf. Matthew 21:12-13. The allusion, of course, suggests a buyer of church office.
[5]The single dove is the dove of the Holy Spirit; the chairs are those of the sellers of doves in the Temple.
[6]John 17:22.
[7]I Corinthians 12:4 and 11.
[8]Hebrews 1:8.
[9]Psalms 131:11.

Taking account of these things and not being ignorant of the unity of the head and the body,[10] I wished to usurp nothing in the body, because whatever thrusts itself in from elsewhere is certainly not in agreement with the head, and no one can doubt that the head does not know what is not approved in the body. Those who will say, "Have we not prophesied in Thy name and cast out devils?"[11] are especially apostate, I should say, and not fellow-members, and therefore they hear it said, "I never knew you,"[12] as if He said, "I know they are not in My body, because they do not live from Me." Therefore a hope, sorry though it was, eased my distaste, and I prayed to Thee, O God, that if ever what was being attempted in my behalf should come to pass, it should be by Thy doing alone, and I was vexed because I heard through others that my relatives were seeking things for me, whereas others were chosen by the simple working of God and with no earthly influence. My kinsmen, who were looking out not so much for me as for themselves in this business, did not deal with me at all in the matter, being plainly unwilling to stir up my youthful feelings over it. At last, God being unwilling that I should any longer be deceived, He inspired my supporters to go abroad for the salvation of their souls,[13] and it became necessary for the monks of certain abbeys, who were depending on them to secure my election, to turn elsewhere.

O God, I thank Thee that then my childish desires entirely withered away and that it no longer pleased me to long for any earthly dignity. Thou didst then scourge me and throw me to the ground, O Father, O God, Chastener of my desires and vanities, and didst bring me back to reflection, binding me within so that my vagrant mind might have no escape, but should yearn from its inmost being for simple humility and sincerity of heart. Then I first began to try, O Lord, for that pious solitude of the mind in which Thou art wont to abide, to approach the Mother of the heavenly kingdom, Mary, Mother of God, my only refuge in every

[10]Cf. Colossians 1:18, and see Otto Gierke, *Political Theories of the Middle Age*, trans. F. W. Maitland (Cambridge, 1913), p. 22.
[11]Matthew 7.22.
[12]Matthew 7:23.
[13]Guibert probably means that they went on crusade.

need, and to aim at her the embracing love of my inward fervor. I heartily desired to be in a modest position; I wholly dreaded higher rank and the empty shadow of a great name in this world. Then, by the sweet savor of Thy close friendship, I first learned the true meaning of singleness of will, of its purity, of an unbending resolve to be forever humble. What shall I say, Lord, of how fleeting was the existence of that paradise, how short the period of calm, how brief and uncertain the taste of such sweetness?

I had scarcely known the foretaste of such happiness for a few months, and Thy good spirit, which had led me into the right land,[14] had scarcely dwelt for a little in my enlightened reason when suddenly Thou seemed to say," When you wished it, I did not. Now you do not wish it and it displeases you. You shall have it, whether you wish it or not," and my election came about, made by men from afar who were utterly unknown to me.[15] But what a choice they made! In truth I should confess myself marked out from other men, since by Thy testimony, O God, of all who were opposed to me I was judged more vile, indeed the worst of all. The blotted appearance of a scholar, to use their word, and the little learning I had attained had made my electors blind or shortsighted. Gracious God, what would they have said if they had then seen my inner self? What would they have thought if they had known what sort of head over them I would be? Thou Who in Thy inscrutable wisdom didst ordain this knowest how I disdain myself, how I detest sitting first among better and more worthy men, in a complete reversal of what is proper. Thou Who seest beforehand into the heart and loins[16] knowest that I by no means coveted such things; rather, I wished to be despised and shamefully rejected and I prayed to Thee with all my heart that I might be excused from this work, so that I might not take up a dreadful burden, which I feared beyond measure, nor in my weakness be found wanting through a proof of my insufficiency.

It was not hidden from Thee, my God, how vexed and displeased my mother was at my promotion. What seemed to others

[14]Psalms 142:10.
[15]Guibert was elected abbot of Nogent-sous-Coucy (80 miles from Saint-Germer) in 1104.
[16]Cf. Psalms 7: 10.

an honor was to her an intolerable sorrow. She wished that no such thing had fallen to my lot, for she feared that my lack of knowledge might be harmful, chiefly because I was entirely ignorant in legal matters, which I had never made any effort to study, being then devoted to letters alone. Yet she and almost all who knew me intimately used to predict often that I should not long be without promotion of some kind. O Lord, Thou knowest with what inward sight she used to speak of the good and ill that would befall me if I should be advanced. I now experience these things, and they are hidden neither from me nor from others. By many visions, in which I and others figured, she foresaw things that would happen long afterward, some of which I see are surely coming to pass or have already come, and the rest I as certainly expect to befall. But about these I deliberately intend to say nothing.

O God, with what warnings she urged me to keep worldly lusts out of my mind, foretelling with certainty the ill chances of adversity which I have suffered, bidding me always be on my guard against juvenile instability, to bridle the mind wandering through mazes of thought. Discussing these matters, she might have been thought some eloquent bishop rather than the illiterate woman she was.

Now, the monastery I was chosen to rule is named Nogent, and it lies so close to the border of the diocese of Laon that a nearby small and sometimes stagnant stream called the Ailette is the boundry between this province and that of Soissons. I intend to discuss its antiquity in this work, if God gives me the strength.

CHAPTER 20

But before going on to Nogent, since I said that I was raised in the church of Fly, under the patronage of God the Father and of St. Germer, the founder of the place, let me pass on as worthy of memory some of the things I heard there or saw happen.

After this church was restored following its destruction by the Danes,[1] a certain monk named Suger, who held the office of prior there, a man of good life, lay ill of a mortal sickness. He was, if

[1]See above, p. 74, n. 3.

I am not mistaken, a brother of the old woman who was associated with my mother at the beginning of her conversion. As he lay there, the Devil stood before him holding a book in his hands and saying, "Take, read; Jupiter sends it to you."[2] Since he was horrified to hear that accursed name, the Devil said further, "Do you love your house?" "I do," said he. The other replied, "You should know that it will lose all the severity of its rule and after a time it will fall into complete disorder." After the monk had confounded the words spoken by Satan with the proper forswearing, the visiting Enemy departed, but the monk, after relating what he had seen, turned mad and had to be put under restraint. Before he expired, however, he regained his wits and, making a good confession, passed away. Since we know that the Devil is "a liar and the father thereof,"[3] we should believe that he spoke out of his usual envy; otherwise, God forbid that this should come true. For the fortunes of the church improved afterward and are still doing so.

CHAPTER 21

In our own time, I saw an elderly monk there who had been a knight, a plain man, it was believed, who had been appointed by his abbot to a certain small house of the monastery in the Vexin, because he was a native of the region.[1] With the consent of his prior, he proposed to repair the foundation of the public road, which was in very bad shape. He carried out this work with the help of the gifts of the faithful, and when it was finished, he kept some sums that were left over from the offerings. After that

[2]The Latin is "Accipe, lege"; the command heard by St. Augustine (*Confessions,* VIII, 12) was "Tolle, lege; tolle, lege."

[3]John 8:44.

[1]The Vexin, which took its name from the Celtic people called Veliocasses, was a district of Frankish Gaul lying north of the Loire to the west of Paris. The Scandinavian occupation of Normandy in the early tenth century split the district at the Epte River into the Norman Vexin and the French Vexin. Saint-Germer was in the district (*pagus*) of Beauvais just to the north of the border with the French Vexin. It had a priory in the French Vexin at Laillerie near Chaumont in the eleventh century; see Ordericus Vitalis, *Ecclesiastical History,* ed. Marjorie Chibnall (Oxford, 1969-), II, 154.

he was seized with a mortal sickness, and yet he did not by any confession reveal what he wickedly kept hidden. Taken to the monastery to which he belonged, he confessed neither to the abbot nor to the prior, although he suffered terrible torments, the heralds of death, but he entrusted the sum of silver to a certain servant who attended the sick.

And so as the dead of night drew near, he lost all feeling of pain and lay stretched as dead on the ground. Summoned by the beating of the wooden signal, we went through the psalms, prayers, and all that can help those about to die. After we had done this, we left the man lying on a sackcloth, as is the monastic custom, since he seemed to be breathing his last gasps. None of us believed he would live, but all expected the final washing of his dead body.[2] Immediately after our departure, he recovered his breath, called for the prior (since the abbot was absent), and told him of the theft he had committed and to whom he had entrusted the stolen money. A little after he said this and had received absolution from the prior, the rattling in his throat came back and he breathed his last. The prior at that time was my teacher, whom I have often mentioned. Behold the multitude of the "mercies of the Lord, that we are not consumed,"[3] for whomever he will he sets "at large out of the narrow mouth."[4]

After the man had been taken from this world, the whole of the inquiry about the money turned upon the servant. Now, he had hidden the sum in the straw of his child's cradle. At night, when the child was put to bed, suddenly devils like little dogs leaped upon it from the side and behind, beating on it here, there, and all around, sometimes nipping it, and making it cry out and weep. When both parents asked why it was crying, the child said it was being eaten up by little dogs. Then the mother, who had been my mother's maid and at one time her attendant, ran to her mistress—that is, my mother—and told her of the stolen money

[2]*The Monastic Constitutions of Lanfranc*, ed. and trans. David Knowles (London, 1951), pp. 122-124, describes the beating of a board to summon the monks to the bed of a dying brother, the prayers they should say there, the laying of the body on sackcloth and ashes, and the ceremony of the final ablution.
[3]Lamentations 3:22.
[4]Job 36:16.

wickedly placed in her charge and of the child's danger of being torn to pieces by the dogs. My mother said to her, "You should know that they are devils who are rejoicing over that devil's money, and they are at hand because they know it is their own." When the husband knew this, although he was unwilling and suffering from a great plague, as I would put it, he gave up what was demanded under compulsion or entreaty or in secret, and he talked freely of the persecution of the devils which he had suffered for it.

We have heard that God "hath mercy on whom He will," and we may gather from this subject that "whom He will, he hardeneth."[5] O wonderful judgments of God! He of whom we have told this tale had passed his whole life in knightly exercises and the foul company of harlots; but he of whom I am about to speak had been apathetic for some little time, though nothing else dishonorable had otherwise come to light about him. Clearly this vice of avarice is the more harmful to monks because it is forbidden by their rule, so that scarcely any crime can be found in which the Devil ensnares so many as that of pilfering.

CHAPTER 22

Another of our monks, a man in priest's orders with whom no fault could be found except his great love of riding, had received two sous[1] from a certain noble lady; soon afterward he fell sick of dysentery at Saint-Quentin of Beauvais.[2] When this was known at Fly, by the order of the abbot he was carried back to his own church. Since he was eating a good deal and immediately passing it on undigested, his abbot, who was about to go on a journey, came to speak to him, fearing that the man might die while he was away. At the moment the abbot came, however, the monk had yielded to the call of nature. Since he could not walk, a cask had been brought for him, and the abbot saw him, in a disgusting condition, sitting on it in pain. After they had stared at one another, the abbot was ashamed at meeting the man in such

[5]Romans 9:18.
[1]That is, 24 silver pennies, worth about the value of a pig.
[2]The abbey of Saint-Quentin of Beauvais was founded in 1067 by Bishop Guy of that city.

circumstances, and so the wretched man was unable to make his confession or to be absolved of his crime, and indeed he was not disposed to do so. The abbot retired, and the monk, rising from the cask, went to his bed to lie down, and he was then strangled there by the Devil as he lay on his back. You could see his chin and throat horribly flattened on his breast as though pressed down violently. And thus he died, unshriven, unanointed, and without making disposition for his cursed money. When his body was stripped for washing, a purse was found hanging from his shoulder under his armpit. When this was found, the man who discovered it, dashing the purse on the ground in a rage and beating his hands together, ran to the monks and poured this extraordinary tale into their ears. Certainly it was unheard of for one of their brothers to die in this fashion.

The man was sent after the abbot, who had begun his dinner at a certain house of his two miles beyond Beauvais. Through another messenger who had reached him, the abbot had already heard that he was dead, but the first man knew nothing and had said nothing about the money. The messenger who came on behalf of the brothers consulted the abbot about what ought to be done, and whether it was lawful for a monk who had so miserably withdrawn from their community to be buried with the others. When the abbot had taken counsel with wise persons, he ordered his burial to take place out in the fields without prayer and psalms, and that the money should be laid on his breast. The brothers did not fail to offer private prayers, however, and they were the more eager to do so since they knew he needed it more. The sudden death of this man made the rest more rigorous in the matter of private possessions. Let us hear further how at other times they were chastised for other offenses.

CHAPTER 23

A few weeks afterward, the night before the feast of the martyrs Gervasius and Protasius,[1] there was a little thunder and occasional lightning with thick clouds and tempestuous winds. In the morning when we rose, the summons for the first hour had just sounded;

[1]June 19th.

we assembled in the church with unusual quickness, and after we had said that very short prayer, "O God, come to my assistance,"[2] and were about to begin what follows, with a burst of thunder a bolt from heaven broke into the church with the following results.[3] The cock over the tower and the cross and the staff were either shattered or burned, and the beam on which they stood was weakened. After half burning and tearing up the shingles nailed to the roof, the bolt passed through the glass of the western window of the tower. The image of the crucified Lord standing beneath was broken rather than consumed, the head being shattered to pieces and the right side pierced, while the right arms both of the cross and of the figure were so burned and maimed that with the exception of the thumb no one could find a single piece of the whole arm, as when the shepherd is smitten, the sheep are scattered abroad with blows and death.[4] Passing to the right through the arch under which the stricken image stood, the bolt descended the stone of the arch in a two-forked black furrow and, entering the choir, struck two monks standing on either side of the arch and killed them instantly. Sweeping to the left on one side, it stripped off the coloring from the surface of the masonry, not continuously but in steps, as if a stone had been rolled over it, and crushed a monk standing there, although neither in this case nor in that of the two others was there any mark of injury to be seen on them, except that on the upturned eyes of the last one there appeared some dust fallen from the arch. It was indeed remarkable that the dead men remained sitting, but we, who were stupefied and half dead from the shock of the bolt, fell headlong on one another. Moreover, some of us who fell down lost all feeling in the body from the waist down; some were so hurt that, fearing their death, we hastily anointed them with holy oil. In some cases the flame darted under the robes and, scorching the shameful pubic hair

[2]According to the Benedictine Rule, ch. 18, the monastic offices were to begin with this versicle, Psalms 69:2.

[3]Albert Besnard argues convincingly in "L'Eglise de Saint-Germer," *Congrès archéologique de France*, LXXII (1905), 407-499, that the present church building dates from the twelfth century, well after Guibert's day. The statements Guibert makes about the form and appearance of his church do not therefore refer to the magnificent church now standing.

[4]Cf. Matthew 26:31.

and that growing in the armpits (which is called "goatlike"), passed out through the extremities by boring through the sandals.

It is impossible to describe with what discrimination the punishment of heaven then raged, by what bends and turns it ran about, what it damaged, what it burned, what it broke. Nobody has heard of anything like it happening in France in our generation. After the hour in which these things happened, I call God to witness that I saw the image of the Blessed Mother of God, which stood below the crucifix, looking so disturbed and changed from her usual calm that she seemed quite a different person. Not trusting my own eyes, I found out that the same thing had been noticed by others. When we had recovered from the amazement which had fallen on us through this event, after making confession, we sadly began to consider why we had suffered for our sins beyond human expression, and, being brought by God face to face with ourselves, by looking into our consciences we discovered how justly we had been punished. Thereupon we saw the face of the Holy Mother changed to a tranquil expression. The grief and shame which we felt for some time are truly beyond belief.

A few years later, when the memory of this event had almost been wiped out of our minds, God gave us another warning of the same kind, except that He hurt no one.[5] One night a peacock had perched to rest against the chimney of a certain room, pressing itself tightly into the chimney as it slept. It was both the feast of St. James the Apostle and a Sunday.[6] In the night a heavy crash of thunder was heard and a bolt of lightning rushed into the chimney, demolishing the part projecting from the room, but the peacock sitting on it remained undisturbed and a young monk sleeping below was not even roused from his sleep. A servant, however, was severely struck with the loss of his wits and of the use of his limbs. According to St. Augustine, God does not idly strike mountains and things inanimate, but He does so to make us reflect that in striking at things that do not sin, He signifies a great judgment on sinners, and Augustine cites as an example

[5]Since Guibert tells later in the paragraph of the injury of a servant, this sentence shows how his sense of humanity was limited by his sense of social position.

[6]The feast is July 25th.

the nurse who strikes the ground with a stick to stop the naughtiness of the child.[7]

When relating the earlier misfortune, I failed to speak of the character of the three men who were killed. Two, being novices, had scarcely completed eight months in the monastic life. One of these had a serious demeanor but was inwardly not so good; the other, under an appearance of levity, was within, as far as we could tell, not so bad a man. The day before they suffered, they had clearly displayed the division of which I have spoken. On the morning of the event, when the one who was outwardly jocose heard the sound of the thunder, he began at once to say silly things and, immediately on entering the church, was struck down by the lightning at which he laughed. The third man, named Robert and known in the world as "the Dove" because of his simple sincerity, was a youth just entering puberty. He was known for his thorough honesty, and he was so active and wise in the offices of the church and brotherhood that he served everyone almost every day. Moreover, he had a good knowledge of grammar. That morning in the very hour that brought his death, when as usual he went ahead of me, who was then arising, to sit in the cloister, he showed me that he was suffering from acute pains in his knees and the rest of his body. Immediately afterward he saw the disturbance in the heavens from which he soon died. See how before their destruction the hearts of two of them were puffed up; for these men, as we believe, in the judgment of God their future sentence was soon more severe. But for the other, humility preceded his glory,[8] for no one doubted that a high place in heaven would be his. Someone soon saw in a vision that these three were journeying together to St. Peter at Rome, two in a shadowy form that could hardly be seen, but the third, clad in white, with his usual good sense was hastening along in a lively fashion.

Some years afterward when we had forgotten these things and had become sluggish and careless, there came a third punishment; this was after I had left that church. One morning when there was stormy weather, they had gone in procession to the high altar to

[7]*Enarratio in psalmum CXLVIII*, ch. 11, ed. Eligius Dekkers and J. Fraipont, Corpus Christianorum, 40 (Turnhout, 1956), p. 2174.
[8]Cf. 2 Paralipomenon 32:25-26.

sing the litany—for they were afraid to remain in the choir where the first bolt had fallen—when suddenly a flame from heaven rushed down and, according to the testimony of those who saw it, striking to the very base of the altar, filled the air around it with a foul stench like that of brimstone. A monk in priest's orders was blinded, and two boys who were stretched out with their heads toward the pediment of the altar—one was a converted Jew, but faithful in heart—were caught up by this bolt without knowing it, carried some distance, and left with their feet toward the altar and their heads against the wall of the apse. The lightning entered the strongbox behind the altar, breaking it in places, and although the greatest part of the church's treasures was there, the only thing hurt was a chasuble, which was considered very costly. Here is the reason for these remarkable events.

This chasuble was sought expressly from the English king, a very lawless man and an enemy of the Church, called Rufus because he was red-haired, whom God slew on a hunting trip by the arrow of his own favorite.[9] Since he did not wish to drain his own treasury, he sent the monk who was engaged on this business to the abbot of Battle Abbey, ordering the abbot to give fifteen marks of silver to the monk.[10] When the abbot refused, the king had the monastery despoiled by force, and soon, against his will, the abbot redeemed the loot for fifteen marks. Through such unholy deceit that chasuble was bought, or rather through a series of unholy means. It was put together with no less deceit, so that in its acquisition, in its purchase, as in its manufacture, it was manifestly compounded of wickedness. After the lightning stroke, when the pieces were sent for examination, it proved to be worth less than half the price. The great deceit of the one who purchased it was then revealed by the actual composition of the chasuble. While the other vestments were uninjured, this one was thus rightly condemned, although the merchant may seem to have escaped a similar punishment.[11]

[9]William Rufus became king in 1087 and was shot by his companion, Walter Tirel, August 2, 1100.

[10]Battle Abbey was founded by William the Conqueror on the site of his victory over Harold near Hastings. A mark of silver is two-thirds of a pound.

[11]The story of this affair is related from the other side in *Chronicon monasterii de Bello* (London, 1846), pp. 44-46; Eng. trans. by Antony Lower,

Before that event, the following vision appeared to a monk who had an uneasy conscience. The image of the crucified Lord seemed to come down from the cross, blood dripping from His hands, side, and feet. Going through the middle of the choir, He was heard to say, "If you will not confess, you will die." When he awoke, the monk was in great fear, but before he confessed, he underwent this danger with all the rest. When he confessed, he fully proved the justice of the judgment. Because of the danger that had fallen on them, on every anniversary of the day this first happened there has been instituted forever a fast with almsgiving, and a daily mass to the blessed Mary, and besides this a mass for the Nativity of the Lord at the altar of St. Michael every Sunday. But now let us hasten on to other matters.

CHAPTER 24

In the year after the first disaster—in fact, four months later—a monk in priest's orders, formerly a secular chaplain of my mother, a man who was at that time outwardly religious, but then and afterward was hopelessly given up to monstrous vices from which he could be kept by no human care, began quickly to grow feeble. Brought close to an unexpected death in two days, he began to cast vicious glances in all directions. When he was asked by those who knew his real character what he saw, he replied, "The house is full of savage men." When they perceived that those whom he saw threatening him were devils, they began to urge him to make the sign of the cross and to call with confidence on the Blessed Mother of God. "I should have hope and confidence in her," said he, "if these barons did not press upon me." It is remarkable that he called them "barons," because its Greek etymology means "heavy";[1] and oh, how sorely heavy were those who had been unable by penitence or some sort of prayer to remove their

---

The Chronicle of Battel Abbey (London, 1851), pp. 48-51. The abbot of Battle at the time was Henry, who took office in 1096, and the monk of Fly was named Richard. The transaction with William probably occurred in the spring of 1097, and in any case between 1096 and 1100, while Guibert was still at Fly. After the time of Guibert's death, Richard and Abbot Eudes of Fly made a trip to Battle to apologize.

[1]In his *Etymologies* (IX, 4, 31), Isidore of Seville derives *barones* from Βαρμ́ς, meaning heavy.

burdens! At last they asked what was his greatest trouble. He replied that he felt as if an immense bar of wrought iron, red-hot from the forge, was burning through his throat and chest. Then, although the night was at its stillest, so that not even a breath of wind was heard, the shutters in the house began to be thrown back against the walls and to be shaken again and again as if by a crowd of people entering. While the others in the house slept, two monks watched beside him, and, knowing that such things had no good origin, they became anxious. Among the things he said were the words we have mentioned. He was a man addicted to many shameful acts, and consequently such a life was closed by such an end.

In the cemetery of that church, a burial was once being prepared for a dead monk, and the gravedigger could not remember whether he had made a grave before in that spot. He continued his digging and when he had gone farther down, he found the plank which is usually placed over a coffin.[2] When that was removed, he found the grave nearly empty except for a hood, commonly called a capuchin, with the head left inside it, and sandals stuffed with hay (which was formerly done at the time of burial to make them fit better on the feet) at the foot of the tomb, but nothing at all in between. When some people had seen this and had reported it to us, we expressed our wonder at the incomprehensible judgment of God, perceiving that these things occurred with such secret and subtle meaning. In this miracle, it is noteworthy that the head was left there but the body had been carried away from its place wherever God pleased.

I learned something similar to this from Archbishop Manasses, of pious memory, who died in the faith some years ago,[3] and in fuller detail from the monks of Saint-Remi in the city of Reims.[4] Artaud, an archbishop of this diocese, had been buried at the feet of St. Remi. A long time later he was disinterred because of the reconstruction of the buildings, and when his grave was opened,

[2]Cf. Louis Gougaud, *Anciennes coutumes claustrales* (Ligugé, 1930), p. 89.
[3]Considering Guibert's remarks about Manasses I (above, p. 59), this must be a reference to Manasses II of Reims, archbishop from 1096 to 1106. In his *Gesta Dei*, Guibert made use of letters sent to Manasses II by Anselm of Ribemont.
[4]This ancient and distinguished Benedictine abbey was the burial place of St. Remi, bishop of Reims, who died in 533.

absolutely nothing of his body was to be found there, and of his garments the only thing left was his chasuble, which showed no signs of decaying with the body, since it appeared quite unmarked.[5] Clearly, if his body had rotted away, the decay would have affected the chasuble. In our own times, we see the renewal of the judgments of God, cited by St. Gregory,[6] on the corpses of the wicked who are evidently buried improperly in holy ground.

In the Abbaye-aux-Dames at Caen, built by the English queen Matilda, wife of William the Conqueror, who became king after being count of Normandy, there was a nun who had fallen into some foul sins and could not by any admonition be induced to confess.[7] She then happened to die without changing her mind, saying nothing on her deathbed that would do her any good. One night when one of the sisters was sleeping in the cell where she had died, she saw in her sleep great fires burning in the fireplace of the house, and the dead nun was in the middle of it, not only burning but being beaten by two wicked spirits on either side with two hammers. As she gazed at the dreadful torments of that wretched woman, a spark seemed to dart into her eye from the stroke of a hammer. So it came about that she awoke from the burning pain of the spark that had settled in her eye. What happened here is that what she had seen in spirit she suffered in her body, and the real evidence of the hurt agreed with the truth of the vision.

CHAPTER 25

There was a certain monk of Fly called Otmund, who had given much to the monastery while still a clerk, and in the end entered it himself. After taking the habit, he regretted his good beginning and was extremely bitter about what he had done. Soon God

[5]Artaud was archbishop of Reims from 932-961. He may have been disinterred at the time of the building of the Romanesque abbey church, which was dedicated in 1049.

[6]Gregory the Great, *Dialogues,* Bk. IV, chs. 51-54.

[7]The church, also known as the abbey of the Trinity, was founded in 1060, at the same time that Duke William founded the Abbaye-aux–Hommes. The usage of the title of duke or count for the ruler of Normandy was not yet standardized in the eleventh century.

chastened him with bodily infirmity, however; he then learned and did what was more for his good, and now kept his holy profession through choice and not through compulsion. He was made custodian of the church, and since he was quicker to anger than was reasonable, one day he expelled from the church a poor man, who was importunately begging him for alms, more harshly than he ought. On the following night as he was going to open the doors to ring the bell for vespers, suddenly he met the Devil in the shape of the poor man whom he had harshly driven out the day before. Raising his stick, the Devil rushed at the monk as if to strike him. The monk had opened the doors in the screen that separates the clergy from the people and was going on to open the others through which the people enter, when suddenly, although the outer doors of the front of the church were barred, the man leaped out from the nave, threatening to strike him. Otmund retreated in alarm, thinking it was the man whom he had driven out the day before, but at last he recovered himself. Remembering that the exterior doors were closed, he finally realized that it was the Devil, who by this sign called attention to what he had done to the man.

In the wintertime when Otmund got up to answer the call of nature, being too lazy to put on the usual clothes, he clad himself only in his cowl and, staying there too long, caught a deadly chill. Not long after, being brought near death by the swelling of his limbs, he was in greater dread than he should have been of the very mention of death. Wailing continually with great anguish, he approached his last hour. Then after he took the sacrament, and by the grace of God retained it—for he vomited up all other food—he was laboring to set free his spirit. Meanwhile, in the first hour of the night, when the sacristan, a worthy man, had gone to bed, he suddenly heard in the nearby cemetery of the monks a countless host of devils gathering together. Although his mind was free to perceive all this, his speech and movement were paralyzed by the power of some spirit. The demons entered the church and, passing before the sacristan's bed, rushed on between the choir and the altar and made their ways to the dormitory where the sick man lay. Seeing this happen with his mind's eye, the sacristan prayed to God in spirit that he might be saved from them, knowing full well that this troop had assembled for the man's death. As soon as they reached the cell of the suffering man, the brothers in attendance on the dying monk beat the board in the customary fashion to call together the others.[1] While they were assembling, his quick dissolution took place. Now, I have related this not because I believed that he departed to the abode of the wicked but to remind all men to reflect with me that the prince of this world once came to the Son of God, against whom he had no claim.[2] And if he came to Him, how much more certain it is that the Devil in his rage summons his volatile passions against us, over whom he has an almost complete claim.

At that monastery, I saw a woman who in her outrageous anger with her little son, among other abuses which that foulmouthed person hurled against the innocent child, even cursed his baptism. Instantly seized by a devil, she began to rave madly and to do and say horrible things. After she had been brought to the church and shown to the brothers, and had been restored to her senses by prayers and exorcism she learned from her torment not to curse the Lord's sacraments.

I also saw there a girl possessed of a devil who was brought to the shrine of St. Germer the Confessor. After she had stayed there for some days, she was led by her parents to the altar. Sitting near it, she turned her head toward the choir and saw the young monks standing behind her, and said, "My God, what handsome young men, but there is one among them who ought never to have lived with them." When we heard that, we were astonished by what such a statement might mean. Shortly thereafter one of them fled, and after he had broken his vows, his wicked life was broken off during his flight.

CHAPTER 26

Since we have begun to deal with devils, we may add certain things we consider proper as a warning to avoid their pronouncements and the counsels of those who converse with them. For they

[1]Cf. p. 103, n. 2.
[2]Matthew 4; Mark 1:13; Luke 4.

admit no one to instruction in their magic except those whom they rob of the honor of all their Christianity by a horrible sacrilege.

In a certain famous monastery, a monk had been brought up from childhood and had attained some knowledge in letters. Directed by his abbot to live in an outlying cell of the abbey, while he was staying there he fell ill of a disease. Because of this, to his sorrow, he had occasion for talking with a Jew skilled in medicine. Gathering boldness from their intimacy, they began to reveal their secrets to one another. Being curious about the black arts and aware that the Jew understood magic, the monk pressed him hard. The Jew consented and promised to be his mediator with the Devil. They agreed upon the time and place for a meeting. At last he was brought by his intermediary into the presence of the Devil, and through the other he asked to have a share in the teaching. That abominable ruler said that it could by no means be done unless he denied his Christianity and offered sacrifice to him. The man asked what sacrifice. "That which is most desirable in a man." "What is that?" "You shall make a libation of your seed," said he. "When you have poured it out to me, you shall taste it first as a celebrant ought to do." What a crime! What a shameful act! And he of whom this was demanded was a priest! Thy ancient enemy did this, O Lord, to cast the dishonor of sacrilege on Thy priesthood and Thy Blessed Host! "Hold not Thy peace, and restrain not" Thy vengeance, O Lord![1] What shall I say? How shall I say it? The unhappy man did what was required of him, he whom Thou hadst abandoned, oh, would it had been in time! And so with that horrible libation he declared his renunciation of his faith. Let us give one instance of the magic which he learned by this accursed bargain.

He was in the habit of having intercourse with a certain nun from a well-known family. Now, he lived in a small cell with one monk as his companion. His companion had outside duties to perform, while he remained at home with leisure for his follies. One day he and the nun were sitting in the cell when his companion returned from his business, and when they saw him in the distance,

[1]Psalms 82:2.

there was no escape open to the woman, as her flight would bring her into the path of the returning monk. Seeing that the woman was in a fright, the novice sorcerer said, "Go to meet the man as he comes, looking neither to the right nor to the left, and fear nothing." The woman trusted him and went. He stood in the doorway and, with an incantation which he had learned, turned her into a monstrous dog. When she came near the returning monk, he said, "Ha! Where did such a big dog come from?" She passed him in great fear and knew from these words in what form she had escaped. When the monk finally came to the house, he asked where a dog of that immense size might have come from. "He belongs to that neighbor of ours," said he. "Have you not seen him before?" And so the other was silent, guessing the truth.

After living for a long time without God, in the end, thanks be to God, he was stricken with a severe illness, and against his will confessed what he had done. The matter was referred to the judgment of wise men and especially to Anselm, afterward archbishop of Canterbury, and at that time abbot of Bec. By his inflexible judgment, that most filthy profaner of the divine mysteries was cast out from administering them. Although he was placed under this proscription, nothing could clear his mind of the belief that he would soon be made a bishop. He had no doubt taken this hope from the demons, who are liars in all things and in this, too, since when he died a few years later, he was not only not a bishop but an unfrocked priest forever.

I will give another instance which had a similar beginning but a happier end. I knew personally a clerk from the district of Beauvais who lived by doing copying, for he had been brought to Fly to do this very work. Afterward, when talking with a sorcerer at the castle of Breteuil,[2] he was told something of this kind: "If it were made worth my while, I could teach you something by which you might get gifts of money every day without any human assistance." He asked what he must do for it. The sorcerer said that he must propitiate the citizen of the lower world; that is, the Devil. "With what victim?" he said. "With a cock," said the other; "but the egg from which it was hatched must have been laid by the hen on

[2]The castle of Breteuil, 17 miles north of Beauvais, was held by a family to which Guibert was related; see above, pp. 54-57.

Jove's day in the month of March.[3] After roasting the cock, take it in the beginning of the night, just cooked and with the spit still in it, and go with me to the nearest fishpond. But whatever you hear, see, or feel there, do not dare to call upon God or the Blessed Mary or any of the saints." "I will do so," said he. Then a marvellous thing happened. They came to the place at night, bringing with them a victim suitable for such a god. As the sorcerer called on the Devil by name and his wicked pupil held the cock, the Devil in a whirlwind suddenly stood by them and seized it. Then the man who had been taken there called upon St. Mary in his fright. When the Devil heard the name of that powerful Lady, he fled with the cock, but he was unable to carry it off, and the next day it was found by some fishermen on an island in the fishpond. O royal, sweet name, so dreaded in the wicked regions! The sorcerer, of course, was angry with the clerk for calling on so great a woman in such a matter. But the clerk was driven by repentance to Archdeacon Lisiard of Beauvais, my uncle, a man who was learned in every branch, wise, courtly, and well-known.[4] After confessing what he had done, he did penance, as Lisiard ordered, with fasting and prayer.

These instances of what I saw and heard in that monastery should be sufficient. And now, since I earlier discussed the nature of my election, in the beginning of the next book let us treat that other monastery to which, by the will of God, I was translated, its location, how it was founded, and what antiquities it had.

[3]That is, Thursday (French *jeudi* from Latin *Jovis dies*) in the month of Mars.

[4]Lisiard was one of the three archdeacons of Beauvais about 1100.

Book II

CHAPTER 1

The place is called Nogent. As a residence for monks it is new, but its use for worship by worldly society is very old. Even if this opinion were unsupported by any written tradition, it would be sufficiently proved by the discovery of a number of tombs which are clearly foreign and, we believe, not Christian in their arrangement. Around it and in the church itself, there has accumulated from ancient times a great quantity of tombs, and the countless number of corpses piled together is evidence of the great fame of a place so sought out. Since the graves are not arranged in the order usual with us, but many graves are placed around a central one in a circle like a chorus around its leader, and since in these graves are found certain vessels the reason for which is unknown in Christian times, we cannot help believing that they belonged to pagans or are very ancient Christian tombs made in the pagan fashion.[1] Moreover, in the same church there is a

[1]Casual excavations made in 1880 and 1884 provide confirmation for Guibert's acute archeological observation. The proprietor informed Abel Lefranc that the graves were arranged in a circle, and the report of the local schoolteacher, which gives the measurements of one of the stone tombs, describes them as Celtic. Unfortunately the destruction of World War I has prevented more

Eighteenth-century drawing of the abbey of Nogent-sous-Coucy, seen from the hill on which the castle of Coucy stands. The stream in the background is the Ailette. Reproduced with the permission of the Archives départementales de l'Aisne.

composition in verse. I should have no authority for resting a case on this, except that very recently I have seen the manifestation of certain things which greatly strengthen my belief in it. This history is related as follows by the text of this writing.[2]

Before the assumption into heaven of the Incarnate Word, it is said that a certain king lived among the English, who anciently were called Britons, and not English, which is a more recent name taken from some of the Saxons who later seized their land.[3] This king of Britain, an oceanic island, was sustained by a great wealth of poetry and philosophy, and besides, by a naturally good disposition, he was given to works of mercy. Since he behaved generously to the poor, not out of consideration for God, of whom he was ignorant, but impelled by the exceptionally humane feelings in which he abounded, it was fitting that to the working of a good heart there should be added the gift of a clearer understanding. Pondering very precise arguments, he began to examine what sure divinity he ought to expect in the many forms taken by the gods. He considered what unity in the government of heaven and earth there could possibly be among those who in their marriages, while they lasted, practiced such undoubted unchastity and brawling, and whose earthly dominion revealed cruel hatred of one another, sons against fathers and fathers against sons, going so far as usurpation, exile, and murder. Since the things related about almost all of them were worse than those told about mortals, he thought it complete madness to ascribe to them rule over the earth, much less over the heavens. Who would hand over the disposal of things on high to those whose miserable power could

---

scientific investigation. See Lefranc, "Traité des reliques," pp. 292-293, and the report of the teacher of Auffrique and Nogent for February 3, 1884, Aisne, arch. dép., coll. Piette, dossier de Coucy-le-Château.

[2]Guibert's statements here suggest that the verse composition *(literae metro compositae)* in the church was a document which gave the following story in full. His words could also apply to an inscription which supported the story without going into detail. In his history of Nogent, written in 1665, Dom Victor Cotron reported that there was a stone, originally in the wall before the middle of the altar, which appeared very old and which was inscribed with square-cut letters: "HIC EST ARA VIRGINIS PARITVRAE" (Here is the altar of a virgin who will bear a child); Aisne, arch. dép. H 325, fol. 5v; or Paris, Bibl. nat. ms. lat. 17775, fol. 12.

[3]Cf. Bede, *Ecclesiastical History*, Bk. I, ch. 15.

not control the smallest portions of the earth without disgraceful deeds?

While the man pondered these and similar things, shutting out of his heart the images of these vain gods, as he thought them, he turned to the worship of one incomprehensible Being, Who ought to be adored under no form, Who alone with single concord governs all things, Whose invisible things he had understood through the things that are made.[4] When in the course of these profitable reasonings he still hesitated in some doubt, God, Who declares better things to men of good will, sent a voice from heaven to urge the man to go to Jerusalem, where he would hear what ought to be believed about God, how the Son of God proceeded from God and lived among men for their sake, what He endured, what became of Him, and what vicars of His divine name He left behind as models. He was told that when he had gone there, the Mother and all the Apostles would explain these great mysteries to him.

After this trustworthy prophecy had been delivered to him, the British king put aside his possessions and his kingdom and determined to hasten to put what he had learned to the test. And so he left the country, prepared a fleet, crossed the channel, passed through the territory of many towns and cities, and came to the borders of the province of Laon. In the rural locality we previously called Nogent, he stopped for hospitality. Now, Nogent lies below a castle named Coucy, which was built recently because of foreign invasions, reportedly by the countryfolk of the region, very proud and wealthy people.[5] The castle, therefore, has no ancient history at all. The place of which we are speaking at that time lay near woods full of wild beasts for hunting and the river we mentioned above, the Ailette. This river is of greater value than size, for it surpasses other, more famous streams in its wealth of fish and it is not confined within the passage of its channel, like other rivers, but spreads out into wide, stagnant pools like fishponds. The slopes of the hills that rise on both sides are covered with vineyards, and since the soil is suitable for both Bacchus and Ceres, the land

[4]Cf. Romans 1:20.

[5]Guibert's assertion that the castle of Coucy which dominated his abbey was built by *rustices* minimizes the importance of the family of the powerful lords of Coucy.

is praised for producing all sorts of good crops, while its productive stream is admired for its pleasant meadows stretching far and wide.

According to an old tradition which is firmly established, there was in that place a very ancient temple, not dedicated to the name or honor of any existing god but consecrated to a woman not yet born who should bear One both God and man. It was therefore dedicated to the future Mother of God, yet to be born.[6] No wise man thinks this absurd, for since they worshipped an unknown god at Athens,[7] they were certainly aware that He would be born of a woman like their ordinary gods, whose mothers they name. And if a shrine was dedicated to One about to be born, His mother, like those of the others, was not likely to be deprived of a similar honor. What should be believed in the case of the One to be born could also happen to His mother. To this place the British prince happened to come, and, thankful that he had reached so pleasant a country, he decided to rest himself and his followers there, worn out as they were by the hardships of their journey, and he gave the pack animals a week to regain their strength in the neighboring pastures.

Going on from here and covering great distances by land and sea, at last he entered the walls of Jerusalem. Recently the Saviour had suffered, risen from the dead, and ascended into heaven, and the Holy Ghost had been given; he therefore found the city divided into opposing factions, some being angered at what had happened and others rejoicing. He had no difficulty in finding those whom he sought, for the great publicity given to the matter readily revealed those who were spreading the new law. At this point, they were not held in the usual imprisonment, and the fear of Jewish treason did not prevent them from bearing witness to the Lord, but he looked upon them as outstanding among the people, so that the evidence of their status fulfilled the authority of the Word. Why prolong the story? He found Peter and the eleven among multitudes of people, with a very large gathering of disciples attending them,

[6]The better-known story of the foundation of Chartres as a pagan temple dedicated to the Virgin does not appear before the fourteenth century; see *Dictionnaire d'histoire et de géographie ecclésiastique*, XII, 550.
[7]Acts 17:23.

along with Mary, that mirror of all our faith and glory, who was graciously present there and bore testimony to the Divine Incarnation. Addressing them and the Virgin Mother, the British king, who was soon to offer first fruits to God, thus set forth the reason for his journey.

"You see, Fathers and Lords, that I have come from the remotest ends of the earth to listen to you. Following in the right line of succession, I have till now ruled over the Britons. Although up to now I observed those customary rites which through the ages of their error they have regarded with veneration, I have recently abandoned those observances for the following reason. When I considered those whom the ages had honored by ascribing to them divine being, reasoning it out that they were the worst of mortals and that after their monstrous abominations they had paid the debt of nature, by reasonable conjectures I concluded that men who had lived poorly on earth, exalted above others by reputation alone, as gods could in no way have created the heavens and the earth and all the things therein which manifestly have waxed strong in this world from the mildness of the sky and weather and the abundance of the earth. After reason had destroyed their divinity, at last I reached the settled conviction that since they had finally been deprived of their divine authority, the unique creation and rule of one God could exist, and that as all things come from Him alone, so He, containing all things in Himself, holds the universe together, and that this ought to be believed. After my mind had become fixed upon one God, and I had scornfully rejected the temples and their idols forever, my heart seemed to be cleansed from the filth of idolatry, and the celestial purity of the unique true religion shone forth in it. Soon a voice from heaven ordered me to come here, where in the dispensation of God the Son, Who has recently suffered, I have been promised that you will deliver to me the truth of the only faith. By this Mother of the Light which was announced to me, whom I see present, and by your offices, I beseech you to instruct me in the mysteries of this new birth."

Hearing this, Peter and his rejoicing colleagues, along with Mary, who shed glory on that heavenly assembly, worshiped the greatness of God and the Son of Man, Who had just bestowed salvation at the world's center[8] and had not yet scattered abroad the interpreters of His grace, but now so suddenly poured out the declaration of His new bounty to the limits of its western parts. When the rule of faith had been delivered to the man and he had next been washed in the water of baptism, he received the name of Quilius. He was then confirmed by the schooling of these great teachers in the understanding of that sacrament which he had received. When he was about to leave them and return to his own country, he begged them with a faithful heart for the sacred pledges of relics; that is, some of the things which he had learned had touched the body of the Saviour. With pious devotion he asked for and took portions of the cords by which he knew the Lord had been fastened to the whipping post, of the scourges with which wicked hands had furrowed His blessed body, of the crown of thorns which had circled His holy head, of the very wood of the Cross on which He had hung, of that garment of the Mother of God in which it is said she had brought forth the Lord, and of the clothing of all the Apostles.

Treasuring these things in a small reliquary which he carried with him, he faced the difficulties of the return trip. After he had passed through the intervening regions, he came to that countryside where he had stayed to rest before. There he was suddenly seized by an unexpected illness, and when he had taken to his bed, it was revealed to him in a dream that in that place the end of his present life was at hand. He was also told that his body must be buried here, and that the relics which he had received from the holy Apostles at Jerusalem were to be buried under the same turf. On awakening, this warning of his death turned the man's thoughts from everything else to this one subject, and he busied himself with the last needs of his dead body in the hope of the glory soon to follow. And so he died there that day and surrendered without loss to Him Who gave it that which had been entrusted to him. There under the soil of the tomb where his body was put to rest, the coffer of relics found a place beside him. Long afterward, by God's care, the box was taken out and enclosed by some faithful persons in a costly shell of gold of ancient workmanship, its visible

[8]Medieval maps commonly showed Jerusalem at the center of the world; cf. Ezekiel 5:5.

evidence descending to this age to provide fresh testimony for the old story. These are said to have been the origins of the place.[9]

CHAPTER 2

Aided by the growing strength of the Christian law, this fine little church shone forth from ancient times under the name of the Mother of God. Situated below the stronghold of Coucy, which I have mentioned before, and closely surrounded by very rich manors of great antiquity, the church is revered and greatly aided by its neighbors. It was also said that while it was only a small place, it was frequently illumined by light from heaven and often honored by miracles; indeed, it was not injured, since among men it modestly maintained a lowly position. The lordship of the castle itself extended far and wide under extremely prosperous leaders, and its barons were endowed with great generosity and wealth. On the advice of the faithful and because of the fame of the place, whose renown for the most holy sanctity was everywhere in good odor, it was decided to transfer its care to monks in order to have there a full offering of the divine offices.[1] Since with such a beginning there was no expectation of greater growth—for the income provided for the monastery seemed little more than sufficient for the support of six monks—some unskilled and uninstructed people began to renovate the church by some sort of construction or enlargement. Since they had no director or instructor with any ingenuity in building, the work done was very jagged, and something more

[9]Guibert's remarkable story about King Quilius does not appear elsewhere in the abundant literature of the legendary kings of England, and even his name is unknown away from Nogent. That Guibert embellished the tale, if he did not invent it out of whole cloth, is suggested by the fact that all the relics Quilius was said to have brought to Nogent were noncorporeal, a matter of considerable importance to Guibert (see the Introduction, p. 29). By the thirteenth century, Quilius was considered a saint at Nogent; in 1228, the counterseal of the chapter of Nogent bore the inscription "SANCTVS QVILIVS REX." See Germain Demay, *Inventaire des sceaux de l'Artois et de la Picardie* (Paris, 1877), no. 1330.

[1]With this indirect account, Guibert veils what the abbey owed to the family of Aubry of Coucy, who established the monastery in 1059 in what had apparently been a secular church in his possession.

compact, useful, and suitable could have been made from the same material.

At a time when there was a greater abundance of wealth than now, the little monastery was growing from the gifts of the barons of the castle; the liberality of the lords in granting the small tithes was pre-eminent, and it was assisted by the generosity of others. Then, by the counsel of the brotherhood and their patrons, very fitting measures were taken to choose as head of that small abbey a very distinguished man, Henri, then abbot of Saint-Remi, who for some time had presided over the monastery of Homblières.[2] He was famous neither for his learning nor his birth, but he was so outstanding in the management of secular business that his concern for the proper care of the internal health of the monastery became equally outstanding. Presiding over these three monasteries, from the abundance of the two richer ones he supplied the needs of the third, which was beginning to thrive. Among the many acts of generosity which he directed toward that church, he put together a great banquet at his consecration, at which he was inaugurated by Hélinand, bishop of Laon, a man abounding in wealth and with the greatest solicitude for the founding of churches and their adornment.[3] He also enriched the church by many of his privileges, by grants of income and exemptions from dues, and by noteworthy gifts.

But since this abbot was elderly and blind, he devoted himself to the richer two abbeys which could more easily be governed by his own powers; the third, which could not be administered without a great deal of work, he decided to relinquish. Although he tried to induce the monks of the abbey to entrust it to a certain monk who was his nephew, he failed to get what he wanted. To his annoyance, the election fell upon a young man named Godfrey, a native of these parts and a monk of Mont-Saint-Quentin near Péronne.[4] When that very perceptive old man saw the votes of the

[2]Henri was abbot of Homblières before 1059 and became abbot of Saint-Remi of Reims about 1074. He died in 1095.

[3]Hélinand was bishop of Laon from 1052 to 1098. On him see below, pp. 146-147.

[4]The life of St. Godfrey of Amiens by Nicholas of Saint-Crépin (*Acta Sanctorum,* Nov., t. III, 905-944) relates a different picture and suggests that Guibert's account falls far short of doing justice to a man of principle and

electors going to another man, he abandoned the place, which he had maintained most worthily and with indulgent generosity, and legally transferred it to the man whom they had chosen.

After Godfrey's election and advancement to the charge of that monastery, as he behaved with great caution and the people and nobles alike had both the will and the power to enrich the churches, much wealth in lands and revenues subsequently poured into this one. He knew how to adapt himself to the manners of the outside world, being courteous and liberal in his dealings with others and in the management of secular affairs, to the mastery of which he devoted a great deal of effort. It is also true that at the time of which I spoke at the beginning of this book,[5] men with a generous desire to found monasteries bestowed on them lands and money, spending their substance on such works more freely and gladly than their sons today favor us with good words. Since in the nearby monasteries there was less zeal for religion than there should have been, while he and his monks seemed to be very active in such matters, so in a comparison of which church officers had excelled in displaying their discipline, the obedience of those under his rule had a favorable setting, like a tiny light standing out in the midst of the darkness.

He forbade any buying or selling of offices in that church; he ruled out purchase and followed his discretionary judgment alone, regarding both the fact and the name of filthy lucre as accursed. Since this man was considered shrewder than most of his fellow-abbots in legal business and was therefore better known in the

---

ability. Godfrey was born into a noble family near Soissons. At the age of five he entered the abbey of Mount-Saint-Quentin, where his godfather Godfrey was abbot, and there he became infirmarian, hospitaler, and bursar. His election as abbot of Nogent took place about 1085. In 1097, he was offered the abbey of Saint-Remi of Reims and answered that he did not wish "to spurn a poor bride for a richer woman." But in 1104 he was forced to accept his election as bishop of Amiens by the pressure of the Council of Troyes and King Philippe. At Amiens he accepted the demands of the burghers for a commune (see below, p. 200), thus winning the scorn of Guibert and making his life miserable. In November, 1114, he set out for La Chartreuse, intending to end his days there, but after a few months he was required by the Council of Soissons to return to his see. He died at Amiens on November 8, 1115.

[5] Above, pp. 62-63.

castles and cities, first there was talk of one of the richer abbacies for him, and later measures were taken to get him a bishopric. At that time, the bishopric of Amiens had been vacant for about two years,[6] and the abbot had declared himself the advocate of an archdeacon of that city, who was seeking the office with the support of a certain part of the clergy and people. Then his worldly shrewdness and the fact that he was a monk brought a demand for his own election while he was seeking it for another. With the authorization of Richard, formerly bishop of Albano and at that time papal legate in France, who had summoned a council at Troyes,[7] he was made bishop of Amiens and translated from Nogent.

Since he acted there with great glory and felicity and was held in such general esteem that even the prelates who ranked above him regarded him with special respect, and, to be brief, since he was everywhere venerated as the mirror of all religion, he thus suddenly attained either what he desired or what he feared, God knows which. Now, I have learned that an inheritance eagerly desired at the outset may prove no blessing in the end. Although his earlier career was clearly attended with the usual plaudits and for years his fame had been his herald, now, as it appears, whatever splendor had seemed to glow within the man burned low and was even extinguished. On the first day of his reception in the city, using an elevated place for a pulpit to address the people, he declared that in the same way he would aim for the heights, not wishing the words of the poet to be aptly applied to his failure:

The mountains labor—and bring forth an absurd little mouse.[8]

These words, true prophecy of what would follow, sank into the minds of all, and his reputation, beginning rapidly to decline without any check to its decay, began to render his promise worse and worse. But let us say no more of these things for the present, at I intend to come back to him later.[9]

[6]Bishop Gervin of Amiens died in 1102.
[7]Richard had been deposed as bishop of Albano in 1079 by Gregory VII, and in 1087 he became a schismatic and was excommunicated. In the same year, however, he was relieved of his sentence and sent to France as papal legate. He presided at the Council of Troyes in 1102 and died in 1113.
[8]Horace, *Art of Poetry,* l. 139.
[9]Below, pp. 200-207.

CHAPTER 3

To the place he left, which he had filled competently and properly, and where, if he wished to be content with his condition, he might have gone on living in the greatest happiness and independence, obligated to no one, it was my lot to be called, after an election as I said above.[1] Whether my election was against the will of God or with His approval, I do not know. This only I freely declare, that neither by solicitation nor with my knowledge nor through the seeking of my kinsfolk was the office procured for me. In this respect all went well. But considering the other side, that none of them knew me and I did not know any of them, the reader would understand if matters did not follow profitably or properly. I am not certain myself that, coming as a stranger to them and they to me, we might not have taken a dislike to one another for that very reason. Some people think so. This has happened elsewhere or could occur, but in no way can I affirm that it occurred in this instance. Now, no one can doubt that acquaintance with a man and familiarity commonly breed boldness, and boldness easily breaks out into rashness.[2] Certainly we usually show greater respect for those we know less, although when I entered that monastery, they did not at all hide their innermost feelings from me. By faithful confession they revealed their hearts and by revealing them became one with me to such a degree that I, who thought I had seen something of monks elsewhere, knew none to be compared with them in this respect.

Thou knowest, most merciful God, that I began this work not in the spirit of pride, but wishing to confess my wickedness, which I would plainly acknowledge specifically if I did not fear to corrupt the minds of many of my readers by my horrible acts. I confess my wickedness, I say, and much more rightly Thy mercy, which is determined not by my iniquity but by Thy grace within me. And if I happen to speak of anyone, I will set forth his character and what

[1]P. 100.

[2]"Familiarity breeds contempt" is a classical proverb which appeared in the collection of Publilius Syrus in the first century before Christ.

eventually happened in order to show Thy judgments. Thou knowest that in these homilies that are Thine and dedicated to Thee, I do not utter destructive and hateful words with pleasure, and that I have undertaken to tell the tale of my fortunes and misfortunes for what help it may be to others.

On the day of my installation, while the monks were preparing to meet me in procession, one monk with a good knowledge of Scripture and curious, I suppose, about my future, purposely opened the Gospels on the altar, meaning to take the first verse to meet the eye as an omen concerning me.[3] Now, the book had not been written in pages but in columns. In the middle of the third column, his eye fixed on the passage which ran as follows: "The light of thy body is thy eye."[4] And so he told the deacon, who was to carry the Gospels before me in the procession, that after I kissed the silver image on the cover, he should put his finger between the pages at the place which he had marked and suddenly open the volume before me, noting carefully where my look fell. He opened the book, on the outside of which I had according to custom pressed my lips, and while he was slyly observing where my glance would fall, I looked neither at the beginning nor the end of the page, but bent my eyes to that very verse. The monk who was the diviner of such things, and who saw that I had unwittingly done what he had intended, came to me some days later and told me both what he had done and that my action had been wonderfully in harmony with his. O God, who lightest the lamps of all that believe in Thee,[5] Thou knowest how Thou didst bestow on me the light of intention and how amid the troubles they laid on me, my will toward them is good. And although with respect to myself my activity—that is, my heart—is foul and wretched, yet Thou knowest how much my soul yearns for the well-being of those whom Thou didst put under me. The more I reflect on my evils, the more

[3]Guibert refers several times to this form of divination, which was widely practiced even thought it was often condemned. St. Augustine disapproved of "those who read fortunes from the pages of the Gospels" (Letter 55, ch. 20), a capitulary of Charlemagne of 789 condemns the practice, and Gratian declared that fortune-telling is prohibited to the faithful because of the danger of falling back into paganism (*Decretum*, C. 26 q.2 c.1).
[4]Luke 11:34; Matthew 5:15.
[5]Cf. Psalms 17:29.

I am cheered by their good works, if they have been pleasing. I know that I shall have freer access to the throne of Thy grace the more I have shown myself gracious to the endeavors of men of good will.

After being taken on by them and brought before the assembled chapter, I preached a sermon on the oracle of the prophet, and since it was the Sunday before Christmas, at the time when Isaiah is read,[6] I said: "Isaiah the prophet says what you have just heard: *A man shall take hold of his brother, one of the house of his father, saying: Thou hast a garment: be thou our ruler: and let this ruin be under thy hand. And he shall answer, saying: I am no healer and in my house there is no bread nor clothing: make me not ruler. For Jerusalem is ruined, and Judah is fallen.*[7] The *man* is one who is not effeminate in the face of the Devil. He *takes hold of his brother* when he unites himself to one born of God. He ought also to be *one of the house of his father,* because he who is taken for the office of a pastor ought not to be found ignorant of the mysteries of the house of God. He who does not know the sacraments of the church is unworthy of its administration, because 'a scribe instructed in the kingdom of heaven,'[8] 'faithful' in preserving its mysteries, 'wise' in expenditure cannot be ranked as a 'servant.'[9] And how shall he preside over the church, when he does not know the church? Therefore let him be *one of the house.*

"What is meant by *a garment* but the fine dress of outward works? And let one who *has a garment* be called as *ruler,* since it often happens that he is sought for rule who by his gait, word, and deed reveals that he is one who chastises. *Ruin* is said to be *under his hand,* because whatever is found among the ruled is discerned as coming into the reckoning of the ruler, as if he were to say, 'You seem to be fair to the eye, yet see by what merit you are preeminent within.' Knowing in particular that you must hold up the ruins of all, he therefore replies more cautiously. '*I am,*' he says, '*no healer* having the power to resist the growing ruin of disease for

6That is, it was December 18, 1104. On the reading of Isaiah see Dom Bruno Albers, *Consuetudines Monasticae,* II (Monte Cassino, 1905), 35.
7Isaiah 3:6-8, slightly altered.
8Matthew 13:52.
9Matthew 24:45.

so many. You are looking at the outer *clothing,* which is not *my house,* because the dress of the soul is not the same as that of the body.' In this way he acknowledges that he is *no healer,* for it is difficult to penetrate to the causes and effects of any vice or virtue by the keenness of the discernment. And this might be the result of his poverty, because there is not *in the house* the daily *bread* of Him Who is today sought from God,[10] the comfort of His divine refreshment which is poured in spiritually, or the strengthening of that love in the inner man, without which there is never good rule.

"And so he, to whom the spirit imbued with powers from on high supplies but little help, declines to be made *ruler.* For *Jerusalem is ruined;* that is, the experience of inner peace has perished. Also *and Judah is fallen;* that is, after the loss of internal tranquility, the confession of sin, which is the closing point of all evil, has broken down in utter despair, providing a good reason for refusing the office of pastor. For when the mind is disquieted by the appearance of vices, the attack on it is very foul, nor does the mind when evilly blinded by these vices forswear them by confession. When it has no strength to rule itself, it is rightly prevented by others, and more rightly by itself, from being the shepherd of other men."

In this way I spoke to them, now explaining, now using more extensive exhortation, and again adducing examples from Scripture to support the argument.[11]

CHAPTER 4

Since I have for some time said nothing about my mother, who was my sole personal possession among all the goods I had in the world, it is proper that I should briefly touch upon a good life's better end. She had surmounted a good many years, as she used to say herself, with the strength of her spirit unbroken, and there

[10]Luke 11:3.

[11]Guibert's sermon is typical of many directed at monks in quoting a passage of Scripture and then commenting on it phrase by phrase. Characteristically for him, Guibert here holds to the tropological level of interpretation; that is, he draws a moral significance of current application from the text. Much of what he says is highly conventional; for instance, peace is the standard etymology of Jerusalem and confession is the meaning St. Jerome gives for Judah.

was in her spirit no slacking of the love of prayer, although her body was becoming exhausted. Kept from sleep by the weakness of her lungs, with a mournful sound she nightly repeated the name of Lord Jesus a hundredfold. Consequently, at last overcome by disease, she took to her bed. At that time my brother and I were busy at Nogent; if I am not mistaken, this was two years before that return to Fly which I have mentioned above,[1] a very thoughtless act indeed, but one which by the power of Him Who uses our misfortunes for good, turned to a much happier issue than might have been believed, for God spared her weakness, so that a heart which loved God so well might not undeservedly be hurt by the sword of that ignominious return.

When she was at the point of death and my master sat weeping by her side, he said, "Behold, the sons of your master[2] are gone, and perhaps you will be grieved, and they will be even more grieved, if you should die in their absence." She gave him a reproachful look and said, "Even if they had remained as before within the neighboring cloister, God knows I should have wished neither them nor any other of my kin to be present at my death. There is one, however, whom I desire with all the strength of my soul; may that one alone be present!" Those were her words, and that night, at the hour when the sending of the angel Gabriel is sung and celebrated,[3] she departed to her greatly beloved and longed for Lady, about whom I have written before, to be received, we believe, with a glad welcome.

A few years before her death, she conceived a strong desire to take the sacred veil. I tried to dissuade her, putting forward as authority the passage where it is written, "Let no prelate attempt to veil widows,"[4] saying that her most chaste life would be sufficient without the external robes, and Anselm, abbot of Bec and afterward archbishop of Canterbury in England, that wonderful man with

[1]Guibert's memory apparently tricked him into thinking that he had already recounted an event which embarrassed him greatly. There is no earlier mention of a return to Fly, though Guibert does refer to it later (p. 168).
[2]Cf. Genesis 24:51.
[3]At the evening Angelus at sunset.
[4]This decretal of Pope Gelasius was included in both the *Decretum* of Burchard of Worms (VIII, 36) and that of Ivo of Chartres (VII, 55); cf. Gratian, *Decretum,* C. 20 q.1 c. 11.

whom I dealt earlier,[5] had also forbidden this to her in the past. She was the more stirred up, however, and by no reasoning could be driven from her resolve. So she prevailed, and during the ceremony, when she gave satisfactory reasons for this act in the presence of Jean, the abbot of that place,[6] whom she had raised as a boy, in the end she proved that in this matter she had been guided by God.

She said she had seen in a vision a Lady of great beauty and authority, having about her an abundance of ornaments, who offered to her a costly robe, as though entrusting it to her for safe-keeping, like a deposit, to be repaid at the proper time. On hearing this tale we all agreed without hesitation, the more because we knew her consecration was invited by signs from heaven. She faithfully guarded this holy veil to the best of her powers for almost three whole years, and on that day she carried it back to the Lady who had entrusted it to her and whose happy omen of Annunciation, which brought eternal bliss, she most joyously heard. To the prayers of all faithful people who read these words, I commend her who certainly never excluded any of the faithful from her own constant prayers. I have said these things of her as in the presence of God, with the true testimony of my heart, inventing nothing at all.

Since we have made a return trip to the church of Fly, it is right that we should stay a little while before retracing our footsteps to the sands of Laon.

CHAPTER 5

In the monastery of Fly, there was a monk who was a Jew by birth. When the beginning of the pilgrimage to Jerusalem began to resound through the Latin world, he was rescued from his superstition in this way. At Rouen on a certain day, the people who had undertaken to go on that expedition under the badge of the cross began to complain to one another, "After traversing great distances, we desire to attack the enemies of God in the East, although the Jews, of all races the worst foes of God, are before our eyes.

[5]Above, pp. 89–90.

[6]Jean was abbot from 1100 to March, 1107. He may have been the infant whom Guibert's mother raised at Saint-Germer (above, pp. 96-97).

That's doing our work backward."[1] Saying this and seizing their weapons, they herded the Jews into a certain place of worship,[2] rounding them up by either force or guile, and without distinction of sex or age put them to the sword. Those who accepted Christianity, however, escaped the impending slaughter. During this massacre a certain nobleman, seeing a little boy, compassionately rescued him and took him to his mother.

She was a lady of very high station, formerly the wife of the count of Eu.[3] Eu is the castle on which the abbey of Saint-Michel by the sea, known as Le Tréport, looks down.[4] This excellent woman received the child, asking him in a kindly way if he would like to come under Christian law. When he did not refuse, thinking that otherwise he would certainly be put to death like his people, whom he had seen slaughtered, they hastily made the necessary preparations for baptism and came to the font.[5] After the holy words had been said and the sacrament performed, when they came to the part where a candle is lighted and the melted wax is dropped on the water, a drop of it was seen to fall separately all by itself, taking the shape of a tiny cross on the water so exactly in its minute substance that no human hand could have made a similar

[1]This statement of motive is remarkably similar to that reported by the three Hebrew chroniclers of the First Crusade. In *A Social and Religious History of the Jews*, IV (2nd ed., New York,, 1957), 102, Salo Baron translates a conflation of their quotations in this way: "We are marching a great distance to seek our sanctuary and to take vengeance on the Muslims. Lo and behold, there live among us Jews whose forefathers slew him [Jesus] and crucified him for no cause. Let us revenge ourselves on them first, and eliminate them from among the nations, so that the name of Israel no longer be remembered, or else let them be like ourselves and believe in the son of [Mary]."

[2]From what follows, clearly a synagogue.

[3]Hélisende, daughter of Richard, the viscount of Avranches, was the second wife of Count Guillaume II of Eu, who was blinded and emasculated in 1096 for treason against William Rufus and probably died shortly thereafter. His son Guillaume, who figures in this story, was a younger brother of Count Henri I of Eu.

[4]The abbey of Saint-Michel of Le Tréport, now totally destroyed, was founded in 1059. It served as a citadel beside the sea from which one could see down the valley of the Bresle to Eu, about four miles away.

[5]According to Christian teaching, Jews were not to be converted by force. For a history of the prohibition against forceful conversion, see Solomon Grayzel, "The Papal Bull *Sicut Judeis*," in *Studies and Essays in Honor of Abraham A. Neuman* (Leiden, 1962), pp. 243-280.

one so small.[6] I was told this by the countess herself, who was so well-known and close to me that she always called me son, and by the priest, both solemnly protesting by God that the tale was true. I should have treated the incident less seriously had I not seen without any doubt the remarkable progress of the boy. The name of the countess was Hélisende. Her son, who rescued him from death and stood godfather to him, was named Guillaume. He gave this name to the boy.

When he was a little older, he was transferred from the study of Hebrew, which he had first been taught, to Latin, with which he soon became familiar. Since he feared that he might be recovered by his family and returned to his earlier condition, he entered him in the monastery of Fly.[7] In fact, they did try for some time to recover him, but they had no effect on him. Once he was assigned to the monastic discipline, he showed such love for the Christian life, drank in whatever divine learning he could acquire with such keeness of mind, endured all that was put on him by way of discipline with such calm, that the glory of the victory over his worthless nature and his recently disturbed character drew from all the greatest respect. He had assigned to him during his boyhood as a secret guard a teacher of grammar, a very religious man who considered that a knowledge of our law was necessary to one born to a new life already formed, and took pains in teaching him which were well rewarded. His naturally acute intellect was so sharpened daily that although many well-educated men flourished there, not one was thought to show greater distinction of understanding. Although many feel this way, he turns no one to envy or backbiting, since his behavior always appears cheerful and of special purity. To increase the strength of his unbroken faith, I sent him a little treatise which I had written about four years ago against the count of Soissons, a Judaizer and a heretic.[8] He was so delighted with this, I hear, that he matched my little work with a devout compilation

[6]On the lighting of the candle, see Honorius Augustodunensis in Migne, *Patrologia latina,* t. 172, 673.

[7]Guibert's vague use of pronouns here makes the text ambiguous as to whether it was Guillaume of Eu or the boy who feared the recovery.

[8]On his *Treatise on the Incarnation in Answer to the Jews,* see p. 237. Guibert comes back to the count of Soissons on p. 209.

of arguments for the faith.[9] Therefore the cross at his baptism seems to have been formed not by chance but by Providence, as a sign of the future religious faith of a man of Jewish origin, which in our days is unusual.

A priest of a very benign and simple nature, with his son who was also a cleric, gave himself up to the monastic life in the same place.[10] In taking after his father, the son proved himself in many ways still more outstanding, since his youth made him more robust and he had some learning. While the father was in the secular clergy, he had been charitable with his fortune to the poor. The Devil was not only envious of this good man but suffered greater pain because of his perfect renunciation of the world. One night when this novice was sleeping with the rest, suddenly there appeared to him in a dream a swarm of demons, carrying their scrips slung over their haunches in the manner of Scotsmen.[11] While he was approached by one of them who seemed a kind of chief and go-between for the others, the rest stayed behind. The leader said, "Give us charity." The monk replied, "I have nothing I can give you, or any man" (for indeed he was mindful of the fact that he was a monk). But the Scot said, "I never saw a charitable priest." Saying this, he furiously snatched up a stone and hurled it with great force. The monk's chest where the blow landed pained him so much that forty days of continuous suffering brought him almost to the point of death, as if the Scot had really struck him with a rock.

A long time later when the monk had recovered from this, or rather, when he saw that he was not about to get better, the Devil tracked him down one night after the others had retired when the monk was sitting alone answering the call of nature. Taking the guise of a monk with a cowled head and shuffling his feet on the

[9] On the known works of Guillaume of Fly, *ex Judaeo conversus,* see Jean Leclercq, "Prédicateurs bénédictins aux XIe et XIIe siècles," *Revue Mabillon,* XXXIII (1943), 59-65.

[10] That is, the abbey of Saint-Germer, the site of the remaining stories in this chapter.

[11] Guibert is the earliest author known to refer to the wearing of the sporran; see Archibald A. M. Duncan, "The Dress of the Scots," *Scottish Historical Review,* XXIX (1950), 210-212.

floor of the stalls as monks customarily do when requesting permission to make a call at night, he struck such terror into the man that, rushing from the place and moved by fear, the monk dashed against the door with a blow, striking the lintel overhead. So, by means of an injured forehead, the Devil once again caused ill to this man, whose soul he had desired to harm. Powerless against his spirit, he attacked his body.

Another man, who was by birth a noble of Beauvais and held land at Noyon as well, was advanced in years and worn out in body, having—what is deadly for such men—a wife with greater vigor in the office of the marriage bed. This man abandoned both his wife and the world, and professed himself a monk there. Persisting in almost unceasing tears and endless prayers, never absent from the hearing of God's word, he made himself respected by all of us. Since he was always eager to keep the rule strictly, when he heard at the chapter meeting that no one was allowed without good reason to enter the infirmary in which he was living, he carefully remembered the order that had been given. One morning as he lay half asleep with his eyes closed, suddenly two devils, who looked like members of that religious sect commonly called Deonandi,[12] sat down on the bench which stood near the bed. Awaking, the old man turned his eyes to the head of the bed and was surprised to see strange people there in a familiar fashion. One of those who sat there had his head uncovered, a short beard, and red tonsured hair; his feet were bare, as is usual with wandering monks of this type, and he had straw bunched between his toes, so that it looked as if he had recently been tramping on it. The other was so hidden behind the first that his features could not be made out, but he had a habit reaching to his ankles and on it a black hood.

Seeing these unknown persons in his presence, he accosted them in great anger: "Since you are laymen and strangers, how can you have the impudence to come at this hour into this place, where no cloistered monk would dare to come without strong reason?"

[12]Scholars have disputed the meaning of this word, which is otherwise unknown. From the context it appears to refer to a wandering sect, quite possibly heretical. The Chronicle of Vézelay refers to some dualist heretics called *Deonarii* who were rounded up in 1167. See Du Cange, *Glossarium*, s. v., Deonandi, Deonarii (ed. Henschel, t. II, 803).

The man replied: "I had heard, master, that there are religious men in this monastery, and I came to learn their religion. I beg you not to be angry."

"The monastic life and the rule are not learned here," said the monk, "but if you wish to be taught, go to those who are in the cloister. There you will find the force of training and the rudiments of holiness. Get away from here, since a place which is out of bounds for such lords as the monks is much more surely forbidden for you."

When the man was going to repeat what he had said and to stay all the same, the monk broke out at them with still more thundering words and compelled them to leave the building. After they had gone to the door, they halted on the threshold. Looking at the old man, the spokesman turned back and said:

"I would prefer you to turn me out of doors if you were clearly not willing to keep me with you. One of your people is guilty of theft, and if he dared to deny it, I would have challenged him to battle and thereby brought you much profit."

When he heard this, the old man chuckled and said, "Now we have certainly picked out the danger from your talk, for while telling me you came here for the sake of religion, you admit you are a fighter. Therefore for your lies you deserve neither to be heard nor to be kept here." Much annoyed that such people had been admitted into the house, the old man got up and went as far as the porch, and, finding some sick brothers who were staying there with him, he hotly rebuked them for allowing such strange men to enter. They were surprised at this and, believing him to be raving, declared they had seen no one. When he told them who the men were, how they had behaved, and what they had said, fixing the time as well, then he discovered from his own testimony and that of the rest that he had been deceived by devils. For some devils are intent on sport alone, while others have some cruel intention and are hurtful. We now give as illustrations two cases from outside the monastic community.

CHAPTER 6

At the castle of Chauny, there was a certain servant of the household of Guascelin, lord of this castle, whose duty it was to act as sentinel to guard the castle at night.[1] In the evening when it was growing dark, being afraid he would miss his supper, which was now due, and being on the other side of the river, he shouted out for a boat to be brought by someone on the far bank. And when no one paid any attention to him, flying into a rage the man said, "You devils, then, why don't you take me across?" At once a devil appeared, saying, "Come aboard, I will take you." Thereupon, to his misfortune, the unhappy man got aboard. Within an hour of taking him, the Devil brought him down in Italy in the outskirts of a city called Subtura,[2] and deposited him with such good will that he broke his hip. This city is about a day's journey on this side of Rome. While visiting the home of the Apostles, the man's lord had left the city the day before and stayed for the night at Subtura. He arose just before dawn, as is usual with travelers in winter, and, coming with his people to the fields outside the city, he heard someone groaning not far from the high road. They searched, and the man was found and recognized by his voice alone, since his voice was known to his lord. When they asked him how he had come there, he told them that he had been at Chauny in the evening, and how he had been carried away by the Devil and had fallen down there. The lord, more than a little surprised, took the man to the next city and paid money from his own purse to take care of his injury and his return. From what he suffered, this man learned and taught others to call on God and not the devils to do anything.

There was also a man at Saint-Médard who performed the same office in that abbey.[3] After passing part of the night over the tower gate on the side of the fishpond, springing rattles, singing out, and blowing on a horn, as watchmen do, at last he went down to

[1]Guascelin was the castellan of Chauny, which was under the control of the counts of Vermandois. Chauny is on the right bank of the Aisne.
[2]Possibly Subura, an ill-famed district of Rome in classical times.
[3]The abbey of Saint-Médard was founded at Soissons in the sixth century. It is on the right bank of the Aisne.

walk about on the edge of the water. As he stood there, the forms of three women appeared. One of them said in his hearing, "Let us enter into this man." Another replied, "He is poor. He could not feed us very well." Then the third said, "There is a clerk here called Hugues, gross and fat, with an abundance of everything. He would easily nourish us. It would be good to attack him."

After they vanished into thin air, the man recovered his senses and realized that they were the three better-known types of fever,[4] which with sneering nicety despised him as a thin man and made for one whose flesh and property could hardly be consumed. Without waiting for the morning, he went to the nearest monks he could find, and after telling them what he had seen and heard, he asked to be sent to the said Hugues to see his condition. He was sent to him and found Hugues in a high fever. From this it is conjectured that by the judgment of God such kinds of sickness are administered by devils. In the same way the woman in the Gospel, bent double for seventeen years, is said to have been bound by Satan.[5] Also the man who suffered from epilepsy—that is, the falling sickness—is said to have been dashed upon the ground by a foul spirit, to foam and gnash with his teeth and to lose his senses, and this condition, it is asserted, can only be cured by prayer and fasting.[6] Job also was assailed by the enmity of devils within and without; that is, in body and property.

Who can stop when he once begins a tale? Let me finally put in writing a fourth case which comes to mind. A certain clerk, who provided a fearful warning for our times, lived at Reims, a mediocre scholar but skilled in painting. Becoming afraid because of the many frivolities in which he had been engaged, he became a canon regular in the abbey of Toussaints at Châlons-sur-Marne.[7] After he had lived there for some time and daily lost some of his first fervor as the heat of his early emotion grew cold, he abandoned the rule

[4]Malarial fevers were for a long time easier to classify than to cure or prevent. When the cycle of attacks (caused by the life cycle of the parasite) was every 72 hours, the fever was called quartan. One which came every 48 hours was called tertian. A daily attack, resulting from a double infection, was called quotidian.

[5]Luke 13:11. Guibert gives 17 years instead of the 18 found in the Bible.

[6]Mark 9:17 and 28.

[7]This Augustinian abbey was founded by Bishop Roger II in 1042-47.

which he had accepted, returned to Reims, and married. After fathering several children, he was stricken with a disease sent by God for his correction. Yet before he was prostrated by this illness, he had the intention of following the expedition to Jerusalem, which at that time was on the lips of everyone.

After he had suffered from this illness for a long time and his discomfort grew worse, he returned to his senses. Addressing entreaties to Jean, the abbot of Saint-Nicaise at that time,[8] he begged him to come to him, promising to renounce the world and begging to be clothed in the holy habit. The abbot was clear-sighted and suspicious through experience of the man's lightness of character; he put him off by refusing to give him the habit which he desired, but he had the sick man carried into the heart of the monastery. Feeling his disorder becoming worse, he assailed the abbot with repeated complaints and induced him against his will to grant him the habit of a monk. Relieved at getting his wish, for a very brief space he seemed to be calmer than before. Then suddenly under some impulse from God, summoning the abbot, he said, "Order your monks to care for me diligently, father, for be assured that in a few days the manifest judgment of God is coming upon me. If perhaps you and your monks suffer great inconvenience on account of me, I beg you not to be troubled, knowing it will not be for long." Hearing this, the abbot ordered resolute and watchful men to be chosen to watch him. Soon swarms of devils rushed upon him from all quarters, tearing him and dragging him prostrate over the floor and striving with mad violence to pluck his holy habit from him, while he held on to the hood with his teeth and clasped his arms to prevent its being torn off. He was hard pressed by this dreadful misery mostly at night and uttered pitiful cries, but sometimes in the day when they left him, he was able to rest for a little while. Then he could be plainly questioned how it was going with him in that stormy business. At those times, he spoke often about the spirits of men whom he had known and whom those present suggested to him, as though he saw them quite clearly.

When a widowed woman, who feared for the peril of her husband's soul and prayed for him far too little, heard about this, she

[8]The ancient abbey of Saint-Nicaise was restored by Philippe I in 1066. Jean is known to have been abbot in 1093

asked him whether she might pray for her husband and if he knew how he was doing. And he said, "Why not? Pray confidently for him; for a little while ago he was here." After being delivered up to these torments for many days, at last he was restored to perfect peace. Although at times there seemed to be a pause in his sufferings, yet soon swarms of demons seemed to burst forth from the walls, the ground, and every place, and to rush on him to tear him to pieces. At last when the evil spirits were gone and when the mercy of God's judgment had been granted to him, he called for the abbot and spoke to him in this way: "See, lord, God repays me for my sins. You may be sure, therefore, that after this trial my end will quickly follow. Grant me such absolution for my wrongdoing as you can and anoint me with the sacred oil to crown its remission." The abbot did this quickly and with devotion. The man received it lovingly and gratefully, and, having by punishment in this world wiped away all stain of sin, he passed free and joyful through death and entered into life.

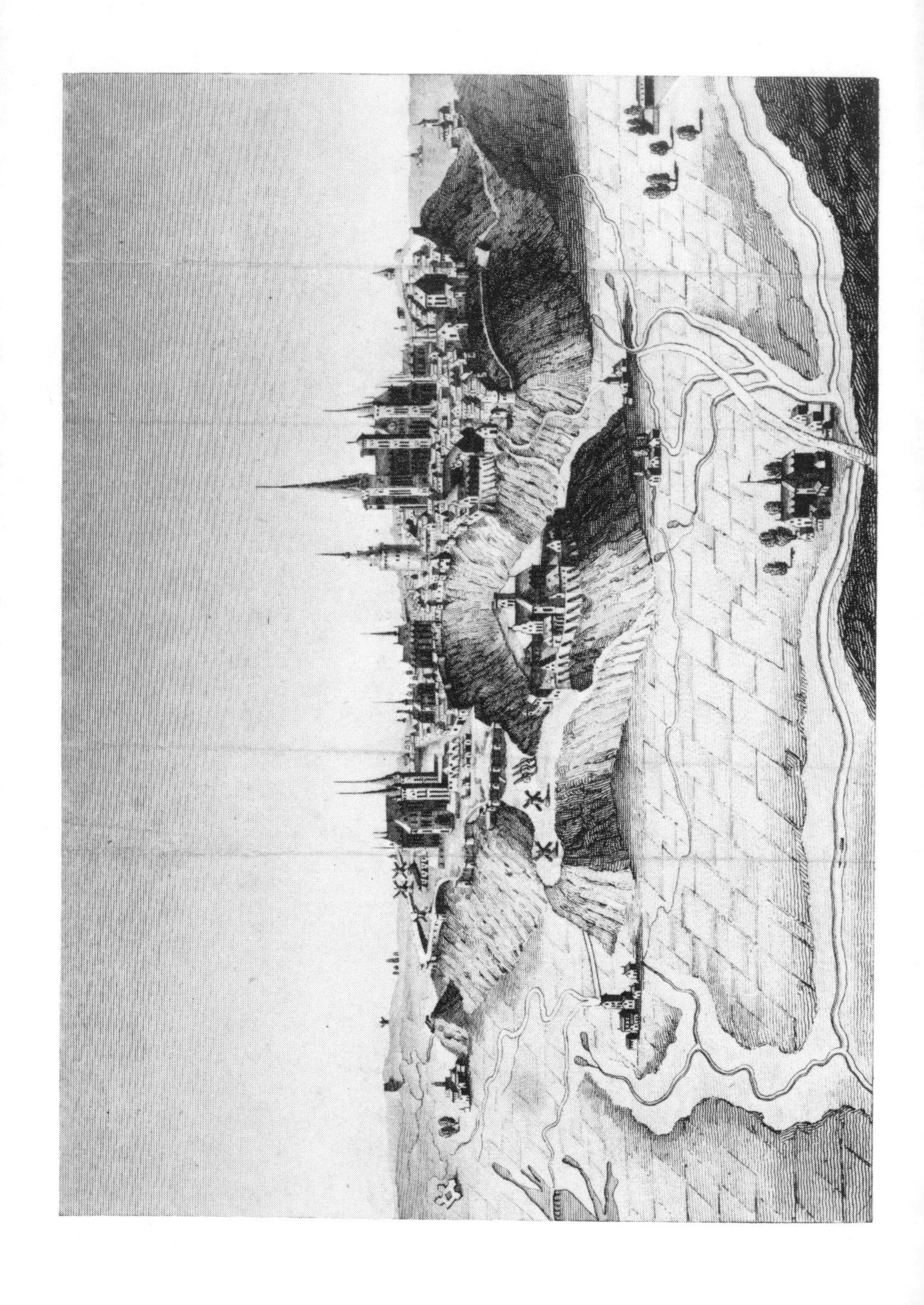

Book III

CHAPTER 1

As I promised to tell the story of the people of Laon, or rather to present their tragedy on the stage,[1] I must first explain that in my opinion the origin of all the trouble came from the errors of the bishops of Laon. Although its existence goes a very long way back, the record of Ascelin, also known as Adalbéron, ought to be woven into this work.[2] We find that he was a native of Lorraine, wealthy in goods and lands, who sold out everything and took huge sums of money to the see over which he presided. He adorned his church with excellent furnishings and greatly increased the prosperity of the clergy and the bishopric, but he defiled all those benefits by his most extraordinary wickedness. For what could be

[1]The rhetoric is classical; tragedies were not staged in Guibert's day. His intention was announced on p. 134.

[2]Adalbéron was bishop of Laon from 977 to 1030 or later. His betrayal of Charles of Lorraine in order to advance the interests of Hugh Capet was recorded by the tenth-century monk Richer. On his career, including his benefactions to the church of Laon, see Robert T. Coolidge, "Adalbero, Bishop of Laon," *Studies in Medieval and Renaissance History*, II (1965), 1-114.

Early seventeenth-century drawing of Laon, seen from the southwest. The tallest building is the Gothic cathedral. The abbey of Saint-Jean is the cloister within the walls of the city between the cathedral and the viewer. The abbey of Saint-Vincent is on the opposite spur of the mountain of Laon. Reproduced from the frontispiece of Jacques Devisme, *Histoire de la ville de Laon* (Laon, 1822).

more wicked or a greater disgrace to him that his betrayal of his lord the king, an innocent boy, to whom he had taken an oath of fealty, and his diversion of the succession of the line of Charlemagne to another family? He committed this crime on Maundy Thursday, imitating Judas.[3] In overthrowing the reigning monarch and his descendants, he certainly did not foresee that the change would later be useful, but looked to the fulfillment of his own wicked will at the expense of the innocent. Nevertheless, in spite of this, worldly prosperity attended the city and the city's bishop, God putting off the day of punishment.

CHAPTER 2

A later bishop, Hélinand, was a man of quite a poor family and humble origin, with scanty education and of little worth as a person.[1] Through his acquaintance with Gautier, the old count of Pontoise, from whose county he came, he won the favor of Edward, the king of England, whose wife had established some sort of connection with that count, and became the king's chaplain.[2] Because he had mastered French courtly manners, the English king often made him his envoy to Henri, the French king. Since Henri was very avaricious and given to selling bishoprics, Hélinand obtained from him, by lavish bribes in the form of presents, a promise that on the death of any French bishop he should succeed to the episcopal insignia. In his position as chaplain to the king and queen, he had accumulated huge mountains of money, since England abounded in unlimited wealth at that time. Basking in favor because of this bribery, he gained the ear of King Henri. And so it came about. After he was installed at Laon, as he knew he would have no influence through respect for his family or his knowledge of

[3]Guibert here differs from Richer and Adhémar of Chabannes, who place the treason on the evening before Palm Sunday (March 28, 991). He may have changed the record here to fit his own later story; see below, p. 171.

[1]Hélinand did not follow Adalbéron directly, but was bishop from 1052 to 1098.

[2]Gautier III of Mantes was the son of Goda, the sister of Edward the Confessor, and Dreux, count of the Vexin; it was through this connection that Hélinand of Pontoise came to the English court. Perhaps Guibert confused Goda and Queen Edith, the daughter of Earl Godwin.

letters, he placed his hopes on his wealth, of which he had stored up a great amount and which he had learned to distribute with great prudence, and on his liberality.

And so he turned to the establishment and building of churches, and while seeming to do much for God's glory, he gave indisputable proof that he was only seeking popularity and the spread of his own fame by those good works. By such artfulness, he got possession of the archbishopric of Reims, which he obtained after its great revenues had been squandered for two years by King Philippe, a man most mercenary in what belonged to God, and he then received word from the lord pope that anyone having one wife could under no circumstances take another.[3] To someone who asked directly why he was striving for this, he said that if he could also become pope he would certainly not conceal it.

Whatever he was personally with respect to self-seeking or any other human passions, all honor is certainly due to him for having splendidly guarded the liberty of the church and for his advancement through his generous bounty both of the see and of the churches attached to it.[4] And it was right that as wealth flowed in to him from outside, he should expend it on the embellishment of the houses of his demesne.

CHAPTER 3

After his end came Enguerrand, who surpassed the aforesaid bishop both in nobility and learning, but in guarding the rights of the church granted to him he was much worse.[1] With entreaties and gifts, Hélinand had extracted from King Philippe certain revenues

[3]When the archbishopric of Reims fell vacant in 1067, the revenues went to King Philippe. Hélinand's claim was disputed by Manasses I of Reims, who was supported by the reform party at Rome and was installed as archbishop in 1070. The statement of the pope, Alexander II, asserts that a bishop is married to his see and cannot be translated without papal permission. See John R. Williams, "Archbishop Manasses I of Rheims and Pope Gregory VII," *American Historical Review*, LIV (1949), 805-807.

[4]In 1089, Hélinand granted to the monastery of Nogent the control of three neighboring churches; *Gallia Christiana*, IX, 525.

[1]Enguerrand of Coucy became bishop of Laon in late 1098 or early 1099, and died in 1104.

which had earlier been seized from the see by royal force, and the return had been confirmed by the king's charter and the bishop's seal. To his own ruination, Enguerrand gave everything back to the king at his accession, and during the rule of three succeeding bishops this income has been lost to the church and perhaps will be forever.[2] In my opinion, in this way he involved in this simony all succeeding bishops who take up the office with such fear of the king as to shrink from demanding restitution of that which he damnably gave for being made bishop. Bereft of all love of God himself, he made a mockery of thrift and the religious rule, indulging in foolish prating and wanton talk, worse than any common soldier or entertainer. In his day the reasons for the destruction of that city and its churches and the whole province began to emerge, with issues far from happy.

A man with the same given name, Enguerrand of Boves, who was closely related to him, was very generous, bountiful, and courteous, treating the churches with very great respect and munificence, at least those where he knew religion was observed, but, on the other hand, he was so abandoned in his love of women that he kept all sorts around him, both the proper kind and mercenaries, and hardly did anything except at the dictation of their wantonness.[3] Since he was most unlucky in his matrimonial fortunes, he began to stray among other men's wives and secretly set out to have the wife of his kinsman, Count Godfrey of Namur. The woman whom he had seduced in secret he then united to himself openly in marriage.[4] This union, condemned by many anathemas and declared accursed

[2]Philippe's charter, issued in 1071, is printed in Maurice Prou, *Recueil des actes de Philippe Ier* (Paris, 1908), pp. 160-163. Louis VI restored these rights to the bishopric of Laon in 1121; see Achille Luchaire, *Institutions monarchiques de la France* (2nd ed., Paris, 1891), II, 335-336.

[3]Enguerrand of Boves was a first cousin of Bishop Enguerrand, since both were grandsons of Aubry of Coucy. He became count of Amiens in 1085 and lord of Coucy in 1086, and by his first marriage he was lord of Marle. He died in 1116. As Guibert says, he made numerous donations to local churches, and he had the charter of Nogent confirmed in 1095. He divorced Adèle of Roucy, the mother of Thomas of Marle, on charges of adultery, leading Guibert to say throughout this work that Thomas was Enguerrand's "reputed" son.

[4]Throughout his book, Guibert never refers to Enguerrand's wife Sybille by her given name.

by the protests of councils,[5] they might both have readily renounced through the pressure of shame had not Enguerrand's kinship and the craft of the woman's flatteries softened the bishop. This weakness so encouraged their adulterous embraces that it gave secret absolution to what had been forbidden to all and publicly excommunicated. Oh, shame! Surely those to whom he falsely gave assurance of absolution never dared to consider themselves absolved.

Meanwhile, since "out of the root of the serpent comes forth a basilisk"[6]—that is, when evils are nourished they burst out into something worse—how shall anyone tell of the slaughter with which Godfrey, robbed of his wife, raged against the county of Porcien? The woman in question was the daughter of Roger, count of Porcien, and his youngest child. Setting aside the sons and daughters begotten of a wife of much nobler birth, and excluding his firstborn heirs on the demand of their stepmother, the count had married this daughter of a mother of less noble birth to a Lorrainer, Count Godfrey of Namur, granting his county as dowry.[7] While her husband was engaged with certain of his enemies in Lorraine, his wife, by his orders, stayed at the castle of Tournes in Porcien.[8] Would she have kept herself in check if he had paid her the marriage debt as often as she desired? This alone can be said with certainty, that she would never have fallen into such manifest and monstrous shame had there not been a gradual descent through hidden acts of wickedness, especially as she had come to her husband already pregnant by intercourse with another. The notoriety of her past lasciviousness was such with all who knew her that we are ashamed to relate or even to remember it.

Godfrey was a young man who was handsome in every feature,

[5]There is no other evidence that this particular marriage was condemned by a church council. Guibert probably means that adulterous marriages had been often condemned in general. For texts see Gratian, *Decretum*, C. 31, q.1.

[6]Isaiah 14:29.

[7]Guibert's contemporary, the author of the history of the monastery of Saint-Hubert-en-Ardennes, supplies quite a different motivation for Roger's action. According to this account, Roger gave his daughter in marriage to Godfrey of Namur and sold his county in 1087 only after he had been imprisoned and deposed. See *Monumenta Germaniae historica, Scriptores*, VIII, 601; cf. Gaston Robert, *Documents relatifs au comté de Porcien* (Monaco-Paris, 1935), p. vii.

[8]The castle of Tournes is in the Ardennes near Renwez.

but Enguerrand to whom she went was advanced in years. Such a mad war began to rage between the two that all of Enguerrand's followers captured by the Lorrainer were either hanged on the gallows or had their eyes put out or their feet cut off, as is plainly apparent today to anyone visiting the county of Porcien. I have heard for certain from someone who was present at such an execution that about twelve men taken in this war were hanged from the gallows in one day. Some of the foremost men in Porcien were go-betweens and principals in this desertion, and on account of it they have become infamous in life and death. Thus Venus, who did not conceive from the fires of Vulcan, passed on to Mars; the heat of lust, that is, boils over into cruelty. Who can tell of the looting and the burning that broke out on both sides and the other things that such a storm usually brings forth? They were so monstrous that they strike dumb those who would relate them.

And the lord bishop in his madness gave absolution to that devilish union.

Much that might be told of the behavior of the bishop would be better left unsaid, most notably that by no realization of his sin did he show his penitence before God. At last he was attacked by illness and yet was no less attached to his folly because of that illness. He fell into a stupor and was so suddenly wrapped in the shadow of death that he was unable to speak rationally. Confession, anointing, and the sacrament were forced upon him by the care of others and not by his request. When his tongue and eyes had become almost useless in death, that other Enguerrand, whom he had bound to him by his wicked absolution, appeared, although the clergy had shut him out of the house as if he were excommunicated so that they could proceed with the anointment. Addressing the bishop with tears, he said, "Lord bishop, see, it's me, Enguerrand, your kinsman." Although he had not been conscious enough to ask to be confessed or anointed or to take the sacrament, he threw his arm around the neck of this man and drew him forward to kiss him. Everyone was scandalized at this, and afterward nothing came from his lips but the ravings of delirium until his last breath. The very woman for whose love he had done that often told about this publicly to show that the evil which he had done in his lifetime lay on him like a stone of wickedness. See, thus "the heavens reveal the iniquities" of some, so that "the earth rises up against them,"[9] and they displease those very persons whom they desire to gratify by foul means.

CHAPTER 4

After he had died in this manner and the bishopric had been vacant for two years, at last we met together to choose a successor.[1] Among those present was the same Enguerrand, who by his appeal to the king had obtained the confirmation of the previous bishop when the king had sworn not to accept him in the episcopal office because of his frivolities. It was clear that he was making every effort to see that the man who was elected bishop would be obligated to him. The king and the clergy most strongly favored one candidate, who as a consequence of the favor would be less likely to dare to oppose the king's union.[2] Thus, to the ruin of the city and the detriment of the whole province, they chose a certain Gaudry, chancellor of the king of England, who by report was rich in silver and gold.[3]

Before this election the two archdeacons of the church, Gautier and Ebal, had been elevated to the chair by contending parties of supporters. They were unseated by the decision of the Apostolic See. For Gautier had always been more of a soldier than a clerk; the other was more than averagely incontinent with women. When these two had been rejected, a third bright light of the church who wished to thrust himself upon them approached the court and, under color

[9]Job 20:27, slightly altered.

[1]The see was vacant from 1104 to 1106. Not until the Fourth Lateran Council in 1215 was the election of a bishop restricted to the cathedral chapter. Guibert was present as one of the abbots of the diocese. The role in episcopal elections of eminent laymen like Enguerrand of Coucy was vigorously debated in the early twelfth century; St. Norbert, who had lived in the diocese of Laon, defended their participation. See Robert L. Benson, *The Bishop-Elect* (Princeton, 1968), pp. 263-267.

[2]Contrary to his promise to Pope Paschal II, King Philippe was still living with Bertrada of Montfort.

[3]Gaudry became the chancellor of Henry I in 1102. According to Ordericus Vitalis, *Historia ecclesiastica,* XI, 20, ed. August Le Prévost (Paris, 1838-55), IV, 230, he took Duke Robert of Normandy prisoner at the battle of Tinchebrai on September 28, 1106, and for this reason was rewarded by Henry with the bishopric of Laon.

of wishing to plead for another, he drew the recommendations of the priesthood upon himself. Why do I go on? He promised to give the king great presents. Swollen with expectations, he embraced the hope and promise of wealth, but not wealth itself. Returning home, he was expecting his installation by the royal deputies on the following Sunday, when suddenly God (Who places deceits before such people, Who casts them down when they are lifted up)[4] struck the proud man with a deadly disease, and his corpse was placed in the church on the day when he thought he would receive his installation from the clergy and people. After he had been placed there, I have been told, wind soon broke from his body and a great cloud of evil stench pervaded the place as far as the middle of the choir. But let me return to the point where I digressed.

After the clergy in a vain hope of profit had chosen Gaudry, by the efforts of Enguerrand in the first place and with the aid of the rest to their own harm, he was sought, contrary to canon law, from the English king at his court at Rouen.[5] He was by no means doubtful of this election, although he was on the rolls of no church and had been admitted to no holy orders except those of a clerk, but he used his influence to be made a subdeacon on the spot and to be admitted as a canon in the church of Rouen, since up to this time he had lived nothing but the life of a soldier. When everyone had approved his accession, the only dissent to his election came from Master Anselm, who in the liberal arts and in serenity of character was the light of all France, or rather of the whole Latin world.[6] He was aware of his character from well-established testi-

[4]Psalms 72:18.

[5]Henry was in Normandy from July, 1106, to April, 1107; on canon law see below, p. 154, n. 12.

[6]Master Anselm was dean and chancellor of the cathedral of Laon, and about 1116 he became archdeacon, replacing the murdered Gautier. He died in 1117. A distinguished theologian and a leading Biblical commentator, he was probably the compiler of at least part of the *Glossa ordinaria* of the Bible. He and his brother Raoul conducted a famous school at Laon (which Guibert does not mention at all). Among his pupils were Guillaume de Champeaux and Gilbert de la Porrée. Abelard came to Laon to study with Anselm in 1113 or a little after, but quickly came into conflict with him. On his place in the world of scholars see Beryl Smalley, *The Study of the Bible in the Middle Ages* (2nd ed., Oxford, 1952), pp. 49-51.

mony, whereas we were unwillingly supporting a stranger. There were some of us, it is true, who did not approve of him, but wrongly afraid of others who outranked us, we followed the lead of the powerful.

After being received with a great show of empty pomp and coming into the city, the bishop-elect soon asked us to go with him to Rome. Paying our expenses, he induced Adalbéron, the abbot of Saint-Vincent, a native of Soissons, and a well-educated man; the abbot of Ribemont, also an educated person; and me, who was junior to both in learning and age, to go with him.[7] After setting out and arriving at Langres, we were informed that the lord pope Paschal had just before left Rome and was approaching the borders of that diocese.[8] We stayed in that town eight days.

When the lord pope had come to Dijon, the clergy of Laon, a great number of whom the bishop-elect had brought with him, went out to meet the pope and plead the cause of their candidate before him in the castle where he was staying. With many to tell him, the pope was soon acquainted with the facts and promised to act in accordance with the wishes of his petitioners. Their plea was that his election was within the law if exception were made for some provisions, which Anselm had brought to the attention of the pope. But members of the curia, specifically the pope's intimates, discovering how wealthy the man was, made themselves agreeable to him and flattered him. For it is the way of the world to become pleasant on the mention of gold.

After the pope had been received in the city of Langres, the next day he dealt with our case. When I had read before him the report on the election in which more than enough was said about the life and character of the bishop-elect, the pope summoned us abbots who were present and certain priests of the cathedral who

[7]Adalbéron became abbot of Saint-Vincent of Laon before 1081 and died in 1120; according to another source, he was a native of Switzerland. The abbey of Ribemont (or Saint-Nicolas-des-Prés) was about 20 miles north of Laon. The abbot at this time was named Mainard.

[8]In early 1107, Pope Paschal, embroiled with Henry V of Germany over the problem of investiture, set out to try to reach an accord wiith the king of France. He had spent Christmas at Cluny, was at Beaune on February 12th, reached Dijon on the 16th, and was at Langres on the 24th. Paschal had not, in fact, recently left Rome, but had spent the fall in northern Italy.

had come with him and began to address us, taking for his subject the report of the election brought to him. The assembly was full of very distinguished persons, Italian bishops and our own, besides cardinals and other very learned men. The pope then first asked why we had chosen a stranger.[9] As none of the priests made any reply to that (for they scarcely knew the rudiments of Latin), he turned to the abbots.

Now, I was sitting between the other two abbots. They both remained silent when addressed, but from either side began to urge me to speak, and I, abashed because of my immaturity[10] and afraid to be branded with rashness in a place and matter of such consequence, was so awed that I hesitated to open my mouth. The question was not being debated in the mother tongue but in the language of the learned. Blushing and embarrassed, I said what I thought fitting in reply to his question. In careful phrases I expressed myself with moderate warmth and not deviating very far from the truth, that we did not have an intimate personal knowledge of the man, but had accepted as true the testimony of others who had spoken of him with good will. And when he had attempted to weaken that statement by adducing the testimony of the Gospel, "He that saw it has given testimony,"[11] and had raised the objection, but not in very plain terms, that he had been elected from the king's court, I soon put aside useless evasion and admitted that I could not refute his words.[12] With that he was much pleased. He was less learned than he should have been in his office. Then when I saw that my indirect defense in reply to his first question carried little weight, although I had much pleased him by it, I passed on to the pressing need of the church and replied briefly to the objection that the man's personal qualities were not suitable for the bishopric.

[9]Canon law warned against choosing as bishop an unknown person from outside the diocese; see Gratian, *Decretum*, D. 61, c. 12.

[10]Although he was over 40 at the time, Guibert refers to his *iuventus*. The word does not carry the modern connotation of "youth"; St. Augustine called himself a *iuvenis* at age 45. See Joseph de Ghellinck, "Iuventus, gravitas, senectus," *Studia medievalia in honorem Raymundi Josephi Martin* (Bruges, 1949), p. 41.

[11]John 19:35.

[12]Several canons oppose making clerics out of courtiers or seeking a candidate from a court; see Ivo, *Decretum*, VI, 95 and 349 (Gratian, *Decretum*, D. 51, cc. 2-3).

Finally, he asked what orders he had, and I replied that he was a subdeacon.[13] Then he inquired in what church he had served. On this point I hesitated, fearing to lie, but my fellow-abbots suggested to me that it was in the church of Rouen. To this, however, I added truthfully that it was recently. Lastly, he asked whether he was of legitimate birth; he had clearly been told he was a bastard.[14] On that head, as I was firmer than on other points and especially since I spoke without equivocation, the pope said, "Do you bring proof of this?" I said to him, "On the other points I am silent, but on this I confidently affirm that he is neither a bastard nor illegitimate." This objection the lord pope withdrew in the fashion we have noted. But the reason he raised these points one after the other was not to prevent his appointment, but because Master Anselm, who had made all these charges against him, was present, so that what he had said privately he might have the opportunity to bring up before the man's face.

But the Master, having seen more deeply into the solicitation of the curia (I do not say of the lord pope), thought it a difficult matter to wrest the club of Hercules from his hand.[15] Seeing the lords arguing against each other, that teacher declined to struggle with the lord pope and, if I may dare to say so in jest, with me. And so the debate fell to the ground, the bishop-elect was brought forward, and the pope granted permission for his consecration. After the meeting had broken up and the pope had gone, a group of cardinals then approached me with great warmth and said to me, "Your speech gave us much pleasure." Which pleasure, Thou knowest, my Lord God, arose not so much from my eloquence as from the very good hope they had of the money with which the bishop-elect had come stuffed. Both I and my fellow-abbot, Adalbéron of Saint-Vincent, were each of us carrying twenty pounds of that money, with which perhaps the wide chasm of their expectations was filled, and for that reason they were glad to back him and his backers.

[13]A canon pronounced by Urban II permitted exceptionally well qualified subdeacons to be elected bishops; see Ivo, *Decretum*, V, 72 (Gratian, *Decretum*, D. 60, c. 4).

[14]The Gregorian reformers made illegitimate birth a bar to entering orders; see *Dictionnaire de droit canonique* (Paris, 1924-65), II, 253-255.

[15]A common classical allusion, used by Suetonius, Macrobius, Cassiodorus, and Isidore.

Lastly, when they were gone, the papal chamberlain, Pierre, a monk of Cluny, who had made the acquaintance of the bishop-elect at Rouen when we were seeking him from the king of England, secretly accosted me with these words: "Since the lord pope has accepted your recommendation of the person you desire, and has graciously listened to you, you should now suggest to your bishop-elect that he obey the commands of the lord pope in all things and defer so much to him in his affairs that, if need arise, he may again willingly listen to your requests, whether for your bishop-elect or for others." See the honey smeared over the lip of the poisonous cup! For what could be better than to obey the admonitions of the pope, what worse than to defer to men for the favors granted by God? I was greatly horrified at being made the go-between in such a business.

When he received the sacrament of episcopal consecration at the church of Saint-Ruf of Avignon,[16] a gloomy omen was discovered in the Gospel. It was this: "Thy own soul a sword shall pierce."[17] It is true, however, that at Langres after his acceptance by the pope, when he went to the altar of the martyr Mamertus with the clergy singing the *Te Deum laudamus,* on opening the Gospels for divination and taking the first verse that met his eye, he read, "Woman, behold thy son."[18] Of this he soon made a great display, showing it round everywhere. In word and in manner he was remarkably unstable, remarkably lightweight. He took delight in talk about military affairs, dogs, and hawks, as he had learned to do among the English. On one occasion when he had dedicated a church, and I was riding in attendance with a young clerk of good disposition, he came on a peasant with a lance. Snatching this up, still wearing the miter, which he should have held sacred, and spurring on his horse, the bishop couched it as if to strike an opponent. To him we said, the clerk in commonplace and I in poetic fashion:

[16]St. Ruf was the legendary first bishop of Avignon and gave his name to an important abbey of that town. We have no indication of why Gaudry should have gone further south for his consecration, but no church near Langres or in the diocese of Laon was dedicated to St. Ruf.
[17]Luke 2:35. On divination from the Gospels, see above, p. 130.
[18]John 19:26. The cathedral of Langres is dedicated to St. Mamertus (St. Mammès).

They do not go well together nor stay in the same place,
The miter and the lance.[19]

Meanwhile that great wealth of English money, cups, and vessels, which had been wickedly gathered together, was quickly squandered. I have certainly heard from Master Anselm, who had traveled with him after he became bishop when he went back to England, that on his arrival such great complaints broke out wherever he turned, some claiming money, others vessels, that it was plain to the Master that his ostentatious riches had been stolen from others and not acquired by honest means.

CHAPTER 5

About three years after his ordination, the bishop gave the following sign, as it were, to his time. One of the barons of the city was the castellan of the nunnery, named Gérard, a man of great power.[1] Although in appearance he was short in stature and lean of body, he had so lively a mind and tongue and such energy in the pursuit of war that he compelled the provinces of Soissons, Laon, and Noyon to fear him, and won the respect of a great many men. Although he was known far and wide as one of sterling character, sometimes he made biting jests in filthy language against those about him, but never against people of good character. He therefore took it upon himself both to speak ill in private and to show open displeasure against that countess to whom some reference was made before.[2] In doing this he acted in a very wrongheaded manner, because he was attacking Enguerrand, this woman's consort, who had with his great wealth advanced Gérard's fortunes. Before

[19]Guibert is playing with a well-known reference of Ovid's to the incompatibility of royal authority and love in *Metamorphoses*, II, 846.

[1]Gérard of Quierzy was the secular guardian *(avoué)* of the Benedictine convent of Saint-Jean of Laon. He had served with distinction on the First Crusade.

[2]Above, p. 148. Sybille of Coucy is called countess with full propriety, since her husband was count of Amiens. Her successors were to take pride in having no other title than Lord of Coucy, as they proclaimed in their device:

Roy ne sui
Ne prince ne duc ne comte aussi
Sui le Sire de Coucy

taking a wife, Gérard himself had been too intimate with the woman of whom we are speaking. After he had been her lover for some time, when he married he reined in his lasciviousness. Then the women, too, began to attack one another with foul words. They were mutually aware of their earlier looseness, and the more they knew of each other's secrets, the fouler was their abuse. The countess was enraged against the other woman's husband because she had been jilted by him, and against his wife because she knew that the woman frequently abused her with twisted words. Being more venomous than any serpent, her determination to ruin the man grew greater every day.

Because God puts a stumbling block in the way of those who sin willfully,[3] an opportunity for destroying Gérard suddenly occurred in an outbreak of enmity between him and Bishop Gaudry. Gérard said unsuitable things about the bishop and his associates, which the bishop endured silently but not patiently. After plotting with his own people and almost all the leading nobles of the city for the death of Gérard, and after exchanging with them mutual oaths of assistance, to which certain wealthy women were also parties, Bishop Gaudry left the matter in the hands of his fellow-conspirators and went on a journey to St. Peter's at Rome. He was led there by the basest designs, not to seek the Apostle, as Thou knowest, O God, but so that through his absence he might seem uninvolved in such a crime. Setting out about Martinmas,[4] he arrived at Rome and stayed there for a while until he learned of the accomplishment of the death of the man he hated, for the less Gérard was hated by all good people, the more hateful he was to the evil.

The deed was done in the following manner. On Friday in the week of Epiphany,[5] in the morning while the light was still faint, Gérard rose from his bed to go to the cathedral of Notre-Dame. When one of the nobles bound by that oath came up to him, he told him about a dream he had the night before, which he said had frightened him thoroughly. He vividly dreamed that two bears were tearing out of his body either his liver or his lungs, I am not sure which.

[3]Cf. Ezekiel 3:20.
[4]November 11, 1109.
[5]January 7, 1110.

Alas, Gérard had had the misfortune not to receive the sacrament for the following reason. A monk living at Barisis-Saint-Amand had undertaken to teach the French language to two little boys who could speak only the Germanic tongue.[6] Now, Barisis with the manors attached to it was under Gérard's protection. Seeing that the boys had fine manners and knowing they were not of mean birth, he seized them and held them for ransom. The mother of the boys sent with the sum agreed upon a fur cloak made of ermine and called a mantle.

Dressed in this mantle over a robe of Tyrian purple, he went on horseback with some of his knights to the church. After entering, he stopped before the image of the crucified Lord, his followers dispersed here and there among the various altars to the saints, and the servants of the conspirators kept an eye on them. Word was then sent to the household of the bishop in the episcopal palace that Gérard of Quierzy (as he was called, since he was lord of that castle)[7] had come to the church to pray. Carrying their swords under their cloaks, the bishop's brother Rorigon and others went through the vaulted ambulatory to the place where he was praying. He was stationed at the foot of a column, called a pillar, a few columns away from the pulpit, at about the middle of the church. While the morning was still dark and there were few people to be seen in the great church, they seized the man from behind as he prayed. He was praying with the fastening of his cloak thrown behind and his hands clasped on his breast. Seizing the cloak from behind, one of them held him in it like a sack so that he could not easily move his hands. When the bishop's steward had seized him in this fashion, he said, "You are taken." With his usual fierceness, Gérard turned his eye round on him (for he had only one) and looking at him said, "Get out of here, you dirty lecher!" But the steward said to Rorigon, "Strike!" and, drawing his sword with his left hand, he wounded him between the nose and the brow. Knowing he was done for, Gérard said, "Take me wherever you want." Then as they stabbed at him repeatedly and pressed him

[6]The monastery of Barisis-aux-Bois, 4 miles north of Nogent, was founded by St. Amand about 664 and was subject to the great Flemish abbey of Saint-Amand. Gérard of Quierzy was the *avoué* or guardian of both Barisis and Saint-Jean of Laon.

[7]Quierzy is 10 miles west of Nogent.

hard, in desperation he cried out with all his strength, "Holy Mary, aid me!" Saying this, he fell in extreme suffering.

The two archdeacons of the church, Gautier and Guy, were in this conspiracy with the bishop. Guy was also the treasurer, and had a house on the other side of the church. From this house, there soon rushed out two servants, who ran up to him and took part in the murder. For by that sacrilegious oath it had been agreed that if those of the bishop's palace took the first step, helpers should immediately come forth from that house. When they had slashed his throat and his legs and given him other wounds, and he was groaning in the nave of the church in his last agonies, a few of the clergy who were then in the choir and some poor women who were going around to pray murmured against them, but half dead with fear, they did not dare to cry out openly. When the murder had been committed, the two carefully picked knights returned to the bishop's palace, and with them, along with the archdeacons, were gathered the nobles of the city, thus betraying their own treason.

At this the royal *prévôt*, a very capable man named Ivo, summoned the king's men and the burghers of the abbey of Saint-Jean, of which Gérard had been the guardian.[8] They attacked the houses of those who had taken the oath to the conspiracy, plundering and burning and driving them out of the city. The archdeacons and the nobles accompanied the murderers of Gérard everywhere, making a display of their fealty to the absent bishop.

CHAPTER 6

The bishop remained at Rome, as if he enjoyed the presence of the apostolic lord, while he listened with eager expectation for some pleasing news to reach him from French parts. At last the fulfillment of his wishes was announced, and the lord pope became aware that a great crime had been done in a great church. The

[8]The *prévôt* was the king's officer in Laon, which was both a royal and an episcopal city. The king's men may have been either noble vassals or royal serfs, more likely serfs. The burghers of Saint-Jean may be thought of as serfs of the abbey who had burgess rights in Laon in return for the dues they paid the church.

bishop had an interview with the pope and by flattering presents warded off suspicion of this infamy. And so, more pleased than ever, Gaudry left Rome.

Since the church had been outraged by that wicked act and needed purification, a messenger was sent to Hubert, the bishop of Senlis, who had recently lost his power on a charge of simony, summoning him to do that work.[1] At the assembly of the clergy and people, I was requested by Master Anselm, the dean of the church, and by the canons to preach to the people on the calamity that had occurred. The following is the general sense of that address:

"*Save me, O God, for the waters are come in even unto my soul. I stick fast in the mire of the deep and there is no sure standing.*[2] If you have had evil of some sort up to this point, now the sword has come *even unto my soul.*[3] You are sunk *in the mire of the deep,* since as the just deserts of your sins, you had fallen into the extreme evil of utter despair. Amid such things *there is no sure standing,* because the honor and power of those to whom you should have recourse in peril—that is, your rulers and nobles—are fallen. Though your bodies were sometimes hard pressed by your hatreds of one another, yet the soul was untouched, since the church, where the desire of salvation remained, rejoiced that it flourished inwardly without any stain. The *waters* and the sword come in *even unto the soul* when tribulations and discords penetrate and pollute the sanctity of the inner refuge. How do you, who are ignorant of spiritual things, think that place can obtain any reverence from you when a man cannot say his prayers there in safety? Behold, God has 'sent upon us the wrath of his indignation: indignation and wrath and trouble, which he sent by evil angels.'[4] There is a wrath of indignation, wrath conceived out of indignation. Indignation, as you know, is less than wrath. Was not God indignant with the transgressions of your sins, when outside your city you

[1]Hubert was bishop of Senlis from 1099 to 1115. Guibert is here bringing up an old charge unnecessarily. Hubert had been driven from his office by his clergy about 1103, although he had the support of the pope and Ivo of Chartres, and he was reinstated at the Council of Troyes in 1104.
[2]Psalms 68:2-3.
[3]A reminder of the prophetic text of Luke 2:35 cited above, p. 156.
[4]Psalms 77:49.

often permitted plunder, burning, and killing? Was He not wrathful when strife from without was brought within this city and civil discord became active in our midst, when with mutual provocations lords moved against burghers, and burghers against lords, and when with improper hostility abbots' men were angered at bishops' men, and bishops' men against abbots' men? But because indignation and wrath brought no amendment from you, at last He brought down tribulation on your stubborn minds. It was not simply any church that was defiled with Christian blood, not anywhere that the beginning of war brought force into the church and destroyed the refugees, but malignant passion conceived with criminal deliberation butchered a man in prayer before the image of Christ hanging on the Cross, not in simply any church, I say, but in the most flourishing of the churches of Gaul, one whose fame has traveled far beyond the Latin world. And who was the man? Was he not one admired for his illustrious birth, whose feats of arms, so remarkable in a man small in size but of lofty soul, made him famous throughout France? Therefore the place, the crime, and the shame will be talked about everywhere. If, then, in your souls, in your innermost hearts, you are not in fear at this mournful moment, if you have no compunction for such dishonor done to a sacred place, be assured that without doubt God will make 'a way for a path to His anger'[5]; that is, to your utter destruction He will openly spread abroad His hidden anger. And how can you think that God will spare the corralling of cattle— that is, of your bodies— when because of your obstinacy in sin He did not spare souls from death?[6] Since divine vengeance with its deadly advance comes on against us step by step, be sure that unless you show yourselves amended under God's scourge, you will fall into a far worse state through those civil conflicts that are arising among you."

Responding to the request of the clergy and the wish of the people, and weaving together these and other remarks, I declared that the murderers of that noble man, their backers in that outrage, and their confederates ought to be excommunicated by Bishop

[5]Psalms 77:50.
[6]*Ibid.*

Hubert, who was reconciling the church, and not less those who had defended or harbored them. And when their excommunication had been pronounced by all of us, the church was duly reconciled. Meanwhile this sentence of anathema was carried to the ears of the archdeacons and nobles, who had withdrawn from the community of the city. Because of the sermon which I preached and the excommunication that was pronounced, all those who had been cut off from the church turned their hatred against me. Archdeacon Gautier in particular was in a frenzy of rage against me. There was indeed terrible thundering to be heard, but out of it, by God's will, no lightning came. In secret they were against me, openly they showed respect. Let me now return to what I have left out.

Armed with bulls and papal rescripts, the lord bishop returned from Rome. After the murder of Gérard, since the king believed without doubt that the bishop was privy to the crime, which under color of absence he sought to conceal, he ordered that all the bishop's palace should be despoiled of grain, wine, and meat.[7] While he was still in Rome, the bishop was aware of the plundering and the cause of it. And so letters were sent to the king, who had determined that he should be kept out of his see and had deprived him of his property, and other letters were dispatched by him to his fellow-bishops and to the abbots of his own and other dioceses. As we have said before, the bridge over the Ailette was on the boundary between the dioceses of Laon and Soissons, and so those archdeacons and nobles whom we had just excommunicated hastened to meet him there when he first set foot on the soil of his diocese. He received them with such loving kisses and embraces that he did not deign to pay a visit to the church of Notre-Dame, which by God's will we serve, although that was the first in his bishopric to which he came, but close to it he had a long talk with those who he thought were the only ones faithful to him. Leaving there, he was entertained at Coucy with all his following.

When I knew this, since I had greatly feared such conduct on

[7]One of the regalian rights claimed by secular lords in this period was the *ius spolii*, or the right to appropriate the personal goods of a dead bishop. The king treated Gaudry's possessions as if he were already deposed for his crime.

his part, I refrained entirely from seeing or saluting him. After three days, if I am not mistaken, he let the madness which he inwardly felt against me seem outwardly to be lulled (for his satellites had bitterly attacked me before him with regard to the aforesaid events), and he ordered me to come to him. When I had presented myself there and had seen his house full of excommunicated men and murderers, I was enraged. He accused me of striving for his exclusion from the church, showing me the pope's letters. I promised what help I could, falsely, as Thou knowest, O God, and not from my heart. For I saw that he was truly in evil communication with those whom his own church had excommunicated and who had so greatly defiled it, since Enguerrand of Coucy was sitting beside him, and he was cherished by the countess, who had sharpened the swords of the two murderers with her own tongue the day before Gérard was killed. Since he was shut out of the city by the king's orders, with exceedingly rash boldness he threatened to enter it with the help of other knights in the city, and declared he would do by force of arms what would scarcely be possible for the imperial Caesars. He collected a troop of knights and spent large sums of what he had accumulated by evil means, but, as was usual with him, without anything coming of it. At length, after gaining nothing but ridicule with so many auxiliaries, with the help of intermediaries and a huge bribe he made terms with King Louis, the son of King Philippe, for himself and his accomplices in the murder of Gérard, that is, the nobles of the city and both the archdeacons.[8]

After entering the city, he held a conventicle at Saint-Nicolas-aux-Bois,[9] and during the mass which he celebrated there, he declared that he was about to excommunicate those who had injured the goods of the conspirators after Gérard was killed and had then left the city. When I heard him say this, whispering in the ear of a fellow-abbot sitting next to me, I said, "Do listen to this absurd twist. He ought to excommunicate those who polluted his church with such a horrible crime, whereas he revenges himself

[8]Louis VI, the son of Philippe I, was sole ruler from 1108 to 1137 and had been associated in his father's rule since 1100.

[9]This Benedictine abbey in the forest of Vois, 8 miles from Laon, was founded about 1080.

on those who inflicted a just punishment on the murderers." The bishop was afraid of everyone with a good conscience, and when he saw me muttering, he thought I was speaking of him. "What are you saying, lord abbot?" he asked. Then Archdeacon Gautier, putting himself forward before he had permission to speak, said, "Go on, lord, with what you had begun. The lord abbot was speaking of other things."

And so he excommunicated those who had harmed the band of sacrilegious slaughterers, an act that was execrated by clergy and people. For a long time the whole city and diocese were embittered against the bishop because he put off for so long excommunication of the murderers of Gérard. At last, seeing himself suspected and almost cursed by everyone, he did excommunicate the guilty men and their accomplices. Moreover, since he had promised much money to the royal courtiers who had helped him and the accomplices of the assassins with the king, when he then began to draw back from his promises, who shall say what taunts he heard in public? None of those who were his accomplices dared to enter the king's court until with much silver and gold they had redeemed their doomed heads from the death threatening them. And yet he could not be accused by the church when it was known that he was excused by the Apostolic See.

CHAPTER 7

Some time after the bishop had set out for England to extract money from the English king, whom he had served and who had been his friend, the archdeacons Gautier and Guy and the nobles of the city devised the following plan. Since ancient times it had been the misfortune of the city of Laon that neither God nor any lord was feared there, but, according to each man's power and desire, the public authority was involved in rapine and murder. To begin with the source of the plague, whenever the king, who ought to have exacted respect for himself with royal severity, happened to visit the city, he was himself first shamefully fined on his own property. When his horses were led out to water in the morning or evening, his grooms were beaten and the horses seized.[1] Also, it was known that the clergy themselves were held in such contempt that neither their persons nor their goods were spared, but the situation then followed the text "As it is with the people, so with the priest."[2] What then shall I say about the lower classes? None of the peasants came into the city (no one who did not have the best guaranteed safe-conduct even approached it) who was not thrown into prison and held for ransom, or, if the opportunity occurred, was not drawn into some lawless lawsuit.

As an example, let me adduce one practice which would be judged as the greatest violation of good faith if it occurred among the barbarians or Scythians, people who have no laws. On Saturdays when the countrypeople from different parts came there to buy and sell, the burghers carried round for sale vegetables, wheat, or other produce in cups and platters or other kinds of measures. When they had offered them for sale in the market place to the peasants seeking such things and the purchaser had settled on a price and agreed to buy, the merchant said, "Follow me to my house to see there the rest of the produce which I am selling you, and to take away what you have seen." The buyer would follow, but when he came to the bin, the honest seller would raise the lid and hold it up, saying, "Bend your head and shoulders over the bin to see that the rest does not differ from the sample which I showed you in the market place." And when the buyer got up on the edge of the bin and leaned his belly over it, the worthy seller standing behind lifted up his feet and pushed the unwary man into the bin, and, putting the lid down on him as he fell, kept him in a safe prison until he ransomed himelf. These things and others like them were done in the city. The leaders and their servants openly committed theft and even armed robbery. No one was safe going

[1]Since Laon was a royal city and the king had the right of compulsory lodging there (see below, p. 172), Guibert's statement that the king had to pay a "fine" and that his horses were seized is probably distorted reporting of some more comprehensible practice. Herman of Laon states that when the king of France was crowned at Laon at the major festivals, he carried a gold crown to the church of Saint-Jean, and that the king and anyone else was required to leave his horses outside the walls of the abbey; see Migne, *Patrologia latina*, t. 156, col. 1004.
[2]Isaiah 24:2.

out at night, for he would surely be either robbed or captured or killed.

The clergy and the archdeacons and the nobles, taking account of these conditions and looking out for ways of exacting money from the people, offered them through their agents the opportunity to have authorization to create a commune, if they would offer an appropriate sum of money. Now, "commune" is a new and evil name for an arrangement for them all to pay the customary head tax, which they owe their lords as a servile due, in a lump sum once a year, and if anyone commits a crime, he shall pay a fine set by law, and all other financial exactions which are customarily imposed on serfs are completely abolished.[3] Seizing on this opportunity for commuting their dues, the people gathered huge sums of money to fill the gaping purses of so many greedy men. Pleased with the shower of income poured upon them, those men established their good faith by proffering oaths that they would keep their word in this matter.

After this sworn association of mutual aid among the clergy, nobles, and people had been established, the bishop returned with much wealth from England. Angered at those responsible for this innovation, for a long time he kept away from the city. But at last a quarrel full of honor and glory began between him and Gautier the archdeacon, his accomplice. The archdeacon made very unbecoming remarks about his bishop concerning the death of Gérard. I do not know what the bishop did with others on this matter, but I do know that he complained to me about Gautier,

[3]Guibert's often quoted definition restricts the purpose of a commune to the limitation of arbitrary payments and servile dues (and perhaps it should be noted that the annual payment of fixed servile dues would not, of course, end serfdom itself). This definition is clearly too narrow, for at the beginning of the chapter Guibert shows that the initiative for the commune came as a reaction against violence, illegality, and arbitrary exercise of judicial authority, and he goes on to call it a "sworn association for mutual aid among the clergy, nobles, and people." For a pioneering study which shows the role of the commune as an institution for establishing peace, rather than an expression of class war, see Albert Vermeesch, *Essai sur les origines et la signification de la commune dans le Nord de la France* (Heule, 1966). For the charter of the commune finally established at Laon in 1128, see *Ordonnances des rois de France* (Paris, 1723-1849), XI, 185-187.

saying, "Lord abbot, if Gautier should happen to bring up any charges against me at some council, would you take it without offense? At the time when you left your monks and retired to Fly, didn't he openly flatter you but secretly raise up discord against you, publicly taking your side but privately stirring me up against you?"[4] Talking like this, he inveigled me to oppose that dangerous man, conscious of the very great weight of the charges against him, and fearful and suspicious of universal condemnation.

Although he said that he was moved by relentless wrath against those who had sworn an oath to the association and those who were the principals in the transaction, in the end his high-sounding words were suddenly quieted by the offer of a great heap of silver and gold. Then he swore that he would maintain the rights of the commune, following the terms of the charters of the city of Noyon and the town of Saint-Quentin.[5] The king, too, was induced to confirm the same thing by oath with a bribe from the people.[6]

O my God, who can describe the controversy that broke out when, after accepting so many gifts from the people, they then took oaths to overturn what they had sworn; that is, when they tried to return the serfs to their former condition after once freeing them from the yoke of their exactions? The hatred of the bishop and the nobles for the burghers was indeed implacable, and as he was not strong enough to crush the freedom of the French, following the fashion of Normandy and England, the pastor remained inactive, forgetful of his sacred calling through his insatiable greed. Whenever one of the people was brought into a court of law, he was judged not on his condition in the eyes of God but, if I may put it this way, on his bargaining power, and he was drained of his substance to the last penny.

Since the taking of gifts is commonly attended by the subversion

[4]See above, p. 133.
[5]The charter of about 1108 by which Bishop Baudry of Noyon announced that he had constituted a commune in his city is very brief and says nothing of the administration of the city; perhaps there was another set of written regulations which has not survived. The charter of Saint-Quentin, issued about 1102, has not survived.
[6]In classical Latin, *largitio* means a bribe; in medieval Latin, it can mean a charter of donation. Guibert is probably punning here, and the phrase could as easily read, "with a charter to the people." It was common to pay for such charters.

of all justice, the coiners of the currency, knowing that if they did wrong in their office they could save themselves by paying money, corrupted the coinage with so much base metal that because of this many people were reduced to poverty. As they made their coins of the cheapest bronze, which in a moment by certain dishonest practices they made brighter than silver,[7] the attention of the foolish people was shamefully deceived, and, giving up their goods of great or little value, they got in exchange nothing but the most debased dross. The lord bishop's acceptance of this practice was well rewarded, and thus not only within the diocese of Laon but in all directions the ruin of many was hastened. When he was deservedly powerless to uphold or improve the value of his own currency, which he had wickedly debased, he instituted halfpence of Amiens, also very debased, to be current in the city for some time. And when he could by no means keep them going, he struck a contemporary impression on which he had stamped a pastoral staff to represent himself.[8] This was received with such secret laughter and scorn that it had even less value than the debased coinage.

However, since on the issue of each of these new coins a proclamation was made that no one should laugh at the dreadful designs, there were a great many opportunities to accuse the people of speaking evil of the bishop's ordinances, and hence they could exact all sorts of heavy fines. Moreover, a monk named Thierry, who had the most shameful reputation in every respect, imported very large quantities of silver from Flanders and from Tournai, of which he was native. Bring it all down to the very debased money of Laon, he scattered it all over the surrounding province.

[7]Many medieval mints used a billon alloy which is approximately one-third silver and two-thirds copper. If this metal is heated in an open flame, much of the copper on the surface is oxidized, leaving a silver-rich layer which will not flake off if the metal is then hammered. Consequently, the routine medieval practice of making coins by heating and hammering produced a deceptively enriched silver surface, though not in a moment. This is probably the "dishonest" process to which Guibert refers, rather than the use of a silver wash on copper coins, which was a practice of Roman days. Since a great many coins of this period are very low in silver, Guibert is misleading in suggesting that a process of debasement which was widespread was peculiar to Laon.

[8]None of these coins is known to survive.

By appealing to the greed of the rich people of the province with his hateful presents and by bringing in lies, perjury, and poverty, he robbed the country of truth, justice, and wealth. No enemy action, no plundering, no burning has ever hurt the province more since the Roman walls contained the ancient and thoroughly respected mint of the city.[9]

Since

> Sooner or later long-hidden sin
> Forces its way through the veil of decency.
> Glistening things cannot be concealed,
> And as bright light pierces glass,
> So sin shows through the countenance,[10]

what the bishop had done to Gérard, secretly and as if he were not responsible, he did some time afterward to another Gérard, giving manifest proof of his cruelty. This Gérard was some sort of rural officer or manorial bailiff of the peasants who belonged to him. The bishop considered him a particular enemy because Gérard inclined toward the most evil man of all we know in this generation, Thomas, the reputed son of that Enguerrand with whom we dealt before.[11] The bishop seized this Gérard and threw him into a prison in the episcopal palace, and then at night had his African man put out his eyes.[12] By this deed he brought open shame upon himself, and the old story of what he had done to the first Gérard was dug out again, both clergy and people being aware that a canon of the Council of Toledo, if I am not mistaken, forbade bishops, priests, and clerks to execute or pass a sentence of death or mutilation.[13] The news of this also angered the king. I do not know whether the story reached the Apostolic See, but I do know

[9]Charlemagne and his successors issued coins at Laon; see Karl F. Morrison and Henry Grunthal, *Carolingian Coinage* (New York, 1967), nos. 127 ff. Carolingian coins had a high silver content and made later billon coinage seem badly inferior in comparison.

[10]These lines of verse are unidentified. Guibert also quoted them in his commentary on Genesis.

[11]The uncertain parentage of Thomas of Marle has been noted above, p. 148, n. 3.

[12]The bishop's man, Jean, is called an Ethiopian here and a Moor on p. 173. Guibert's language indicates that the bishop possessed Jean without otherwise showing his status; he was probably held in personal servitude.

[13]This canon appears in the *Decreta* of Burchard of Worms (II, 149) and Ivo of Chartres (VI, 222); cf. Gratian, *Decretum,* C. 23, q. 8, c. 29.

that the pope suspended him from his office, and I believe he did it for no other reason. To make matters worse, during his suspension he dedicated a church. Therefore he went to Rome, softened the lord pope with gifts once again, and was sent back to us with his authority restored. And so, seeing that masters and subjects were by act and will partners in wickedness, God could no longer restrain his judgment and at last permitted the malice that had been conceived to break out into open rage. When one is driven headlong by pride, through the vengeance of God he is completely shattered by a dreadful fall.[14].

Calling together the nobles and certain of the clergy in the last days of Lent in the most holy Passiontide of Our Lord, the bishop determined to attack the commune, to which he had sworn and had with presents induced the king to swear. He had summoned the king to that pious duty, and on the day before Good Friday—that is, on Maundy Thursday—he instructed the king and all his people to break their oaths, after first placing his own neck in that noose.[15] As I said before, this was the day on which his predecessor Bishop Ascelin had betrayed his king.[16] On the very day when he should have performed that most glorious of all episcopal duties, the consecration of the oil and the absolution of the people from their sins, he was not even seen to enter the church. He was intriguing with the king's courtiers so that after the sworn association was destroyed the king would restore the laws of the city to their former state. But the burghers, fearing their overthrow, promised the king and his courtiers four hundred pounds, and possibly more. In reply, the bishop begged the nobles to go with him to interview the king, and they promised on their part seven hundred pounds. King Louis, Philippe's son, was a remarkable person[17] who seemed well-suited for royal majesty, mighty in arms, intolerant toward sloth in business, of dauntless courage in adversity; although in other respects he was a good man, in this matter he was most unjust and paid too much attention to worthless

[14]Cf. Proverbs 16:18.

[15]Maundy Thursday fell on April 18th in 1112. The proper "pious duty" for that day was for the king to wash the feet of the poor.

[16]Above, p. 146. As noted, Guibert's date differs from that of other historians.

[17]It is hard to judge Guibert's tone in calling *persona conspicuus* a man known to history as Louis the Fat.

persons debased by greed. This redounded to his own great loss and blame and the ruin of many, which certainly happened here and elsewhere.

When the king's desire was turned, as I said, toward the larger promise and he ruled against God, the oaths of the bishop and the nobles were voided without any regard for honor or the sacred season. Because of the turmoil with which he had so unjustly struck the people, that night the king was afraid to sleep outside the bishop's palace, although he had the right to compulsory lodging elsewhere. Very early the next morning the king departed, and the bishop promised the nobles they need have no fear about the agreement to pay so much money, informing them that he would himself pay whatever they had promised. "And if I do not fulfill my promise," he said, "hand me over to the king's prison until I pay it off."

After the bonds of the association were broken, such rage, such amazement seized the burghers that all the craftsmen abandoned their jobs, and the stalls of the tanners and cobblers were closed and nothing was exposed for sale by the innkeepers and chapmen, who expected to have nothing left when the lords began plundering. For at once the property of such individuals was calculated by the bishop and nobles, and the amount any man was known to have given to establish the commune was demanded of him to pay for its annulment.

These events took place on the Parasceve, which means preparation.[18] On Holy Saturday, when they should have been preparing to receive the Body and Blood of the Lord, they were actually preparing only for murder and perjury. To be brief, all the efforts of the bishop and the nobles in these days were reserved for fleecing their inferiors. But those inferiors were no longer merely angry, but were goaded into an animal rage. Binding themselves by mutual oaths, they conspired for the death, or rather the murder, of the bishop and his accomplices. They say that forty took the oath. Their great undertaking could not be kept completely secret, and when it came to the attention of Master Anselm toward evening of Holy Saturday, he sent word to the bishop, who was retiring

[18]Ancient term for Good Friday, from the Greek word for preparation.

to rest, not to go out to the service of matins, knowing that if he did he would be killed. With excessive pride the bishop stupidly said, "Nonsense, I'm not likely to die at the hands of such people." But although he scorned them orally, he did not dare to go out for matins and to enter the church.

The next day, as he followed the clergy in procession, he ordered the people of his household and all the knights to come behind him carrying short swords under their garments. During this procession when a little disorder began to arise, as often happens in a crowd, one of the burghers came out of the church and thought the time had come for the murder to which they were sworn. He then began to cry out in a loud voice, as if he were signaling, "Commune, Commune!" over and over again. Because it was a feast day, this was easily stopped, yet it brought suspicion on the opposition. And so, when the service of the mass was over, the bishop summoned a great number of peasants from the episcopal manors and manned the towers of the cathedral and ordered them to guard his palace, although they hated him almost as much, since they knew that the piles of money which he had promised the king must be drained from their own purses.

On Easter Monday it is the custom for the clergy to assemble at the abbey of Saint-Vincent. Since the conspirators knew they had been anticipated the day before, they had decided to act on this day, and they would have done so if they had not seen that all the nobles were with the bishop. They did find one of the nobles in the outskirts of the city, a harmless man who had recently married a young cousin of mine, a girl of modest character. But they were unwilling to attack him, fearing to put others on their guard. Coming through to Tuesday and feeling more secure, the bishop dismissed those men whom he had put in the towers and palace to protect him and whom he had to feed there from his own resources. On Wednesday I went to him because through his disorders he had robbed me of my grain supply and of some legs of pork, called *bacons* in French. When I requested him to relieve the city of these great disturbances, he replied, "What do you think they can do with their riots? If Jean, my moor, were to take by the nose the most powerful man among them, he would not even dare to grunt. For just now I have compelled them to renounce what they call their commune for as long as I live." I said something, and then, seeing the man was overcome with arrogance, I stopped. But before I left the city, because of his instability we quarreled with mutual recriminations. Although he was warned by many of the imminent peril, he took no notice of anyone.

CHAPTER 8

The next day—that is, on Thursday—when the bishop and Archdeacon Gautier were engaged after the noon offices in collecting money, suddenly there arose throughout the city the tumult of men shouting, "Commune!" Then through the nave of the cathedral of Notre-Dame, and through the very door by which Gérard's killers had come and gone, a great crowd of burghers attacked the episcopal palace, armed with rapiers, double-edged swords, bows, and axes, and carrying clubs and lances. As soon as this sudden attack was discovered, the nobles rallied from all sides to the bishop, having sworn to give him aid against such an assault if it should occur. In this rally Guimar the castellan, an older nobleman of handsome presence and guiltless character, armed only with a shield and spear, ran through the church. Just as he entered the bishop's hall, he was the first to fall, struck on the back of the head with a sword by a man named Raimbert, who had been his close friend. Immediately afterward that Renier of whom I spoke before as married to my cousin,[1] rushing to enter the palace, was struck from behind with a spear when he tried to duck under it while poised on the porch of the bishop's chapel. Struck to the ground there, he was soon consumed by the fire of the palace from his groin downward. Adon the *vidame,* sharp in small matters and even keener in important ones, separated from the rest and able to do little by himself among so many, encountered the full force of the attack as he was striving to reach the bishop's palace.[2] With

[1]Above, p. 173.

[2]A *vidame (vicedominus)* was a lay lord who was responsible for protecting and administering ecclesiastical property. At Laon, Gérard of Quierzy had been *avoué* of Saint-Jean of Laon and was succeeded as castellan of that abbey by Roger of Montaigu (below, p. 180). Adon the *vidame* seems to have been an episcopal officer. Another important noble of Laon who fought

his spear and sword he made such a stand that in a moment he struck down three of those who rushed at him. Then he mounted the dining table in the hall, where he was wounded in the knees and other parts of the body. At last, falling on his knees and striking at his assailants all round him, he kept them off for a long time, until someone pierced his exhausted body with a javelin. After a little he was burned to ashes by the fire in that house.

While the insolent mob was attacking the bishop and howling before the walls of his palace, the bishop and the people who were aiding him fought them off as best they could by hurling stones and shooting arrows. Now, as at all times, he showed great spirit as a fighter; but because he had wrongly and in vain taken up that other sword, he perished by the sword.[3] Unable to resist the reckless assaults of the people, he put on the clothes of one of his servants and fled into the warehouse of the church, where he hid himself in a container. When the cover had been fastened on by a faithful follower, he thought himself safely hidden. As those looking for him ran hither and thither, they did not call out for the bishop but for a felon. They seized one of his pages, but he remained faithful and they could get nothing out of him. Laying hands on another, they learned from the traitor's nod where to look for him. Entering the warehouse and searching everywhere, at last they found him in the following manner.

There was a most pestilent man named Thiégaud, a serf of the abbey of Saint-Vincent. For a long time he was a servant and *prévôt* of Enguerrand of Coucy, who set him over the collection of tolls paid for crossing the bridge at a place called Sort.[4] Sometimes he watched until there were only a few travelers passing and robbed them of all their property; then, so that they could make no complaint against him, he weighted them down and tossed them into the river. How often he had done this, God only knows. Although the number of his thefts and robberies was more than

---

for the bishop was Guimar the castellan. He may have been in charge of the ancient fortress of Laon, though this is not a necessary conclusion from his title. In any case, at Laon there was room for both a *vidame* and a castellan.

[3]Cf. Matthew 26:52. The bishop properly bore the spiritual sword.

[4]The bridge at Sort crossed the river Serre south of Crécy-sur-Serre.

anyone could count, the unrestrained wickedness of his heart was displayed in his hideous face. When he ran afoul of Enguerrand, he committed himself completely to the commune at Laon. He who had before not spared monks or clerks or pilgrims, or, in fact, women, was finally to be the slayer of the bishop. As the leader and instigator of this abominable attack, he searched diligently for the bishop, whom he hated more bitterly than did the rest.

As they sought for him in every vessel, Thiégaud halted in front of the cask where the man was hiding, and after breaking in the head he asked again and again who was there. Hardly able to move his frozen lips under the blows, the bishop said, "A prisoner." Now, as a joke, the bishop used to call this man Isengrin, because he had the look of a wolf and that is what some people commonly call wolves.[5] So the scoundrel said to the bishop, "Is this my Lord Isengrin stored away here?" Sinner though he was and yet the Lord's anointed,[6] he was dragged out of the cask by the hair, beaten with many blows, and brought out in the open air in the narrow lane of the cloister before the house of the chaplain Godfrey. As he implored them piteously, ready to swear that he would cease to be their bishop, that he would give them unlimited riches, that he would leave the country, with hardened hearts they jeered at him. Then a man named Bernard of Bruyères raised his sword and brutally dashed out that sinner's brains from his holy head. Slipping between the hands of those who held him, before he died he was struck by someone else with a blow running under his eye sockets and across the middle of his nose. Brought to his end there, his legs were hacked off and many other wounds inflicted. Seeing the ring on the finger of the former bishop and not being able to draw it off easily, Thiégaud cut off the dead man's finger with his sword and took the ring. Stripped naked, he was thrown into a corner in front of his chaplain's house. My God, who shall recount the mocking words that were thrown at him by passers-by as he lay there, and with what clods and stones and dirt his corpse was pelted?

[5]On this much-discussed passage see Lucien Foulet, *Le Roman de Renard* (Paris, 1914), pp. 75-89.

[6]The Lord's injunction in I Paralipomenon 16: 22, "Touch not my anointed," was a principle of fundamental importance to the priesthood.

Before I go on to other matters, I must say that something he had done recently contributed considerably to his end. Two days, I think, before his death, there was a meeting in the nave of the cathedral of the leading men of his clergy, because the bishop had denounced them to the king when he was recently in the city, saying that the clergy ought not to be respected, since nearly all of them were the children of royal serfs.[7] When confronted with his words, he denied them in this way: "May the Holy Communion, which I have just received at that altar," he said, stretching out his right hand toward it, "turn to my ruin, and the sword of the Holy Spirit strike my soul if I ever spoke such words to the king about you." When they heard this, some were utterly confounded and swore that they heard these things from his own mouth when he was talking with the king. Clearly, the inconstancy of his mind and tongue brought on his ruin.

CHAPTER 9

Meanwhile part of the raging mob made its way to the house of Raoul, who was the bishop's seneschal and had been one of the closest intimates of Gérard of Quierzy, a man of small stature but heroic spirit. Since he was wearing a coat of mail and a helmet and carrying light weapons, he resolved to resist, but, seeing that the numbers were too great and fearing to be thrown into the fire, he cast away his arms and exposed himself unprotected to their mercy with his arms stretched out in the shape of a cross. With no thought of God, they cruelly butchered him as he lay prostrate on the ground.

Before the murder of Gérard in the church, Raoul had the following vision. He seemed to be in the cathedral of Notre-Dame, where a crowd of men of wicked disposition played strange games and presented an unusual show to some spectators. While that went on, other men came out of the house of Guy the treasurer, which was next to the church, bearing cups containing a drink which

[7]Serfs were prohibited from entering holy orders without the permission of their lords. See notably a canon included in their *Decreta* by Burchard (II, 21), Ivo (VI, 41), and Gratian (D. 54, c. 2).

stank so badly that it was intolerable to those who smelled it, and this was carried along the rows of spectators. The meaning of this is clearer than daylight. What horrible and hateful demonic game was played there, what monstrous stench of wickedness poured out of that house in all directions, is now manifest. For the maddened populace first threw their brands into that house, and from there the fire leaped into the church and at last seized the bishop's palace.

He also had another premonition of his coming fate. In a vision, his squire reported to him and said, "Lord, the forequarters of your horse are unusually large, and its hindquarters are so small that I have never seen the equal." He had been a man of great wealth and held in high esteem, but all his prosperity was brought down to the meanness of his wretched death; for the horse signifies the glory of this world.[1]

Chiefly through the sin of one man, that most famous church was brought to miserable ruin. From the house of the treasurer, who by simony was also the archdeacon, the fire was seen to spread into the church. In honor of the Easter season, the church was decorated all about with draperies and the finest tapestries, and when the fire broke out, a few of these hangings are believed to have been stolen rather than touched by the flames. Since the ropes of the pulleys could not easily be released by a few men, some of the tapestries were destroyed by the fire. The gilded panels of the altar and the reliquaries of the saints were rescued, along with the baldaquin,[2] as it is called, which projects above them. The rest, I think, were destroyed by the circling flames. When one of the higher clergy hid under it, not daring to come out for fear of encountering the crowds roaming about, he heard the fire crackling about him, ran to the bishop's chair, kicked at the central window over it, broke through, and so escaped.

The image of the crucified Lord, splendidly covered with gold and adorned with jewels, and the vessel of lapis lazuli hanging

[1]This was one of the meanings given to the horse by Biblical commentators. See Rabanus Maurus in Migne, *Patrologia latina*, t. 111, col. 214, and t. 112, col. 916.

[2]The word Guibert actually uses is a Germanic one, *repa*. Baldaquin comes from Baldacco, the Italian name for Baghdad, bringing to mind the rich cloth of the altar canopies.

before the feet of the image melted and fell to the ground and were recovered with very heavy losses. When the church and the palace were burning, it is astonishing to relate that by the mysterious judgment of God either a brand or a burning coal flew onto the nunnery and set fire to the church of Saint-Jean, burning it to ashes along with the churches of Notre-Dame-la-Profonde and Saint-Pierre-au-Marché[3]

The tale of how the wives of the nobles behaved at such a crisis is not a shameful one. Seeing her husband joining the bishop's party when the rising began, and believing that it meant instant death, the wife of Adon the *vidame* began to beg his pardon for any wrong she had done him. For some time, she clung closely to him with cries of sorrow and gave him her last kisses, saying, "How can you leave me to the swords of the townspeople?" Grasping the woman's right hand and holding his lance, he told his steward (who happened to be among the original traitors) to carry his shield behind him. Not only did he fail to follow with the shield, but, reviling him with curses, he attacked him from the rear.[4] No longer did he acknowledge him whose serf he was and whom he had served a little while before at dinner. After defending his wife through the mobs, at last he concealed her in the house of a certain doorkeeper of the bishop. When she saw the assault and the firing of the buildings, she fled wherever chance took her. Falling into the hands of some of the women of the town, she was seized, beaten with their fists, and stripped of the costly clothes she was wearing; she was scarcely able to reach the abbey of Saint-Vincent clad in a nun's habit.

When my cousin's husband left her, she took no account of her household goods, and, keeping only a cloak for herself, with masculine agility she climbed the wall which surrounded the garden and jumped down from it. Then she took refuge in the hovel of some poor woman, but, perceiving after a little that the flames were increasing, she rushed to the door which the old woman had locked

[3]The Benedictine abbey of Notre-Dame-la-Profonde and the church of Saint-Pierre-au-Marché, both founded in the sixth century, were behind the cathedral to the east.

[4]Guibert's account and chronology are here confusing, since he earlier related Adon's death on a table in the bishop's palace on p. 175.

from the outside and broke the lock with a stone. Thinking that she would be safe among the nuns, she wrapped herself in a habit and veil which she had obtained from a relative who was a nun, but then she saw that the convent of Saint-Jean was on fire and turned back on her tracks and fled to a house farther off. She appeared the next day when her relatives sought her out, whereupon the anguish she had felt through the fear of death was changed to more violent grief for her husband.

The wife and daughters of the castellan Guimar and many more women hid themselves in mean places.

Gautier the archdeacon was with the bishop when he saw the attack on the palace. Since he always knew how to take care of himself, he leaped out through a window of the house into the bishop's gardens and then from the wall which surrounded it into the vineyards. With his head covered he followed an unfrequented path to the castle of Montaigu.[5] When the burghers could not find him anywhere, they mocked him by saying that he had been frightened into hiding in the sewers.

Ermengarde, the wife of Roger, lord of Montaigu, was in the city that day, for her husband had succeeded Gérard as castellan of the nunnery. Along with the wife of Raoul the seneschal, putting on the garb of nuns, if I am not mistaken, she made her way to Saint-Vincent's through the valley of Bibrax.[6] Raoul's six-year-old son was being carried to freedom under someone's cloak when a servant looked to see what the man was holding under his mantle and cut the throat of the boy in his arms.

That day and night, the vineyards between the two spurs of the mountain of Laon were an escape route for both clergy and women. Men did not fear to wear women's dress, nor women that of men.[7] So rapid, too, was the progress of the flames on the other side as the wind drove them in their direction that the monks feared everything

[5]The castle of Montaigu was 10 miles east of Laon. On the position of Roger of Montaigu as castellan of Saint-Jean of Laon, see above, p. 174, n. 2.

[6]According to a medieval tradition, Laon was the site of that Bibrax named in Caesar's *Gallic Wars,* the name being derived from the twin arms *(bina brachia)* of the mountain of Laon; see the anonymous poem printed in *Recueil des historiens des Gaules et de la France* (Paris, 1738-1904), IX, 105-106.

[7]Deuteronomy 22:5 prohibits wearing the garments of the opposite sex.

they had would be burned. The fear of those who had taken refuge there was as great as if a sword threatened their heads. Lucky Guy, who missed this affair! The archdeacon-treasurer had gone before Easter to pray at Notre-Dame of Verdelot.[8] The murderers were especially annoyed at his absence.

After the bishop and the leading nobles had been slain, the assailants turned upon the houses of the survivors. Through the night they attacked the house of Guillaume, the son of Haduin, who had not conspired with the people of the city to murder Gérard, but had gone in the morning to pray with the man who was to be slain. When they had pressed home the assault on the house with firebrands and scaling ladders, tearing at the walls with axes and pikes while those within resisted stoutly, at last he was driven to surrender. By the wonderful judgment of God, although they hated him worse than the rest, he was put in fetters safe and unharmed. The son of the castellan was treated in the same way.

In the same house, there was a young chamberlain of the bishop, also named Guillaume, who won much honor in that defense. When the house was taken, he was questioned by that party of the burghers who had besieged the house if he knew whether the bishop had been slain or not, and he replied that he did not know. For those who slew the bishop were a different party from those who had stormed the house. As they were going around, they found the bishop's corpse, and asked the young man whether he could prove the body lying there was his by any mark. Now, his head and face had been so disfigured by his many wounds that they were unrecognizable. "I remember that when he was alive," he said, "the bishop frequently used to say when talking about military matters, which to his sorrow he much loved, that once in a mock fight he was in sport attacking a certain soldier on horseback, and by a stroke of that knight's lance he was wounded in that part of the neck called the windpipe." And when they looked, they found the scar.[9]

[8]The priory of Verdelot, a dependency of the abbey of Chézy, was over 40 miles south of Laon.

[9]The theme of a corpse stripped and so badly disfigured that it can be recognized only by a secret mark is so common in medieval writing that

When Adalbéron, the abbot of Saint-Vincent, heard that the bishop had been killed and wished to go to him, he was plainly told that if he ventured into the midst of the maddened mob, he would quickly fall by a similar death. Those who were present at these events positively declare that one day continued into the following day in such a way that no sign of darkness marked the fall of night. When I objected that the brightness of the flames was the cause, they swore that the fire was suppressed and burned out in the daytime, which was true. The fire in the nunnery so got the upper hand as to consume some of the bodies of the saints.

CHAPTER 10

Since hardly anyone passed the bishop's corpse without casting at him some insult or curse and no one thought of burying him, the next day Master Anselm, who had hidden carefully when the rebellion broke out the day before, poured out his prayers to the authors of this tragedy to allow the man to be buried, if only because he had the name and rank of a bishop. They reluctantly consented. Because he had lain naked on the ground from vespers on Thursday to the third hour of the following day, treated as if he were a filthy dog, the Master ordered him to be taken up with a cloth thrown over him to be carried away at last to Saint-Vincent's.[1] One cannot describe the threats and abuse that were showered upon those who cared for his burial or count the curses with which the dead man was pelted. Once he was carried to the church, he had at his burial none of the offices that are provided for any Christian, much less a bishop. The earth was only half scraped out to receive him and the body was so tightly packed in the tiny coffin that his breast and belly were crushed near bursting. Since he had such bad

---

one must suspect that Guibert has here embellished his tale. Raoul Glaber told such a story of Eudes of Champagne, William of Malmesbury did the same for Tostig, and a number of authors relate something similar in their accounts of the discovery of the body of King Harold. See Edward A. Freeman, *The History of the Norman Conquest of England* (Oxford, 1870-79), III, 514.

[1]The abbey of Saint-Vincent had the privilege of being the burial place of the bishops of Laon.

undertakers to lay him out, as I said, those who were present have argued from this that they clearly did their job as wickedly as they could. That day there was no divine service by the monks in that church. But why do I say that day? Indeed, there was none for several days, since they were fearful for the safety of those who fled to them and dreaded death for themselves, too.

Next Guimar the castellan was brought in, it is sad to say, by his wife and daughters, a very noble family, who placed his body on a cart and drew it themselves. Behind him came Renier, placed above the axle between the two wheels, his lower parts somewhere in the cart, his upper parts still hissing at the hips from the fire, drawn in the same miserable manner by a peasant of his and a young noblewoman, his relative. For these two "a good word was found,"[2] as the Book of Kings says, since all well-disposed people mourned over their death. They were not evil people in any way, except in their association with the murderers of Gérard. Consequently, they were buried with much more compassion than their bishop. Many days after the rebellion and burning, a few small pieces of the remains of Adon the *vidame* were found; these were tied up in a small cloth and kept until the day on which Raoul, archbishop of Reims, came to Laon to reconsecrate the church.[3] When the archbishop came to Saint-Vincent's, he celebrated the first mass for the bishop and his confederates, although many days had passed since their deaths. Raoul the seneschal, along with his little son, was brought in the same way and on the same day as the others, and was buried by his old mother, and the son was laid on the breast of his father.

After the venerable and wise archbishop had improved the position of some of the corpses, he performed the divine offices in the presence of the grieving relatives and those close to the dead. During mass he preached a sermon about these accursed communes in which, contrary to right and justice, serfs withdraw from the rule of their lords. " 'Serfs,' said the Apostle, 'be subject to your masters with all fear.' And lest serfs plead as an excuse that their masters are hard and greedy, they should hear how it continues, 'and not

[2]III Kings 14:13.

[3]After a contested election, Raoul was confirmed by Pope Paschal and recognized as archbishop by 1108. He died in 1124.

only to the good and gentle, but also to the froward.'[4] In the authoritative canons, those people are damned with anathema who teach serfs to disobey their masters for the sake of entering religion, or to fly anywhere, much less to resist.[5] A further proof of this is the fact that no one is admitted to the clergy or into holy orders or to be a monk unless he is free of servitude; moreover, when so admitted, he may by no means be kept against the demands of his master."[6] Many times he maintained this principle in the king's court and even more often in various assemblies. This we have said by way of anticipation; now let us return to the orderly narrative.

CHAPTER 11

When the wicked citizens had duly weighed the enormity of the crime they had committed, they were consumed with dread, greatly fearing the king's judgment. Consequently, when they ought to have sought a remedy, they only added one wound to another. For they decided to call in Thomas, who held the castle of Marle, the reputed son of Enguerrand of Coucy, to defend them against a royal attack.[1] From the beginning of his adolescence, this man seemed to attain great power for the destruction of many men by preying on poor people and pilgrims going to Jerusalem and by adding to his lands through his incestuous marriages.[2] So unheard-of in our times was his cruelty that men who are considered cruel seem more humane

[4]I Peter 2:18.
[5]Canon in *Decreta* of Burchard (VIII, 25) and Ivo (VII, 45); cf. Gratian, *Decretum*, C. 17, q. 4, c. 38.
[6]See above, p. 177, n. 7.
[1]Thomas had received the lordship of Marle from his mother, whom Enguerrand of Coucy had divorced, and he therefore held a base of power in his own right from which he could oppose Enguerrand. After Enguerrand's death in 1116, Thomas inherited Coucy, but he was unable to acquire the county of Amiens. Denounced by Guibert and Suger, Thomas has often been painted by historians as an example of unmitigated feudal villainy. For a sympathetic study which does as much as possible to rehabilitate him, see Jacques Chaurand, *Thomas de Marle, Sire de Coucy* (Marle, 1963).
[2]Both here and in the *Gesta Dei*, Guibert fails to mention Thomas's distinguished and valorous service on the First Crusade. His first marriage was to Ida, daughter of the count of Hainault. After her death he married Ermengarde of Montaigu; this marriage was annulled on grounds of consanguinity. His third marriage was to Milesende, daughter of Guy of Crécy.

in killing cattle than he in killing men. For he did not merely kill them outright with the sword and for definite offenses, as is usual, but by butchery after horrible tortures. When he was compelling prisoners of any condition to ransom themselves, he hung them up by their testicles, and as these often tore off from the weight of the body, the vitals soon burst out. Sometimes he did this with his own hands. Others were suspended by their thumbs or by the male organ itself, and were weighted down with a stone placed on their shoulders. He himself walked below them, and when he could not extort from them what they did not have, he beat them madly with cudgels until they promised what satisfied him, or perished under this punishment.

No one can tell how many expired in his dungeons and chains from starvation, disease, and torture. It is certain that two years ago, when he had gone to Le Mont de Soissons to give aid to someone against some peasants, three of these men hid in a cave, and when he came to the entrance of the cave with his lance, he drove his weapon into the mouth of one of them with so hard a thrust that the blade of the lance tore through his entrails and passed out through his anus. Why go on with instances that have no end? The two left in the cave both perished by his hand. Again, one of his prisoners was wounded and could not march. He asked the man why he did not go faster. He replied that he could not. "Stop," said he, "I'll fix things so you'll make speed with real trouble." Leaping down from his horse, he cut off both the man's feet, and of that he died. Of what use is it to recount these horrors when later there will be a major occasion for telling them? Let me return to the subject.

This man long gave shelter to the excommunicated murderers of Gérard, and long encouraged them, cherishing none but the worst criminals. The saying of Sallust "He was spontaneously evil and cruel"[3] applies to him better than to Catiline. To set the crown upon their wrongdoing, the burghers turned to him with a request to come and protect them against the king, and when at last he did so, they admitted him into the city. After hearing their pleas, he consulted his men on what he should do. They unanimously replied

[3] *The War with Catiline*, XVI, 3.

that his strength was not sufficient to hold the city against the king. Not daring to make this decision known to those madmen as long as he was in their city, he told them to come out into the open country where he would reveal his advice. When they had gone about a mile outside, he told them, "Since this city is the capital of the realm, I cannot hold it against the king. But if you are afraid of the king's arms, follow me into my land and take me for your patron and friend." At those words they were greatly dismayed. Maddened with fear because of the villainy they had done and thinking the king was a threat to their lives, a countless mob soon fled with him. Thiégaud, the slayer of the bishop, who, sword in hand, had searched the rafters and vaults of the church of Saint-Vincent and the recesses of the cloister to find fugitives to kill, who had displayed the episcopal ring on his finger to prove his right to be their head, he and his accomplices did not dare to return to the city, and followed Thomas almost empty-handed. Moreover, Thomas had freed Guillaume, the son of Haduin, and the other prisoners in the city, for Guillaume had not been involved in the death of Gérard. Rumor then flew abroad with the speed of Pegasus, rousing the men of the neighboring countryside and towns with the tale that the city was emptied of inhabitants. Then all the people of the district rushed upon the deserted city and took possession of the houses, full of property and with no one to defend them. Townsmen who were clearly wealthy disguised themselves in mean dress, for they were afraid to incite the eyes of the nobles against them.

At that time the unlawful and incestuous wife of Enguerrand spurned him because of his age and obesity by appearing to be continent, but she could not give up her old enjoyment of lovers. Since she was in love with a handsome youth and Enguerrand kept her from any discourse whatsoever with him, she suddenly became so mad with lust for the man that she summoned him to her side, established him in her house, gave her little daughter to him in marriage to cover their wicked intrigue, and made him the defender of her land against Thomas, for whom his so-called father cherished an implacable hatred and whom she wished to disinherit.[4] At the

[4]Nothing more is known of this marriage by which Sybille hoped to disinherit Thomas and gain the aid of an ally who would have an interest in opposing him.

time when this man was at Coucy and was declaring that he would oppose Thomas with every means in his power, although he had insufficient resources to venture upon such a difficult task, fortune proved to be his friend.

Learning that Thomas had left the city and had been followed by the people, Enguerrand and Guy (as the man was called) went to Laon and found the houses filled with an abundance of everything but without inhabitants. There was such wealth that if those who were there first had carefully guarded it from the prodigious extractions of the thieves and parasites, they would have labored in vain against this young man bent on wiping it out and he would have felt no want for the rest of his life. Who can say how much money, clothing, and provisions of all kinds were found there, or would be believed if he said it? Since the forces of the peasants and those from near the city and even from Montaigu and Pierrepoint and La Fère got there before the people from Coucy, one marvels to say what the firstcomers found and carried off when our people arriving later boasted that they had found everything in order and almost untouched! But what consideration and self-restraint could there be among brutes and fools? The wine and grain, found again and again, had no value to them, and because there were no means on the spot for carrying them off, the goods were wantonly and shockingly wasted. Then the proceeds of their plundering began to give rise to quarrels, and any booty passed out of the hands of the weaker into the possession of the stronger. If two men met a third, they were certain to plunder him. Such was the wretched state of the city. Those who had fled from it had pillaged and burned the houses of the clergy and nobles whom they hated, but now the remaining nobles seized all the property and equipment of the refugees, even down to the locks and bolts.

Not a single monk could enter or leave the city in safety without being deprived of his horse or stripped of the clothes on his body. Guilty and innocent alike had gathered at Saint-Vincent's with a great quantity of goods. How many monks, Lord God, were threatened by the swords of those desiring their lives as much as their property! Guillaume, the son of Haduin, forgetting the deliverance granted him by God, allowed the supporters of Guimar and Renier, the nobles who had been slain, to take and condemn one of his intimates, to whom he had just guaranteed the security of his life and limbs and had bound to him in fealty. The son of the castellan tied the man's feet to the tail of a horse; his brains were quickly dashed out and he was then placed on the gallows. He was named Robert le Mangeur, and he was a rich and upright man. The steward of the *vidame* of whom I spoke before, who was named Evrard, if I am not mistaken, the serf who killed his lord on the very day he had eaten with him, was hoisted up on high. Others, too, were done to death in similar ways. It is an impossible task to unravel all that happened in all the places where punishment was inflicted on the guilty and the innocent.

It should be known that Thomas entered the city on the day after the slaughter—that is, on Friday—he left on Saturday, and on Sunday God quickly sent punishment on them for their great crime. These events took place in the year 1112 of the Incarnation of our Lord, from the Friday of Easter week to April 29th.[5]

The late bishop was assuredly of unbounded levity, so that whatever foolish and worldly thought he conceived, his tongue quickly released it. I clearly saw that my cousin, whom I mentioned as recently married at Laon, conducted herself with the greatest possible modesty; but he cut her to pieces in my hearing and called her "a shitty peasant," because she held herself back from the talk and sight of strangers, and was far from forcing herself on his notice like other women. As another clear instance, I had written a book on the crusade to Jerusalem, which was sent to him when he asked to see it; he was greatly displeased with it, because he saw in the introduction that it was dedicated to my lord Bishop Lisiard of Soissons.[6] After that he deigned to read no more, although he had valued my other little works more than I deserved. And although he seemed successful in gathering wealth, he quickly squandered the whole of it on useless causes. Both these evils came to early fruition in his own days.

It should be known that these evils did not arise in him alone, but resulted from the great wickedness of others, too; in fact of the

[5]The Friday of Easter week was April 26th; April 29th (*tertio calendas maii*) fell on Monday.

[6]The *Gesta Dei* bears an introductory letter to Lisiard of Crépy, who became bishop of Soissons in 1108 and died in 1126.

whole population. In all of France, there nowhere occurred such crimes as among the people of Laon. A very little time before these things happened, when a certain priest was sitting near the fire in his own house, he was struck from behind and killed by a serving boy with whom he had been too familiar. Taking up the body, the boy hid it in a more secret chamber and locked it up. When the neighbors had not seen his master for some days and asked the servant where he had gone, he lied to them, saying the man had gone on some sort of business. And when, because of the unusual stench, the body could no longer be hidden in the house, he collected his master's property, laid the body face downward on the ashes in the fireplace, threw the shelf hanging above, which is called the drying shelf, down upon him, to make it appear that its fall had crushed him, and then fled away with the goods.

Just before the first of the month, the rural deans used to hear the cases of the priests in their districts. When a certain Burgundian priest, who was overly talkative and quick, had accused the priest next to him of some trifling matter, the dean fined him sixpence for the offense. More than a little annoyed at the fine, the priest who had lost the money lay in wait for the Burgundian when he was returning home at night. And when the Burgundian was climbing the steps of his house with a lantern, he struck him from the rear on the back of the head with a club, and the man died without giving alms for his soul.

Another time, when a priest found a priest whom he hated celebrating mass before the altar, he ordered his attendant to shoot him down with an arrow.[7] Although he did not die of the wound, the man who was the instigator and cause of it had the intention of killing the man and was not guiltless of the crime of murder and a sacrilege unheard of among Christians. Other such acts are related, done at the same time and in the same district.

Visions foreshowing the evil I have described also appeared. One man saw a moon-shaped ball fall over Laon, which meant that

[7]The sentence is deformed in some way. D'Achery and Bourgin read the word *Exosimi* as the name of the place from which the priest came, and Bourgin suggested that it was Essommes, which is not, however, in the province of Laon. This translation is based on an emendation to *exosum*, "hated."

a sudden rebellion would arise in the city. One of our monks also saw before the knees of the crucifix in the church of Notre-Dame three great beams opposite in a row. Moreover, the place where Gérard died seemed to be covered with blood. The crucifix signified someone high up in the church, who was truly opposed by three bars, his evil entry into office, his sin against Gérard, and, lastly, the one he committed against the people, which stood out as the stumbling block that brought about his end. The place in which Gérard had perished was covered with blood because the wickedness done there was wiped out by no punishment.

Moreover, I learned from the monks of Saint-Vincent that a tumult of evil spirits (as they thought) was heard, and flames appeared in the air at night in the city. Some days before, a boy was born who was double down to the buttocks; that is, he had two heads and two bodies right down to the loins, each with its own arms; double above, he was single below. After he was baptized, he lived three days. In short, many portents were seen to occur which left no doubt that they presaged the great disaster which followed.

CHAPTER 12

After the storm had died away into a calm for a little while, the church began to be restored gradually by the zeal of the clergy. Since the wall near where Gérard was killed seemed to be more weakened by the violence of the fire than the rest, at great cost they built some arches between the middle wall that had been most damaged and the outer structure. One night, with the sound of a great crash, it was so shattered by a thunderbolt that the arches joining the wall were torn asunder and the wall, partly inclined out of the perpendicular, had now to be pulled down to the foundations. O wondrous judgment of God! What judgment must Thy stern wrath pass on those men who in any way attacked a man standing in prayer to Thee, when the material wall near which that act was done was not permitted to go unscathed! Nor was Thy displeasure at such a wrong itself a wrong, O Lord. Assuredly, if my enemy lay prostrate before my knees to ask pardon and were slain by his enemy at my feet, at such an insult put upon me my wrath against the first would certainly be laid at rest. Thus it is with us men, and Thou art the very source of mercy, O God! If Thou dost crown those little children that in Herod's time were utterly ignorant of Thee, just because Thou didst cause their destruction, must we believe Thou couldst harden Thy heart against him, sinner and undeserving as he was, who was killed in contempt of Thy name? Such is not Thy way, Infinite Goodness.

Meanwhile, following the customary way, such as it is, of raising money, they began to carry around the feretories and relics of the saints.[1] And so it came to pass that the Gracious Judge, Who comforts with His pity in heaven those whom He reproves below, showed many miracles where they went. Now they were carrying, along with some box of undistinguished memory, a splendid little reliquary which contained parts of the robe of the Virgin Mother and of the sponge lifted to the lips of the Saviour and of His Cross. Whether it contained some of the hair of Our Lady, I do not know. It was made of gold and gems, and verses written on it in gold told of the wonders within.[2]

On their second trip, coming to the district of Tours, they reached the town of Buzançais, which is held by a certain robber.[3]

[1]The money-raising travels of the canons of Laon and the miracles associated with them are known from three sources: Guibert's account; the *Miracles of Notre-Dame of Laon,* by Herman of Laon (printed in Migne, *Patrologia latina,* t. 156, cols. 963–1018), written shortly after 1145 but apparently containing a report written soon after their return by those who made the journey; and the *Miracles of Notre-Dame,* by Gautier of Coincy, a work written about 1220, based on Herman and without independent historical value. Because Herman's work contains an important early reference to a Cornish belief that King Arthur was still alive, it has been subjected to close scrutiny by J. S. P. Tatlock, "The English Journey of the Laon Canons," *Speculum,* VIII (1933), 454–465; see also Simone Martinet, "Le voyage des Laonnais en Angleterre en 1113," *Mémoires de la Fédération des Sociétés d'Histoire et d'Archéologie de l'Aisne,* IX (1963), 81–92.

[2]Guibert's reluctance to accept as authentic any corporeal relics, and particularly those of one who had ascended into heaven, is noted above, p. 29. According to Herman, the reliquary bore the inscription: "May I be consecrated by the sponge and the cross of the Lord, with the cloth of Thy face and the hair of Thy Virgin Mother" (Bk. II, ch. 1).

[3]Buzançais is on the Indre near Châteauroux, on the route to Tours. This trip to the Touraine was made in 1112, not long after the burning of the cathedral.

There they preached to the people, among other things, about the disaster to their church. When our clergy saw that the lord and his garrison were listening to them with evil in their hearts and were planning to plunder them as they left the castle, the man who had the responsibility of speaking was placed in a difficult position. Although he did not believe his promises, he said to the people standing there, "If there is any infirm soul among you, let him come to these holy relics, and, drinking the water which the relics have touched, he will assuredly be healed."

Then the lord and the men of his castle were glad, thinking they must be caught for liars out of their own mouths, and they brought forward to him a servant about twenty years old, who was deaf and dumb. At that the danger and dismay of the clergy cannot be described. After they had prayed with deep sighs to the Lady of all and her only Son, the Lord Jesus, the servant drank the holy water and the trembling priest asked him some question or other. He immediately replied, not with an answer to the question but with a repetition of the exact words which the priest had used. Since he had never before heard what was said to him, he was ignorant of any words but those just used. Why prolong the story? In that poor town their hearts suddenly became larger than their means. The lord of the town immediately gave the only horse he had, while the liberality of the rest went almost beyond their powers. And so the men who had planned to be their attackers became their advocates, with many tears praising God as their helper, and they freed the youth who had been cured so that he could stay with the holy relics forever. I saw this man in our church of Nogent, a person of dull intellect, awkward in speech and understanding, who faithfully carried round the tale of such a miracle and died not long afterward in the discharge of that duty.[4]

In the city of Angers, there was a woman who had married as a little girl, and had worn the ring placed on her finger at that early age day and night, as she said, without ever taking it off. As

[4]In Herman's account, the deaf-mute cured at Buzançâis was the son of the lord of the town, about 15 years old. He says that a second deaf-mute was cured at Tours, and that the young man lived with Guy the archdeacon at Laon for about seven years (Bk. I, chs. 5 and 8). Cf. Hugues Farsit, *De miraculis B. Mariae*, ch. XI, Migne, *Patrologia latina*, t. 179, cols. 1785–1786.

years went by and the girl grew larger in body, the flesh rising up on each side of the ring had almost covered the metal, and consequently she had given up all hope of getting it off her finger. When the holy relics came there and she went with other women after the sermon to make her offering, as she held out her hand to place the money she had brought on the relics, the ring cracked and slipped from her hand before them.[5] When the people, and especially the women, saw that the Virgin Mother had granted the woman such a favor, something she had not dared to ask for, the offerings of money by the people and of rings and necklaces by the women were beyond description. Touraine took much joy from the showering of the sweet odor of the merits of Our Lady, who is common to all, but the people of Anjou boasted that in a special sense they had the Mother of God at hand.

At another place—I cannot exactly say in what town it happened, but in the same diocese—at her own urgent prayer the relics were taken by the clergy to a certain honorable lady, who had long been in the grasp of a lasting and hopeless infirmity. And when she had adored the relics with all her heart and had drunk the holy water prepared from them, at once by Mary's healing she was restored to health. After she had done honor with due offerings to God's sacred relics and their bearer had left the threshold of her house, suddenly a boy came up on a horse, drawing a coach which filled the middle of the narrow lane through which he had to pass. The cleric said to him, "Halt, until the holy relics pass by." And when the bearer had passed and the boy began to urge his horse forward, he was unable to continue his journey. The man who bore the relics then looked back that way and said, "Go on, in the name of the Lord." Once that was said, the horse and cart moved on. See what power Thou dost grant in Mary and what respect she demands for herself!

In the third journey, they came to the castle of Nesle. Now Raoul, the lord of the castle,[6] had in his house a deaf-and-dumb youth who supposedly knew the art of divination, learned no doubt from devils, and whom he was therefore said to love greatly. The relics

[5]This miracle is not reported by Herman.
[6]According to Dr. William M. Newman, whose *Les Seigneurs de Nesle* is in the process of publication, Raoul I appeared as lord of Nesle between 1103 and 1125.

were brought into the castle and honored by the people with quite small gifts. The deaf-and-dumb man, who had been informed by signs of the curing of the other deaf-mute and who now actually saw him, gave his shoes to a poor man and, barefooted and with a penitent heart, followed the relics to the monastery of Lihons.[7] As he lay during the day under the reliquary, it happened to be the hour for dinner; most of the clergy went to their meal and only a few remained to guard the relics. These men went for a short walk outside the church, and when they returned, they found the man stretched on the ground in great distress, with blood flowing from his mouth and ears with a great stench. When they saw this, the clerics called their companions who had gone to dinner to run to the scene of such a wonder. As the man came out of his fit, the clerics tried to ask him somehow or other if he could speak. Immediately he replied in the same words as he had heard his questioner use. They offered praise without limit and indescribable jubilation to God on high. At last by all sorts of prayers they were compelled to return to the town of Nesle, so that the poor first offering to the relics might be amply increased. And that was done to a wonderful degree. Here, too, Our Lady glorified herself, when her Divine Son made whole the gifts of nature which up to then He had held back.[8]

CHAPTER 13

From here they sought lands overseas. When they had traveled to the Channel, they found certain wealthy merchants with ships for that voyage and were carried across calmly, as far as the winds were concerned. But suddenly they saw the galleys of pirates, whom they greatly feared, coming on directly against them. Steering toward them with oars sweeping the waters and their prows cutting through the waves, they were soon scarcely a furlong off. As the carriers of

[7]Lihons-en-Sangterre, a Cluniac priory on the road to the coast 8 miles from Nesle.

[8]Herman (Bk. II, ch. 1) places this miracle during the trip to England in 1113, and says the name of the young man was Jean. What Guibert calls the second and third trips, Herman calls the first and second. Presumably Guibert had in mind a first trip in the environs of Laon, a second to Touraine and Anjou, and a third to England.

the relics were terribly afraid of those marine soldiers, one of our priests arose from their midst and lifted on high the reliquary in which the relics of the Queen of Heaven were kept, forbidding their approach in the name of the Son and of the Mother. At that command the pirate craft immediately fell astern, driven off as speedily as they had with eagerness approached. Then there was thanksgiving among the delivered and much glorification, and the merchants with them offered many gifts in thanks to the gracious Mary.[1]

They had a fair voyage then to England, and when they came to Winchester, many miracles done there brought renown.[2] At Exeter similar events occurred and produced many gifts.[3] Let me pass over the ordinary healing of sickness and touch only on exceptional cases. We are not writing their travel book—let them do that themselves—or what happened to each person, but are picking out examples useful for sermons. In almost all places, they were received with reverence, as was fitting, but when they came to a certain hamlet they were not admitted by the priest within the church, or by the peasants within their dwellings. They found two buildings without inhabitants and in one they bestowed themselves and their baggage and fitted up the other for the holy relics. Since that wicked crowd persisted in their obstinacy against the holy things, the next morning after the clergy left that place, suddenly, with a crash of thunder, a terrible bolt of lightning struck from the clouds and in its descent blasted their town, burning all the dwellings to ashes. But what a marvelous distinction God made! Although those two houses were in the midst of those that were burned, they remained as a manifest testimony by God that those unhappy men had suffered their fire because of the irreverence they had shown toward the Mother of God. The wicked priest, who had inflamed the cruelty of the barbarians instead of teaching them, gathered up the goods he was able to save from the heaven-sent fire and carried them away, either to the river or the sea, intending to cross over. But there all the property he had gathered together to take across was destroyed on the spot by lightning. Thus these countrypeople, un-

[1]According to Herman, the travelers embarked from Wissant on April 25, 1113. This miracle is told in Bk. II, ch. 4.
[2]Herman, Bk. II, chs. 7–9.
[3]Herman, Bk. II, ch. 12.

instructed in the understanding of the mysteries of God, were taught by their own punishment.[4]

They came to another town in which the great fervor of offerings to the sacred relics corresponded to their reputation and the evidence of the miracles. A certain Englishman standing in front of the church said to his companion, "Let's go drink." But the other said, "I don't have the money." Said the first, "I will get some." "Where will you get it?" said he. "I am thinking about those clerics," said the first, "who by their lying and their tricks get so much money out of the silly people. I will certainly manage in some way or other to get out of them the expense of my entertainment." After saying this, he entered the church and went to the consistory, in which the relics were placed, and, pretending that he wished to show his reverence for them by kissing them, he put his mouth against them with his lips open and sucked up some coins that had been offered. Then he went back to his companion and said, "Come on, let's drink, for we have enough money now for our drinking bout." "Where did you get it" said he, "when you had none before?" "I got it," he said, "by carrying away in my cheek some of the money given to those cheats in the church." "You have done something bad," said the other, "since you took it from the saints." "Be quiet," replied he, "and get along to the nearest tavern." Why am I running on? They almost drank the sun down into the ocean. When evening came on, the man who had stolen the money from the holy altar mounted his horse and said he was going home. And when he had reached a nearby wood, he made a noose and hanged himself on a tree. Dying a miserable death, he paid the penalty for his sacrilegious lips.[5] Out of the many things which the queenly

[4]Herman's account (Bk. II, chs. 10–11) rounds out this story. The travelers arrived at Christchurch (Twynham), where there was a priory with a dean and 12 canons, at the octave of Pentecost during the borough's annual fair. The dean told the Frenchmen to move on, since he did not want their competition for the offerings of the merchants. The travelers were well received by one couple, however, exposed their relics, and conducted a service, and even induced a group of merchants to boycott the dean's church and to fine their colleagues 15 shillings if they entered it. Shortly after they left the next day, the town was nearly destroyed by a great dragon breathing fire from its nostrils.

[5]According to Herman (Bk. II, ch. 20), this incident occurred at the castle of Joel of Totnes, whose wife was the sister of Guermond of Picquigny (see below, p. 200). In Herman's version the hanging was accidental.

Virgin did in England, it should be enough to have culled these instances.

After they had returned to Laon from collecting money, I have been told by a cleric of good character, who was given the job of carting wood for the repair of the roof of the church, that in ascending the mountain of Laon one of the oxen broke down from exhaustion. The cleric was exasperated, because he could not find another ox to put in its place, when suddenly an ox ran up to offer itself to him, coming as if it intended to help in the work. When he and the others had speedily drawn their carts right up to the church, the cleric was very anxious to know to whom he should return the strange ox. But as soon as the ox was unyoked, it did not wait for an oxherd or driver, but returned quickly to the place from which it came.[6]

The cleric who told me that also related the following story. On the day Bishop Gaudry set out on his journey to Rome after arranging for the death of Gérard, this man was standing behind the priest at mass (for he was a deacon) when suddenly, although the day was quite calm and no wind was blowing, the gilded eagle standing above the chest which contains the reliquaries of the saints fell with a bound as if violently hurled. From this event they then drew the following inference: that the pinnacle of the place—that is, the bishop—was going to die. But in fact I believe that perhaps this event foretold this and I also think that the honor of the most royal among all the cities of France had fallen, or rather was to fall farther. During that destruction of the city which we recounted, the king, whose greed contributed to it, did not once come back. And the royal *prévôt*, aware of the evil about to be perpetrated, sent his concubine and children on ahead and left the city a few hours before the rebellion held the city in its grip. Before he had gone three or four miles, he saw the city in flames.

CHAPTER 14

After the death of Bishop Gaudry, the clergy began to call upon the king for the election of another. Without any election, the king

[6]The oxen who served to drag material up the mountain of Laon are immortalized by the statues in the towers of the Gothic cathedral.

gave them a certain dean of Orléans.[1] This happened because the king's chancellor, a certain Etienne, who could not be bishop, was seeking the dean's office at Orléans, and when he obtained the bishopric for the dean, he acquired the deanship.[2] When the dean was brought to be consecrated and they took divination about him, they came on a blank page, as if to say, "I will prophesy nothing about him, since his acts will be almost nothing." A few months later he died. He did rebuild parts of the episcopal palace.

When he died, another man was elected lawfully and reluctantly. Lawfully, I say, in this respect, that he took office without paying for it and did not try to have dealings in simony. And yet at his divination the verse of the Gospel sounded harsh, for he had the same one as Gaudry: "Thy own soul a sword shall pierce."[3] God will have seen what misfortune threatens him.

Before we pass on to other matters, we ought to say that Thiégaud, the betrayer and slayer of the bishop, was captured by Enguerrand's knights and brought to the gallows two years after that murder. He was taken in Lent after eating and drinking almost to vomiting. Sticking out his belly and stroking it with his hand, he boasted in the presence of some people that he was full of the glory of God, which is a wicked thing to say. Once captured and thrown into prison, he sought pardon of neither God nor man, and even when brought out for his punishment, he said nothing to anyone, dying with that insensibility toward God with which he had lived. Now let me return to what I omitted.

Thomas, in league with that hateful commune, had supported those wicked murderers, first the killers of Gérard and then of the bishop, his lord and kinsman.[4] As his malice grew unspeakably worse, he was attacked with frequent anathemas by all the arch-

[1]The date of the consecration of Hugues, dean of the cathedral of Orléans, was set for August 4, 1112. He died six or seven months later.

[2]Etienne of Garland was Louis VI's chancellor from 1108 to 1127 and from 1132 to 1137, and his seneschal from 1120 to 1127.

[3]Luke 2:35. The man in question is Barthélemy de Jur, bishop from 1113 to 1151.

[4]The charge that Thomas had supported the murderers of Gérard, also made above (p. 185), is questionable. On p. 164, Guibert names Enguerrand as their supporter, and at that time Enguerrand and Thomas were bitter enemies. The statement that Thomas and Gaudry were kinsmen is otherwise unattested.

bishops and bishops throughout France, not only in councils, synods, and the royal courts, but afterward every Sunday in every parish and see. Now, his stepmother, that woman whom Enguerrand had wickedly taken to himself, had a spirit more cruel than any wild she-bear. Seeing that Thomas was becoming a sort of rival to herself, she induced Enguerrand to forswear all fatherly love toward him and even the name of father. Once she had begun by her woman's cunning to keep him out of his rights and to show herself his open enemy, she then undertook, in the words of the comic poet, to drive him from folly to insanity.[5] Steeped in worse wickedness from day to day, his mind broke out into such rage that he declared it was right and proper if in killing men he treated them no better than beasts. Because he was unjustly disinherited by a loose woman, as he actually was, he and his confederates believed he could justly indulge in an orgy of slaughter. By her ever-changing devices, that savage woman daily procured enemies to offer to him for their destruction; Thomas, on the other hand, never took a holiday from his unceasing pursuit of plunder, burning, and slaughter against Enguerrand. In our generation we have never seen two persons come together anywhere under whose administration we have seen so many evils arise from a single cause. If he was the fire, she could be called the oil.

Clearly such was the character of each that after they indulged in promiscuous acts of Venus, when the opportunity occurred, they immediately became no less cruel; in fact they were even more so. Just as the laws of marriage never restrained him, so his individual wives could not keep him from the rivalry of harlots and the bodies of others. Why say more? Since his stepmother daily spurred him on with her new undertakings and he could not satisfy his rage by the murder of innocent men—so much so that in one day he put out the eyes of ten men, whose fate it was soon to die—it came about that from mutual exhaustion they would make a momentary peace, but after a little when the woman rubbed the old sores again, once more slaughter would break out on both sides.

While the province of Laon was plagued with the quarrels of these two, by the judgment of God the disaster passed on to

[5]Terrence, *Eunuch*, 1. 254.

Amiens. After the fatal event of the destruction of Laon, the people of Amiens won over the king with a bribe and formed a commune, which the bishop ought under no compulsion whatever to have favored, especially as no one pressed him to do so and he was well aware of the miserable end of his fellow-bishop and of the conflict of the unfortunate citizens.[6] Enguerrand, who was count of the city, saw that the sworn association of the burghers was reducing his ancient rights in the county, and attacked the rebels with as much force as he could muster. In this he had the support of Adam de la Tour (for he took his name from the tower) and of the tower which he held.[7] Driven from the city by its burghers, Enguerrand retired into the tower. While the burghers were assaulting the count with repeated attacks, they called upon Thomas, as if he were their more beloved lord, to take an oath to the commune, and incited the son against his reputed father. Since his mother was absolutely shameful, he had therefore always lacked the love of his father. Meanwhile Enguerrand considered that these innkeepers and butchers despised him for the corpulence of old age, and summoned Thomas and made a treaty with him, even reconciling him to his stepmother by taking any number of oaths to this new affection. Truly active on her own behalf, she exacted from him considerable treasure in return for the new peace.

When Thomas had exhausted the great riches that he had accumulated, he also promised help to Enguerrand against the burghers, whom the bishop and the *vidame* were aiding.[8] Thomas and Adam de la Tour therefore began a vigorous attack on the *vidame* and the citizens, and as they charged the bishop and the clergy

[6]The bishop of Amiens was St. Godfrey, introduced above, p. 126. Guibert's statement makes clear that the commune at Amiens was formed by a peaceful agreement of the burghers with the bishop (and his *vidame*); the opposition came first from the count, who felt that he had not received sufficient recompense for the rights he lost, and then from the castellan, Adam de la Tour.

[7]Adam was the castellan of Amiens, an office which apparently descended from that of viscount. According to A. de Calonne, *Histoire de la ville d'Amiens* (Amiens, 1899), I, 132 and 40-42, Adam's tower, named Le Castillon, occupied the site of the present Hôtel de Ville, outside the early medieval walls of the city.

[8]The *vidame* was Guermond of Picquigny.

with taking part with the citizens, as soon as possible Thomas attacked the property of the church. In one of the manors, he established his headquarters, from which he could soon destroy the rest with fire and pillage. After he had carried off from one of them a great company of captives and much money, he burned the remaining people, a large troop of refugees of both sexes and various ages, in a church which he set on fire. Among the prisoners was one man, a hermit who had come to the manor to buy bread, who was brought before him. Now, the feast of St. Martin was close at hand, in fact the next day.[9] When the hermit tearfully declared to Thomas what his profession was, and why he had come there, begging him to have pity on him out of respect for St. Martin, if for nothing else, Thomas drew his dagger from its scabbard and drove it through his breast and heart, saying, "Take that for St. Martin's sake."

Another time he had thrust a leper into prison. When an assemblage of lepers in the province heard of it, they besieged the doors of the tyrant, crying out for their comrade to be returned to them. He threatened that if they did not go away, he would burn them alive. Fleeing in fright, when they had reached a safe place and had gathered together from every quarter, they called on God to take vengeance on him, and, lifting up their voices, they cursed him all together. That same day, the leper died in the prison where he was punished. Also a pregnant woman was put to forced labor in that prison and died there.

When some of the prisoners traveled slowly, he ordered his men to pierce the place under the neck called the windpipe and had cords inserted in five or six people and made them march in terrible pain. After a little while they died in captivity.[10] Why prolong the story? In that affair he alone killed thirty men with his own sword.

[9]Martinmas, November 11th [1113].

[10]This story sounds unbelievable, and Chaurand (*Thomas*, p. 77, n. 1) has a reasonable explanation. In Old French, the word *canole* which Guibert uses in Latin had two meanings: (1) windpipe, and (2) the cord by which the yokes of cattle were tied to their horns. Quite possibly Guibert, unfamiliar with the technical terms of the peasantry, heard a story about Thomas tying yokes to his prisoners and transformed it into the gruesome tale we have here.

His stepmother, seeing Thomas putting himself in such peril and being eager for his destruction, sent word to the *vidame* to keep secret watch on his expeditions. One night when the *vidame* surrounded Thomas with troops in ambush somewhere or other, he was wounded in his arms and legs and was struck in the knee with the lance of an enemy foot soldier. Seriously wounded in the knee and other places, he withdrew from the undertaking against his will.

Before his church suffered such destruction, the bishop was about to celebrate mass on a feast day. But the priest before him, who appeared to be devoted to the religious life, had unwittingly made the sacrament of water alone, and after him the same thing happened to the bishop. And when he had tasted the libation and found it was nothing but water, he said, "You should know for certain that some great misfortune threatens this church." The misfortune that occurred earlier to the priest confirmed this. When the bishop saw that his presence was acceptable neither to the clergy nor to the people, since he could please no one, taking a certain monk of ours as his companion and without consulting anyone else, he gave a bill of divorcement, if I may use that term, to his clergy and people, sent back his ring and shoes to the archbishop of Reims, and declared that he was going into exile and would never thereafter be bishop again anywhere. After he had thus become an ex-prelate, he went to Cluny, and, acting as bishop again by his own choice, he consecrated an altar there. Leaving Cluny, he went to La Chartreuse, about which something was said in the beginning of this little book of ours. Remaining outside the convent in a cell, he kept with him six silver marks of his traveling money.[11] After two months, when he was called back, not by any of his people but by the archbishop, he was not slow to return, for he knew the money would be useful for the return trip. The clergy and people received him with regret, for in his absence they were not sufficiently active

[11]A mark was a measure of weight equal to two-thirds of a pound. This is the sort of detail Guibert could have learned most easily from the monk of Nogent (the bishop's former monastery) who apparently accompanied Godfrey. Actually, as a novice Godfrey was required to keep his possessions until he made his profession at La Chartreuse. See A. De Meyer and J. M. De Smet, "Notes sur quelques sources littéraires relatives à Guigue Ier," *Revue d'histoire ecclésiastique*, XLVIII (1953), 168–172, esp. 172, n. 3.

to choose another as an expression of their great contempt for him. He had started a disturbance which he could not lay to rest.[12]

Once Thomas was carried home and was unable to do anything because of his earlier wound, Enguerrand's foul concubine, who was responsible for that wound, prepared to attack Adam and his tower, because Adam's son, a very handsome boy named Alleaume, had become engaged to Thomas's daughter.[13] Up to this point Adam had steadfastly opposed the burghers in fealty to Enguerrand. Then the king was brought (or brought) in, and he besieged the tower. And Adam had clearly done homage to the king and had not broken it, and the king had received him in fealty.[14]

Even those who were involved in its dangers could not describe the slaughter inflicted on the burghers by the men of the tower, not only before the siege but still more frequently afterward. There was no activity among the townsmen, only passive suffering. At the beginning, before the evil had progressed very far, Bishop Godfrey might have settled the matter easily, as everyone knows, if he had not been afraid of the *vidame,* who always held him in the greatest contempt. It is clearly his practice to respect no one and to do nothing for anyone, except to speak evilly and to act evilly toward him. The man who knowingly placates a treacherous foe through fear of being bitten, by the just judgment of God gets hurt by everyone else and especially by him.

Thomas could not bring help to the tower, into which he had sent his daughter and the most trustworthy of his soldiers. He had done such evil deeds everywhere that the archbishops and bishops complained to the king on behalf of their churches, saying that they would not carry on the services of God in his realm unless he

[12]Godfrey had notified the Council of Beauvais, which met November–December, 1114, of his abdication. He was summoned back by the Council of Soissons on January 6, 1115, and received at the Council of Reims on March 28th. According to his biographer, Nicolas of Saint-Crépin, he was welcomed back with joy.

[13]Calonne, *Histoire d'Amiens,* p. 145, gives a genealogy of the descendents of Alleaume and Thomas's daughter Milesende.

[14]Guibert's charge is that Louis had no right to attack his vassal Adam, since Adam had not broken faith with him. Suger also tells of Louis's attack on Adam in *Vie de Louis VI le Gros,* ed. Henri Waquet (Paris, 1929), p. 178.

took vengeance on him.[15] For at the time when that pestilent man was backing the burghers against Enguerrand, Gautier, about whom we have spoken before—with Guy, his fellow-archdeacon, he was the only one left of the betrayers of Gérard—had gone about the middle of Lent to see that worthy associate of Enguerrand, his own uterine sister, since he had himself forwarded that adulterous connection.[16] When Thomas found this out, he sent a hasty message to a certain Robert, the worst of criminals (for he loves such servants), ordering him and his men to watch for Gautier as he returned from Amiens and to kill as many as they could. After keeping watch from the mountain of Laon itself, Robert and his men attacked him through that dip in the road where it comes down from the mountain. Gautier had sent his company on ahead and was following into the city riding on a mule. Caught in this lonely ambush, he was most cruelly cut to pieces by their swords. After killing him, they merrily returned to Thomas with the mule.

Since the king's ears were continually assailed with the loud complaints of the churches on this and like matters, in Lent of the year following the slaying of the archdeacon he collected an army against Thomas and attacked the strongholds which he had built in the manors of the abbey of Saint-Jean. The king received hardly any hearty help from those of the knightly order, whose numbers, too, were small; but he had a very large force of light-armed troops. Hearing that these men were being raised against him, Thomas could only talk, since he was laid up utterly helpless in bed. Warned by the king to destroy the adulterine castles, he refused with foul language; when help was offered by many close to him, he hissed in derision. Then the archbishop and the bishops, going up on high platforms, united the crowd, gave them their instructions for the affair, absolved them from their sins, and ordered them as an act of penitence in full assurance of the salvation of their souls to attack that castle, which was called Crécy. With wonderful audacity, they assaulted it. Now, the fortress was of unusual strength, so that to many all their efforts seemed ridiculous. In spite of a vigorous defense, the king captured the first

[15]Such was the statement of the Council of Beauvais, in late 1114.

[16]We are now back in Lent, 1114. As the brother of Sybille of Coucy, Gautier was the son (or possibly the stepson) of Roger, count of Porcien.

moat, gained a footing at the gate of the castle, and warned the garrison to surrender it to him. On their refusal, he stretched out his hand and swore that he would not eat until it was taken. Nevertheless he drew back from the assault that day. On the morrow he returned and attacked, although hardly any of the knights were willing to take part. Charging them with open mutiny, he called upon the infantry and was himself the first to attack the moat and to try to get inside. Quickly he forced his way in, an immense quantity of supplies was found, the defenders were taken, and the castle destroyed.[17]

Not far from here was another town named Nouvion. Its keys were given up to the king and the inhabitants fled. At Crécy some of the prisoners were hanged on the gallows to terrify the defenders; others were put to death in other ways. I do not know that any of the attackers perished except one knight. Thomas remained safe at Marle; he paid a money ransom to the king and his courtiers, and came to an agreement for the damage he had done to the churches, thus returning to peace on the one hand and to Holy Communion on the other. Thus the proudest and most wicked of men was now punished through the force of the very poorest people, whom he had often punished and scorned.

I must not fail to mention that when the king came to Laon with his army, the balmy weather turned completely unseasonable. Then the archbishop said to them, "Let us pray God to give us clear weather if He wishes what we have proposed to be done." No sooner was this said than the weather turned fair.

On Palm Sunday,[18] Bishop Godfrey returned from La Chartreuse and began to spread abroad something far different from what he had learned there. He summoned the king, and on that celebrated and awesome day he preached a sermon more like one of Catiline's speeches than one that proceeded from God, inciting him and the assembled populace against the men of the tower and promising the

[17]According to Suger (*Vie*, pp. 174–178), this attack on Crécy took place before the siege of the tower of Amiens, which began in mid-April, 1115. Suger supports Guibert in saying that the estates of Crécy-sur-Serre and Nouvion-l'Abbesse belonged to the convent of Saint-Jean of Laon. But Thomas's third wife was Milesende of Crécy, and he may well have had a claim to the two places through her.
[18]April 11, 1115.

kingdom of heaven to those who should die in the assault upon it. The next day huge siege towers were brought up to the wall of Le Castillon, as it is called, and knights were assigned to them. Those of the castle had earlier protected themselves with curtain walls to prevent the taking of the heart of their defense. The bishop himself had gone barefooted to Saint-Acheul, undeserving of a hearing in this cause.[19] Meanwhile the people of the castle allowed them to approach the walls and to move up the towers. When they were set in place, a man named Aleran, who was very skilled in these matters, placed opposite them two catapults, which he had built, and set almost fourscore women to cranking the stones he had piled up. The knights inside also dueled hand to hand with the assailants. And while the men defended their ramparts with the spirit of Achilles, the women with equal courage hurled stones from the catapults and shattered both of the towers. As the shower of missiles grew hotter, it is said that fourscore were injured, and they even wounded the king himself with a shaft on his mailed breast. Moreover, of those who were pierced with arrows, only one was saved. I heard this from Rohart, a cleric who was the bishop's nephew.[20]

Seeing that they were beaten, the soldiers perched in the wooden towers began to retreat, and at once the rest followed them. Soon after they had been driven back, the defenders sallied out, destroyed the towers, and dragged the timbers inside, watched from afar by nearly three thousand men who had fought before but did not dare to attack now. The king realized that the place was impregnable and retreated, ordering it to be blockaded until the defenders were starved into submission. The siege is still going on, and it is impossible to say how many of the burghers alone perish almost every day. Established outside the suburbs of the city, Adam presses frequent attacks against Enguerrand and the *vidame*. If vexation makes them understand what they hear,[21] they could know that although Thomas was beaten, not all cases are the same and

[19]Saint-Acheul, formerly the cathedral of Amiens, became a priory of Augustinian canons in 1085.
[20]Rohart became dean of the chapter of Soissons. Nicolas of Saint-Crépin wrote his *Life of St. Godfrey* at his request.
[21]Isaiah 28:19.

the judgments of God are not equal for all, giving the bishop license to incite others to murder.[22]

CHAPTER 15

Before we pass on to our neighbors (for we are going to say something about the people of Soissons), you should know that the conduct of the people of Laon surpasses all the provinces of France in its abomination. For besides their murder of priests, a bishop, and an archdeacon, quite recently Raisinde, the abbess of Saint-Jean, a very capable woman from an outstanding family, a benefactor of the church and a native of Laon, was killed by her own serf and bore what she suffered for her loyalty to the church.[1] Why was that church not rendered desolate for the idolaters? The story proceeds in a proper fashion, for the Queen of all did not leave the deed unpunished. The servants in charge of the riches of the church, known as the sextons, began to filch the sacramental vessels, but threw the blame on the clerics in charge of them. Clearly the culprits were laymen. This is the first of several impious acts.

Secondly, a man named Anselm, sprung from the common people of the city, an uncouth and savage man, stole some crosses, cups, and gold before matins during the week after Christmas. After a time, he took a lump of the stolen gold to sell to a merchant of Soissons, revealing the sacrilegious theft he had committed and making the merchant swear an oath that he would not betray him. Soon the merchant heard that those involved in the theft were being excommunicated throughout the parishes of Soissons. Doing his duty, the merchant went to Laon and gave information to the clergy. Why say more? When Anselm was summoned, he denied it. The merchant pledged bail and challenged him to a judicial duel, which Anselm did not avoid. It was Sunday. The battle began, hurried on by some clerics, and the man who had charged the

[22]Suger (*Vie*, p. 178) says the siege went on for nearly two years. Since Guibert makes no mention of the death of Bishop Godfrey on November 8, 1115, he was presumably writing before that time.

[1]Raisinde was killed August 6, 1112.

other with theft was vanquished and fell. From this, one of two things is evident: either the man who broke his oath in giving information of the theft did not act rightly, or, what is much more likely, he was subject to a law that is completely illegal. It is certain that no canon agrees with this law of combat.[2]

Finally, Anselm, feeling safer after this victory, broke out into a third sacrilege. By an unspeakable trick, he burst open the treasure chest and carried off great quantities of gold and jewels. After this theft, when the ordeal of holy water was performed and he was thrown in with the other sextons, he was convicted by his floating on the surface, along with some others who were parties to the first theft. Some were brought to the gallows and others spared. When he was treated in this fashion, he promised to talk, but when set free, he refused. Brought back to the gallows a second time, he swore to reveal the facts. Freed again, he said, "Without a reward I will do nothing." "You shall be hanged," they said. "And you will get nothing by that," said he. Meanwhile he cast endless abuse at Nicolas the castellan, son of Guimar, the outstanding young man who was in authority.[3] The bishop and Master Anselm were asked what to do. "It is better to give him money," they said, "than that so much gold should be lost." They therefore agreed to pay him about five hundred sous.[4] When that promise had been made, he returned a large quantity of gold which he had hidden in his vineyard. He had undertaken to leave the country, and the bishop had guaranteed him three days' grace to do so. Since he wished to get away secretly during this time, he scouted all the exits of the city. Then the appearance of great floods surrounded his manor, completely preventing him from leaving. These invisible streams which had been sent to him compelled him to return openly without stealing away with his gains. Returning, he declared with many furious words that he would not go away, and when the bishop urged him, he began to mutter as if he were out of his mind, saying that he

[2]Guibert's contemporary, the canonist Ivo of Chartres, was generally hostile to ordeals, but he did include some canons which favored them in his collections. See S. Grelewski, *La Réaction contre les ordalies en France depuis le IXe siècle jusqu'au Décret de Gratien* (Strasbourg, 1924), pp. 70–83.
[3]The survival of the castellan's son is recorded on p. 188.
[4]Five hundred sous was equal to 20 pounds, a sum of money which would buy a medium-sized vineyard or five good horses.

knew something more which he had refrained from revealing. When the bishop learned this from the *vidame,* he took the opportunity to deprive him of the money he had proposed to give him, and to throw him into prison, since he had sworn that he knew nothing more. When he was put to torture, he confessed he had in his possession some jewels of filigree work. Taking them to the place, he showed them the jewels in a linen cloth hanging under a stone. With all these he had also stolen some holy reliquaries. As long as he kept them, he was unable to sleep, since the horror of his sacrilege attacked him and the saints struck his bestial mind with holy blows. He, too, was then hanged on high and sent to his fathers, who were certainly the devils.[5]

CHAPTER 16

To turn my pen now to what I promised, Jean, the count of Soissons, was skilled in war and eager for peace, but his only motive was his own advantage. He came by this naturally, for the wickedness of his father and his grandfather was always exerted for the ruin of Mother Church. Moreover, among other exhibitions of her power, his mother caused the tongue of a deacon to be cut out of his throat and his eyes to be put out. No doubt the daring of a parricide emboldened her to do this, for with the help of a certain Jew she had poisoned her own brother through greed for his county.[1] Because of that, the Jew was burned. As for herself, after dining exceedingly well on the first day of Lent, she was stricken with paralysis in the beginning of the night when she went to sleep. She lost the use of her tongue and became infirm throughout her body, and, what was worst of all, after that she had no understand-

[5]The story of Anselm *Beessus* is told in much more detail by Herman of Laon, Bk. III, ch. 28.

[1]The marriage of Guillaume Busac and Alais, daughter of Count Renaud of Soissons, is mentioned in a charter of 1066. Their son Jean is named as count as early as 1082, though Guillaume Busac seems to have been alive in 1098. Nothing is known of the murder Guibert attributes to Alais, through whom her husband acquired his rights to the county. On the family see Edouard de Barthélemy, "Les comtes de Soissons," *Mémoires de la Société des Sciences, Arts, Belles-Lettres, Agriculture et Industrie de Saint-Quentin,* Sér. 3, t. 14 (1876), 131–139.

ing of the things of God and lived the life of a pig. By the just judgment of God, her tongue was almost cut out in an attempt to cure her. So she remained from the beginning of Lent to the week after Easter, when she died. There was not only quarreling but deadly hatred of a very real kind between her and her sons, Jean and Bishop Manasses.[2] For in this family there was mutual enmity. At any rate, after she was carried to her grave and while she was being buried, the count told me what has been recorded above about her, adding, "Why should I lavish money on her soul when she was unwilling to do it herself?"

In the end the count, to whom it could properly have been said "Thy father was an Amorrhite and thy mother a Cethite,"[3] not only became as bad as his parents, but did things much worse. He practiced the perfidy of the Jews and heretics to such an extent that he said blasphemous things about the Saviour, which through fear of the faithful the Jews did not dare to do. How evilly he "set his mouth against heaven"[4] may be understood from that little work which I wrote against him at the request of Bernard the dean.[5] Since such words may not be uttered by a Christian's lips and must bring the horror of detestation to pious ears, we have suppressed them. Although he supported the Jews, the Jews considered him insane, since he approved of their religion in word and publicly practiced ours.

At Christmas and Easter and other holy days, he clearly showed such humility that we could hardly believe he was a heretic. On the eve of Easter, he had gone to watch in the church and had suggested to a certain cleric that he should tell him something about the mystery of those days. When the cleric had explained how the Lord had suffered and how He rose again, the count hissed and said, "What a fable, what windy talk!" "If you regard as wind and fable what I have said," the cleric replied, "why are you watching here?" "I am waiting with pleasure," said he, "for the beautiful women who watch[6] with you here." Although he had a pretty young wife,

[2]Manasses was elected bishop of Cambrai in 1092 and was translated to Soissons in 1103. He died in 1109.
[3]Ezekiel 16:3.
[4]Psalms 72:9.
[5]See Appendix I, p. 237, and above, p. 136.
[6]A pun in Latin, for *coexcubare* also means "to lie outside together."

he scorned her and was in love with a wrinkled old woman.[7] He had a bed in the house of a certain Jew and often had it laid out for him, but he could never be restricted to a bed and, in his raging lust, thrust himself and that filthy woman into any foul corner, or, at any rate, some closet. And he ordered a certain parasite to go and lie with his own wife after the lamps had been put out at night, pretending to be himself, so that he could fasten a charge of adultery on her. But she perceived it was not the count through the difference in bodies (for the count was disgustingly scabby) and hardily felled the rascal by her own efforts and with the help of her attendants. Why say more? He did not except nuns or holy women from his abuse, and he never gave up open rivalry with the holy brothers.

When the Virgin Mother, Queen of all, could no longer endure the blasphemies of this corrupt man, a great band of his brothers, the devils, appeared to him as he was returning from a royal expedition and approaching the city.[8] Coming home with his hair disordered and out of his wits, he repulsed his wife that night and lay with that old woman. That night he fell ill of a mortal disease. When he began to be in great pain, he consulted the cleric with whom he had kept the Easter watch for an examination of his urine. The cleric in reply spoke of his death and reproached him for his lustful acts, to which he replied, "Do you want me to pay up to those lechers?"—meaning the priests. "Not one farthing. I have learned from many wiser persons than you that all women ought to be in common and that this sin is of no consequence." Thus he spoke and all that he said or did afterward was in delirium. In trying to drive his wife away with a kick, he inflicted such a blow on a soldier as to knock him over. The hands of the madman were then bound so that he would not tear himself and his people to pieces, until he became weak and the devils wrested from him a soul that was the enemy of the Virgin Mother and her divine Son.

[7]His wife was Adeline, daughter of Nevelon of Pierrepont. When Jean charged his wife with adultery and proposed that she be judged by the ordeal of hot iron, Ivo of Chartres declared that he must prove his case through the testimony of witnesses (letter 280, Migne, *Patrologia latina*, t. 162, cols. 281–282.

[8]The obituary of the cathedral of Soissons places his death on September 24th. The date of Guibert's book, which was probably composed in 1115, sets a limit on the year of his death.

CHAPTER 17

Since we have in mind the heretics whom this abominable man loved, a certain peasant named Clement lived with his brother Evrard at Bucy, a village near Soissons.[1] As was commonly reported, he was one of the leaders of the heresy. That foul count used to say of him that he had found no one wiser. This heresy is not one that openly defends its faith, but, condemned to everlasting whispers, it spreads secretly. The following is said to be the sum of it.

They declare that the divine dispensation of the Virgin's Son is a delusion.

They consider void the baptism of young children not yet of an age of understanding under any sort of godfathers and godmothers.

They call upon God's own Word, which comes into being by some long rigmarole of talk.

They so abominate the mystery which is enacted on our altar that they call the mouths of all priests the mouth of hell.

If they ever receive our sacrament to hide their heresy, they arrange their meals so as to eat nothing more that day.

They do not separate their cemeteries from other land as being sacred in comparison.

They condemn marriage and propagation by intercourse.

Clearly, although there are few of them in the Latin world, you may see men living with women without the name of husband and wife in such fashion that one man does not stay with one woman, each to each, but men are known to lie with men and women with women, for with them it is impious for men to go to women.

They abstain from all food which is produced by sexual generation.

They have their meetings in underground vaults or unfrequented cellars, without distinction of sex. After they have lighted candles, some loose woman lies down for all to watch, and, so it is said, uncovers her buttocks, and they present their candles at her from be-

[1]Bucy-le-Long is three miles east of Soissons.

hind; and as soon as the candles are put out, they shout "Chaos" from all sides, and everyone fornicates with whatever woman comes first to hand.

If a woman becomes pregnant there, after the delivery the infant is taken back to the place. They light a great fire and those sitting around it toss the child from hand to hand through the flames until it is dead. Then it is reduced to ashes and the ashes made into bread. To each person a portion is given as a sacrament, and once it has been received, hardly anyone recovers from that heresy.[2]

If you review the heresies described by Augustine, you will find this like none of them so much as that of the Manicheans.[3] This heresy, which first originated among the more learned people, filtered down to the country population. These people, who pride themselves on keeping up the apostolic life, esteem only the reading of the Acts of the Apostles.

The two heretics named before were brought for examination to Lisiard, the illustrious lord bishop of Soissons. When they were charged by the bishop with holding meetings outside the church and were said to be heretics by their neighbors, Clement replied, "Haven't you read in the Gospels, master, where it says, 'Beati eritis'?"[4] Since he knew no Latin, he thought this meant, "Blessed are the heretics." He also believed that they were called "heretics" as if they were "heritors," doubtless not those of God. When they were examined about their belief, they gave most Christian answers, yet did not deny their meetings. But since such people deny charges and always draw away the hearts of the dull-witted in secret, they were assigned to the ordeal of exorcised water. As it was being prepared, the bishop asked me to extract their opinions from them privately. When I proposed to them the subject of infant baptism, they said, "He that believeth and is baptized shall be saved."[5] And when I perceived that with them a good saying covers much wicked-

[2]The account in these last two paragraphs seems to be based on the written report of a heresy exposed at Orléans in 1022; see *Gesta synodi Aurelianensis* in *Recueil des historiens,* X, 538.
[3]Augustine, *Concerning Heresies,* ch. 46, in Migne, *Patrologia latina,* t. 42, cols. 34–38.
[4]John 13:17, "You shall be blessed."
[5]Mark 16:16.

ness, I asked what they thought of those who are baptized in the faith of others. They replied, "In God's name do not expect us to search so deeply. When you add to that single verse, we believe everything you say." I then remembered that line to which the Priscillianists formerly agreed; that is, "Swear, perjure yourself, but do not reveal the secret."[6] I said to the bishop, "Since the witnesses who heard them professing such beliefs are not present, sentence them to the ordeal prepared for them." There was in fact a certain lady whose mind Clement had addled for a year, and there was also a deacon who had heard other wicked statements from the man's own mouth.

The bishop celebrated mass, and from his hand they received the sacrament with these words: "Let the body and blood of the Lord try you this day." After this, the pious bishop and Archdeacon Pierre, a man of great honesty who had scorned the promises they had made to escape the ordeal, proceeded to the water. With many tears the bishop recited the litany and then pronounced the exorcism. After that they took an oath that they had never believed or taught anything contrary to our faith. Clement was then thrown into the vat and floated like a stick. At this sight, the whole church was filled with unbounded joy. Their notoriety had brought together such an assembly of both sexes that no one present could remember seeing one like it before. The other confessed his error, but, being impenitent, was thrown into prison with his convicted brother. Two other established heretics from the village of Dormans had come to look on and were held with them.[7]

We then went on to the Council of Beauvais to consult with the bishops about what ought to be done.[8] But in the interval the faithful people, fearing weakness on the part of the clergy, ran to the prison, seized them, placed them in a fire outside the city, and burned them to ashes. To prevent the spreading of the cancer, God's people showed a righteous zeal against them.

[6]Augustine, *Concerning Heresies*, ch. 70 (col. 44). The Priscillianists were a sect formed in the fourth century by Priscillian, bishop of Avila.

[7]Dormans, a village on the Marne, belonged to the count of Champagne.

[8]The Council of Beauvais met in November–December, 1114. The heretics were killed by the mob before the Council of Soissons, January 6, 1115.

CHAPTER 18

At Noyon there is a parish church which Aldouin, a former bishop, dedicated to the honor of St. Nicaise.[1] When his relics were transferred by the people of Reims, they rested there for some time, not in that church, I should say, but in the city. About five years before this, although the priest ordered that the approaching festival of the martyr was to be duly honored with a holiday, that day a poor girl living alone with her mother dared to do some needlework. While she was adjusting the work to be sewn with her hands, drawing the thread over her tongue and lips in the usual way, the knot in the very coarse thread pierced the tip of her tongue like a sharp object so that it was impossible to pull it out. When anyone tried to remove it, the wretched girl was tortured with excessive pain. Accompanied by a crowd of people, the unlucky girl went with her mother to the cathedral to pray for the pity of the Queen of martyrs, but not in spoken words, for with the thread boring a hole in her tongue and hanging from it she could barely speak. Why say more? After the mob of people had in tearful commiseration looked upon the girl in her great and continuing pain, they returned to their homes. That day and the following night she persevered in prayer and remained in the company of her mother. Next day, after assailing the Queen of heaven and earth with heartfelt prayers, the mother speaking clearly and the daughter mumbling (as Anseau the priest, the sacristan of the church, told me), they had rehearsed the litany with remarkable accuracy as if they had been learned; the daughter advanced to the altar of the Virgin Mother and embraced it in tears, and quickly the thread came loose in the midst of her kisses. To the scene of such great mercy the clergy and people flocked in haste, magnifying God and the Virgin Mother in unending praises, since she had proved herself the Queen of martyrs by avenging herself on a crime committed against a martyr, and yet, when satisfaction was given, allowed her wrath in the end to be assuaged. The worth of that martyr shone forth brightly, for by

[1]Aldouin was bishop of Tournai-Noyon from 997 to about 1030.

punishing a poor humble woman he made known how great an adversary he is against the proud who oppose him. This was related to me in the very church where it happened, and the thread of remarkable thickness and the knot with the blood still on it were shown to me by the priest I mentioned before. Something like it occurred in our time on the day of the Annunciation of the Blessed Mary and has been recorded by Radbod, bishop of Noyon.[2]

In this very church of Nogent, in which by God's will we serve, a knight had committed a robbery by carrying off cattle belonging to the brothers. Coming to the castle of Chauny, he had roasted one of the oxen to be eaten, as he thought, by himself and his accomplices.[3] At the first mouthful that he took of the meat, he was stricken by the power of God, and in the midst of chewing both his eyes protruded from his face and his tongue from his mouth. Thus condemned, the man returned the rest of his booty in spite of himself.

Another knight claimed exclusive fishing rights in a part of the neighboring stream, called the Ailette, which has belonged to the brothers of the abbey since ancient times. When the knight drove away one of the brothers while he was fishing in that part of the river and beset the church with many suits over this matter, the man was stricken with paralysis in some of his limbs by the powerful Lady. And after he ascribed this to fortune and not to divine vengeance, as he slept the Holy Virgin stood by him and cuffed him severely in the face. Waking up and being brought to his senses by the blows, he immediately came barefoot to me to beg pardon, showed what the anger of the Blessed Mary had done to him, and gave up his wrongful claims. I have learned this one thing: that no one was an enemy of that church without sustaining certain damage if he chose to persist in it.

At Compiègne a royal *prévôt* opposed the church of Notre-Dame and Saints Cornelius and Cyprian.[4] When the clergy met in the

[2]Radbod II was bishop from 1068 to 1098. His similar story about the cure of a young girl of Noyon in the cathedral of Notre-Dame is printed in *Gallia Christiana,* X, Instr., col. 370.

[3]On Chauny, see above, p. 140.

[4]The church of Saint-Corneille of Compiègne was founded by Charles the Bald in honor of Notre-Dame and contained the bodies of SS. Cornelius and Cyprian.

middle of the market place and in the names of such a great Lady and such great patrons ordered him to cease, he showed no respect for the sacred names and distressed his petitioners with his foul curses. In the midst of his speech, he fell from his horse and in a moment found his breeches badly fouled beneath him by a loosening of his bowels.

As we have begun to speak of the reverence that should be shown to the saints, there is in that region a town called Saint-Just which belongs to the bishop of Beauvais.[5] When an insurrection was stirred up in this town and the dregs of the populace were running riot with the townsmen in outrageous insolence, the clergy of the boy martyr St. Just brought out the relics in the feretory to quiet the people. Some servant, more ready than the rest, stood in their way and irreverently and wickedly aimed a blow with his sword at that most holy feretory. Sooner than one could say it, he fell to the ground and, like the man just mentioned, became putrid with the stinking efflux of his excrement.

In the same district of Beauvais, on a certain manor, a priest held the cure of a church. A peasant pursued him with excessive hatred, which became so strong that he tried to compass his death. Because he could not act openly, the peasant prepared to murder him by poisoning. He therefore cut up a toad and put it in an earthen jar in which the priest used to keep the wine for mass. Now, vessels are made for this purpose with a long narrow neck and swelling belly. When he came to mass, the priest celebrated the holy mysteries with the poisoned wine. At the end of mass, he began to fall into a deadly illness, to loathe his food and to vomit up all he ate and drank, and to waste away. After he had taken to his bed for some time, at last he managed with difficulty to rise and go to the church. There he took the vessel which he knew to be the cause of his sickness, broke its neck with a knife, and poured out the liquid in it on to the pavement. The wine used for the consecration of the mass seemed full of spawn teeming with tadpoles. Knowing now that his inward parts were doomed to mortify and while hopelessly awaiting the fate that threatened him, he received from someone the following advice: "If you wish to cast out the pestilence

[5]Saint-Just-des-Marais is on the outskirts of Beauvais.

that has entered into you, ask to have dust brought to you either from the grave of Marcel, bishop of Paris, or from his altar, and if you swallow that in water you may be confident of your immediate recovery." He at once made haste to do this and swallowed the dust with great affection for the saint. At once he vomited up lumps of countless reptiles with all the poisonous stuff in which they were embedded, his health returned, and his sickness utterly left him. It is no wonder that Marcel, now with God, can do this, since he, when separated from Him by the wall of his flesh, had wrought as great miracles in a similar instance.[6]

CHAPTER 19

The story which I am about to relate, unparalleled in our times, was told to me by a religious and truly meek-spirited monk whose name was Geoffroi; formerly he had been lord of the castle of Semur and other castles in Burgundy.[1] Because his life is apparently a fitting one, I think the story ought to be told in his own words.[2] Now, this is how the story runs.

There was a young man in the upper part of the land adjoining his own who had tied himself to a woman, not by proper but by improper love, or to use a phrase of Solinus, not matrimonially but mercenarily.[3] At long last regaining his senses for a while, he decided

[6]St. Marcel was bishop of Paris in the early fifth century.

[1]Geoffroi III of Semur-en-Brionnais, nephew of St. Hugues of Cluny, succeeded his father as lord of Semur, entered Cluny about 1088, became prior of Marcigny about 1110, and died in 1123. See François Cucherat, "Semur-en-Brionnais," *Mémoires de la Société Eduenne*, N.S., B XV (1887), 296.

[2]With this disavowal Guibert places the responsibility for the grossness of the story which follows on the old soldier Geoffroi. But the Latin words for the male organ, which are of a variety and coarseness not reproduced in the translation, are surely the fruits of Guibert's classical studies. The story itself appears as a poem by Guaiferius of Salerno, an eleventh-century monk of Monte Cassino, *De miraculo illius qui seipsum occidit*, printed in Migne, *Patrologia latina*, t. 147, cols. 1285–1288. The poem says that the miraculous cure occurred near Cluny in the time of Abbot Hugues. It is noteworthy that the theme of sexual mutilation is absent from the poem of Guaiferius.

[3]"Non uxorio sed usurario" does not appear in the extant works of Solinus.

to go on a pilgrimage to Santiago in Galicia.[4] But into the lump of that pious intention some leaven was introduced.[5] Carrying the woman's sash with him, he misused it to remind him of her and was unrighteously distracted in his righteous service. On the way, the Devil found occasion to attack the man; he appeared to him in the shape of St. James the Apostle and said: "Where are you going?" "To St. James," said he. "You are not going properly," said the other, "I am that St. James to whom you are hastening, but you are taking with you something which is a great insult to my dignity. Although up to now you have wallowed in the mire of the worst fornication, you now wish to appear a penitent, and you dare to present yourself before me as though you were offering me the fruit of a good beginning, although you are still girded with the belt of that foul whore of yours." The man flushed at the charge, and, believing the other was in truth the Apostle, he said, "I know, lord, that previously and even now I have behaved very shamefully. Tell me, please, what counsel you will give to one who throws himself on your mercy." "If you wish to bring forth fruit of repentance worthy of the shame you have wrought," he said, "for God's sake and mine cut off that member with which you have sinned—that is, your penis—and afterward take your very life, which you have led so evilly, by cutting your throat." So he spoke, and withdrawing from sight he left the man very distraught.

Coming to the inn that night, he hastened to obey the Devil, not the Apostle as he supposed, who had given him that advice. While his companions slept, he first cut off his penis and then plunged the knife into his throat. Hearing the shriek of the dying man and the splash of the flowing blood, his companions awoke and brought a light to see what had happened to him. They were grieved to see their comrade come to so dismal an end, not knowing what advice he had received from the Devil. Because they were ignorant of how it had happened, they did not refuse him their services in burying him; and although in such circumstances it was not the dead man's due, they had masses celebrated for their fellow-pilgrim, as he seemed to them. When these had been faithfully offered up to God,

[4]The pilgrimage to the church of Saint James of Compostela in northwestern Spain was one of the most important of medieval Europe.
[5]Cf. I Corinthians 5:6; Galatians 5:9.

it pleased God to mend the wound in his throat and through his Apostle to restore the dead man to life. Rising up and amazing everyone inexpressibly at his revival, the man began to speak. When those present asked what he was thinking of in killing himself, he admitted the appearance of the Devil in the name of the Apostle. Asked what sentence of punishment he had received for his suicide, he said, "I was brought before the throne of God in the presence of our common Lady, Mary the Virgin Mother of God; St. James the Apostle was there, too, as my patron. When what was to be done with me was debated before God, the blessed Apostle remembered my intention, sinner and corrupt as I was, and implored that Blessed Lady on my behalf. Out of her sweet mouth she pronounced the sentence that I, poor wretch, whom the malice of the Devil had ruined through a holy guise, should be pardoned. Thus it came about that I returned to life, by God's command, for my own amendment and for the denunciation of the devils." Now, the lord who told me this said he had the tale from someone who had seen the man who came back to life. It was further reported that a plain and distinct scar was left on his throat, which spread the miracle abroad, and where his penis had been cut off he had left a little perforation, if I may put it that way, for passing urine.

There is also a famous tale, which may or may not have been committed to writing, about a certain man who had left the laity, if I am not mistaken, to put on the habit of a holy monk, and had entered a particular monastery and there taken the oath of his profession. Thinking that the rule was kept there with less strictness than he approved, he obtained permission from the abbot and went as a monk to another monastery, and there he lived with the greatest possible devotion. Some time afterward he fell ill and died of that illness. Passing from the present world, he soon became the subject of controversy of opposing powers. While the powers against him charged him with the breach of his first profession, the argument of the spirits of light, which relied on the testimony to his good deeds, was pleaded strenuously on the other side. The case was called up for hearing before Peter, the doorkeeper of heaven, and he immediately referred it to the divine presence. When the case came before Him, the Lord said, "Go to Richard the Justiciar and take his decision for your sentence." This Richard was a man of very great power through his earthly possessions, but much more powerful in his firm adherence to right and justice.[6] He went to Richard, the case was stated, and Richard pronounced his sentence: "Since he has been found guilty of breaking his earlier vow," said he, "it is clear that perjury has occurred and the devils do not have an unjust case, although the very righteous conduct of the man is against them; but my decision, inspired by heaven, commands him to return to the world to amend his faults." Rising out of death into the upper world, he summoned the abbot and told him what he had seen, publicly confessing the offense of desertion and breaking his oath, and returned to his first monastery. Everyone who vows to maintain monastic stability under the name of God at any place whatsoever should therefore know that he should keep the promise made to God and his saints, and that he ought not to change his monastery, unless he is forced to do wrong by those who are in charge there.

Since it is somctimes useful to speak of the characters of dying men, at Laon a certain man was devoted to the practice of usury wherever he could, and his end proves that he had led a life which deserved destruction. When he was near death, he demanded interest from a certain poor woman who had already paid the debt itself. She begged him to remit the interest, calling upon his approaching end, but he obstinately refused to do so. She then brought in and placed on the chest all the agreed-upon interest of that miserable loan except one penny. And when she begged him to remit that alone, he swore he would never do it. Why prolong the tale? She sought for a penny, which she was scarcely able to find, and brought it to him when in the last conflict between flesh and spirit the death rattle was in his throat. Taking it in the moment of death, he placed it in his mouth; while he was swallowing it as though it were the viaticum, he breathed his last and under that protection went to the Devil. Consequently, his body was deservedly buried in banishment from holy ground.

I will add what happened to a man of similar character in Artois. He had over a long time filled his moneybags with ill-gotten gains. At last after heaping up mountains of cash he came to his dying

[6]Richard the Justiciar, duke of Burgundy and count of Auxerre, died in 921.

hour. Suddenly the Devil appeared in the guise of a man driving a black ox before him. Standing by the bed of the dying man, he said, "My lord sends you this ox." The sick man replied, "I thank my lord for the gift." Then he said to his wife, "Prepare a meal for the man who brought the ox, and bring the beast inside and take good care of him." So he spoke and at once expired. Meanwhile, however, the man was called to have his dinner, and fodder was brought for the ox, but neither of them could be found. Everyone was amazed and frightened by what had happened and considered that no good could come of such gifts. When the funeral was ready and the body placed on the bier, there was a procession of the clergy to the house to perform the usual offices for the dead. But the devils who were celebrating the last rites for their servant raised such a storm in the air on their coming that a sudden whirlwind—although the weather was fine—almost blew off the eaves of the house, called the gutter, and lifted up part of the bier placed in the middle of the house. These stories of such devourers of the poor should suffice.

No one should be surprised that wicked spirits have much power at this time to make sport of men or injure them, for without doubt they do these acts as beasts and not in the name of the Lord. For instance, we know for certain that not many years ago in the district of Vexin some of the nobles of a certain place were hunting somewhere in the region. They caught a badger which had failed to escape to its hole and thrust it in a sack, or rather they thought they had thrust it in, when they had really put in the Devil. As night was falling, they began to carry him away, using all their strength and finding him far heavier than is usual with that beast. Suddenly a voice from a nearby hill rang out through the midst of the wood. "Listen," it said, "listen!" A great many voices from the other side shouted in reply, "What is it?" The voice then cried again, "They are carrying off Caduceus here." And perhaps he was deservedly called Caduceus for causing many to fall.[7] Thereupon endless troops of demons from all quarters rushed out as though to rescue him, so that the whole wood seemed to be crowded with their hosts. Throwing down the Devil whom they were carry-

[7]Guibert here associates the *caduceus,* the herald's staff of Mercury, with the verb *cadere,* to fall.

ing, and not a badger, and almost driven out of their senses, they fled. A short time after reaching their homes, they were all dead.

In the same province, a peasant returning from work had taken off his shoes and stockings and sat down at the edge of a stream on Saturday evening to wash his legs. Soon from the bottom of the water in which he was washing the Devil fastened his feet together. The peasant, finding himself bound, called out to his neighbors for help and was carried to his own house by them, where these men of the ignorant class tried every device to break through the fetters. They struggled for a long time in this useless round of efforts, but their labors were unavailing, for "spiritual things must be matched with spiritual."[8] After they had gone around in circles for a long time, they were joined by a pilgrim who rushed upon the fettered man in the sight of all of them and in a moment set him free. After doing this he quickly departed before anyone could ask who he was.

Stories about demons who covet the love of women and even intercourse with them are widely circulated, and if it were not shameful, we could tell a great many of them. There are some who are barbarous in inflicting their wickedness, and others who are content with sport alone. But let me now turn my pen to more cheerful topics.[9]

I heard very recently from a monk of Monte Cassino the story which I now relate.[10] An abbot of that monastery named Desiderius was a candidate for the papacy after Hildebrand, who was known as Gregory VII. Desiderius was one of the cardinals of the Roman Church, and he got the pontificate for himself with money from the vast store of goods that he had stolen away from the church of our lord Benedict. In the first celebration of the mass at which he

[8] I Corinthians 2:13, slightly altered.

[9] Since the rest of the chapter is not composed of "cheerful" material, while Chapter 20 begins with miracles of the saints, the following stories were probably added as an afterthought.

[10] Guibert could have met a monk of Monte Cassino in the entourage of the papal legate at one of the church councils of 1114–1115. In 1057, Desiderius became abbot of Monte Cassino, the mother house of the Benedictine order. He was elected pope as Victor III on May 24, 1086, and died at Monte Cassino on September 16, 1087. Other accounts suggest that he was opposed to simony and had the blessing of Gregory VII. At his death he willed the abbey of Monte Cassino many precious objects.

officiated at the Holy See, when the verse *Pax vobis* was to be said to the people, he fell down and seriously injured his head on the pavement. He was carried from the place, and one night while he slept, St. Benedict appeared to him and said: "Simoniac, how have you dared to come to such a great office? You have indeed committed a hateful sacrilege by stealing my property from me and by usurping an office completely beyond your deserts! Renounce it and devote yourself to mortification for this shameful fall, for if you choose to persist in what you have begun, you will bring upon yourself sudden and terrible retribution." When Desiderius heard this, he feared many punishments for the deception he had practiced—and especially those great punishments which the authority of so noble and powerful a person had threatened the day before. He completely renounced his undeserved office, went back to Monte Cassino, and there soberly lived out a whole year as a humble porter in reparation for the excesses with which he had insanely puffed himself up. On account of his proven humility—for he had indeed made himself very useful—he was raised to become abbot for a second time.

Things went very differently for a certain monk of Fleury, as I have often heard. With money provided by the king of France, this man stole the abbey of Fleury, which is the church of our glorious lord Benedict, out of the care of that most holy and learned man, Abbot Abbon.[11] In pursuing this man, in order to seize him like a sheep that had gone astray and put him under guard, Abbon opposed him vigorously at Orléans. When the simoniac learned for certain of Abbon's coming and could not find an escape anywhere, he repaired to the latrine, pretending that he had to go because of the weight of his bowels. On Abbon's arrival the monk was sought for, but he was nowhere to be found. All that was to be seen was his cowl hanging upon a hook—for the man had disappeared, and the only thing deserving of reverence was his sacred habit.

[11]The abbey of Fleury on the Loire 22 miles from Orléans received the remains of St. Benedict about 672; it is also known as Saint-Benoît-sur-Loire. St. Abbon became abbot in 988. His early conflicts with his monks and the role of the king, Hugh Capet, were passed over by his biographer, Aimon, and Guibert's story was probably part of the Benedictine oral tradition. Abbon was murdered by rebellious monks of La Réole in 1004.

I have also seen Veranus, a relative of mine and a nobleman, devoted to such great wrongs and evil ways of thinking that he was expelled from the rule of his abbey, even though the monarchy was in support. God usually punishes more severely those leaders who turn to crime.[12]

And I have heard that some years ago when those monks at Fleury were straying far from the rule, the most holy Father condemned many of them to loathesome deaths.

CHAPTER 20

In England, King Edmund, the most blessed martyr, has been a great miracle-worker, both formerly and now.[1] I refrain from speaking of his body, still uncorrupted and with the color not of a man but of an angel, which excites our awe because the nails and hair are still growing as if he were alive. But there is this to be said, that being in such a miraculous condition, he suffers himself to be seen by no one. In our time a certain abbot of his monastery wished to know for himself whether the head that had been cut off at his martyrdom had been reunited to the body, as was commonly reported. After fasting with his chaplain, he uncovered him and saw what I described before, that the flesh had nowhere fallen in and he had all the appearance of a sleeper. To his danger, he learned all this by sight and touch; with one at the head and the other at his feet, he pulled to see how he was and determined that the body was solid. But soon after he wasted away with a permanent palsy of both hands.[2]

Let me tell another marvelous tale. The monks in the monastery had reared a young goat from the time it was a kid. When this animal was wandering here and there about the buildings and even

[12]A Veranus was abbot of Fleury in 1080, but it is not certain that Guibert was referring to Fleury in this sentence.

[1]Edmund, king of East Anglia, reportedly was decapitated by the Danes in 870. According to legend, his head was reunited to his body in the tomb. The monastery of Bury Saint Edmunds was built around his shrine.

[2]The tale of Abbot Leofstan of Bury tugging at the saint's head is told by Herman of Bury, who wrote the *Miracles of St. Edmund* about 1100; see *Memorials of St. Edmund's Abbey*, ed. Thomas Arnold, I (London, 1890), 53–54, and the embellished account of Abbot Samson, *ibid.*, 133–134.

the church with the wantonness of its kind, it fell and broke its leg. Limping about slowly on three legs as best it could in its ramblings everywhere, it chanced to enter the church and to make its way to the feretory of the martyr. At once, as it satisfied its animal curiosity, its leg was made whole. What will the good martyr do when faithfully approached on behalf of human-kind, when he thus shows his natural generosity, or, I should rather say, his royal benignity, in the case of a beast?

St. Swithin in the city of Winchester has shown himself potent in wonders up to the present day. Not long ago a monk who had dreadful ulcers on both hands, so that in those members he was worse than any leper, entirely lost the use of them. The saint appeared to him in displeasure because this condition kept him away from the night offices on the eve of the saint's feast, and asked him why he was missing the common chanting of the psalms. Thereupon he gave as the reason for his absence the pain and festering of his hands. "Stretch out your hands," said he. He did so and the saint grasped them both and drew off like gloves the whole of the scabby skin and left it smoother than the flesh of a child.[3]

The arm of the martyr St. Arnoul was kept in the town from which I came.[4] After it was brought to this place by someone, the townspeople became doubtful about it and it was thrown into a fire to test it, but it immediately leaped out. Some time elapsed and then a cousin of mine, one of the nobles of the castle, was stricken with a very serious disease. When the arm of the blessed martyr was laid on him, the complaint shifted its ground at the touch and settled in another part. And when its virulence was put to flight and the touch of the holy arm pressed it hard, in the end after running up and down his face and limbs, the whole force of the disease flowed into the region of the throat and shoulders, the skin being a little raised like a mouse, and gathering into a ball it vanished without any pain. Because of this, every year he gave a sumptuous banquet to all the clergy present at the saint's festival, as long as he lived, and his descendants do not cease to do so to this very day. The arm was covered with thick gold and

[3]Guibert could have heard this tale from the canons of Laon who had recently visited Winchester. St. Swithin's Day is celebrated July 15th.
[4]On the relic of St. Arnoul at Clermont, see below, p. 233, n. 17.

jewels, not by the wife of my grandfather but by a certain woman familiar with such practices who was skilled in worldly things.

The arm of St. Arnoul is also said to be at the castle of Guise in this same district of Laon.[5] Some thieves who had plundered the church wished to steal this, too, and laid their hands on it, but it wrested itself from their grasp and could not be taken anywhere. After these thieves were caught with the rest of their booty, they confessed this at the time when they were to be carried to the gallows. In the gold with which the arm is adorned, there is a spot where no jewel can be fastened securely by any skill of the gem setter. As soon as one was set there, it became loose, and when the workman was changed, neither the new workman nor his work were of any avail.

We know that the martyr Léger is an eminent miracle-worker and a ready helper in need. When I was a little boy living under my mother's authority (although I still remember this clearly), at Easter I was violently ill of a quotidian fever. Below the town, there was a church dedicated to SS. Léger and Maclou, where my mother in humble faith supplied an oil lamp continually burning. When I turned against almost every kind of food, she summoned two clerics, her chaplain and my schoolmaster, and ordered that I should be taken there in their care. In accordance with the bad practice of ancient custom, that church was under her control.[6] The clerics came there and ordered that a bed should be made for me and them before the altar that night. Suddenly, in the middle of the night, the ground inside the church began to be beaten as if with hammers, the locks of the chests were torn off with a loud noise, and sometimes the cracking of sticks could be heard above the chests. When the clerics were awakened by the sounds, they began to be afraid that the fright would make me worse. Why say more? I heard them muttering in low voices, but I was only moderately afraid because of their companionship and the comfort of the shining lamp. Passing through the night this way, I returned safely to my mother as if I had suffered no inconvenience, and I

[5]The arm kept at Guise was transferred to the church of Saint-Pierre of Bucilly about 1570; see *Acta Sanctorum, Julius*, IV, 401–402.

[6]There is a church dedicated to St. Léger at Agnetz, which is about a mile below the hill of Clermont to the west. This church later became the property of the abbey of Saint-Germer.

who had earlier turned from the most delicious dishes was now eager for ordinary food and was just as ready for a game of ball.

King William I of England had a tower built at his expense in the church of the mighty Denis (whose dimensions, had it been finished and still standing, would have been extremely great). Since this work was not well constructed by the masons, during his lifetime it was seen to produce destruction. When Ivo, who was abbot at the time, and the monks were afraid that the fall of the new construction would ruin the old basilica, where the altars of St. Edmund and some others were, the disturbed abbot had this vision.[7] He saw a lady with a very honorable appearance standing in the nave of the church of Saint-Denis and blessing water in the manner of a priest. And while the abbot was wondering at the power of the woman, whose behavior was unfamiliar, he noticed that after the blessing of the water, she sprinkled it here and there, and after the sprinkling she made the sign of the cross all round, wherever she had sprinkled. Suddenly the tower fell, but it harmed no part of the church in its fall. For she who is blessed among woman, the fruit of whose womb is blessed,[8] had protected it with her own blessing seen in the vision of the abbot. In its fall it buried a man walking beneath. When it was discovered that the man was buried under all the stones, out of human concern they began to remove the pile from him. At last when the mountains of stone and rubble had been taken away, they came to him, and it is wonderful to relate that they found him safe and cheerful, as if he were sitting at home. The squared stones had wedged themselves together in a straight line to make a little room for him. Although he was kept there I do not know how many days, neither hunger, fear, nor a very offensive smell of mortar did the imprisoned man any harm.

Let us now place the name of the most excellent Mary, Queen of heaven and earth, together with that of Denis, lord of all France, as a conclusion to this book.

[7]Guibert is the only author to refer to this tower, whose foundations were discovered in 1946. Built against the northwest side of the eighth-century church of Abbot Fuldrad, between the transept and the nave, King William's tower had a square base about 34 feet across. Ivo was abbot from 1075 to 1094. See Sumner McK. Crosby, *L'abbaye royale de Saint-Denis* (Paris, 1953), p. 21 and picture on p. 53.
[8]Cf. Luke 1:42.

Appendix I

Guibert's Birth and Family and the Chronology of His Writings

Readers of Guibert's *Memoirs* have long been troubled by his failure to provide us with such basic details as the year and place of his birth and his family background. He is not responsible for our uncertainty about the year of his death, but that date, too, has been subject to discussion, and the chronology of his writings remains undetermined. The purpose of this appendix is to re-examine these details, of minor importance themselves but basic to our understanding of Guibert's own story of his life.

Dom Jean Mabillon suggested in his *Annales Ordinis S. Benedicti* that Guibert was born in 1053, and that suggestion has been followed to the present day. It is based on the slightest evidence, however; the only support Mabillon gives is that Guibert says he was born on the day before Easter *(vigilia Paschalis)*, a time which he also describes as *iduato ferme aprili*. Mabillon interprets this latter phrase as "a little before the Ides of that month" *(paullo ante idus illius mensis)*. Since in 1053 Easter fell on April 11th—that is, a little before the Ides on April 13th—Mabillon felt that the date was established.[1] It can easily be seen, however, that 1053 is only a possible year, and that without further evidence the date of Guibert's birth remains undetermined. Mabillon was, moreover, too narrow in defining *ferme* as "a little before," since Guibert uses the word to mean "almost"

[1]Ed. Lucca, 1739 1745, IV, 497.

[2]At one point (p. 44) Guibert refers to the time between his birth and his father's death as "about eight months" *(octo fere mensium spatium)*,

or "about."[2] All Guibert has told us in this passage is that he was born the day before Easter in a year when Easter fell "about" the middle of the month of April.

Mabillon's suggestion was called into question by Professor Jan Dhondt in an article on "Les relations entre la France et la Normandie sous Henri Ier."[3] Dhondt was concerned with a passage in which Guibert relates that his father was captured during a conflict between King Henri of France and Duke William of Normandy, and that since it was William's custom "never to hold his prisoners for ransom, but to condemn them to captivity for life" (p. 69), his mother was crushed with despair. Guibert goes on to say that he was not yet born: *necdum enim natus eram, nec longo post tempore fui.* Following ordinary classical construction, Dhondt read this passage to mean "a little before his birth."[4] Others have read the passage in the same way, asserting that William never released Guibert's father and that Guibert was born not long after his capture.[5] Dhondt goes on to conclude that Guibert's father was very likely captured at the battle of Mortemer. Since he dates the battle of Mortemer early in the year 1054, it follows from his reasoning (though he does not say so directly) that Guibert was born in the spring of that year.

Mabillon had not known what date to assign to the capture of Guibert's father, but Dhondt quite reasonably associates it with the battle of Mortemer, which the *Annals* of Saint-Evroult record under the year 1054 and which Ordericus Vitalis says took place "in the winter before Lent."[6] Dhondt's discussion of Guibert's birth is intended to show that the *Annals* began the new year at Christmas rather than in the spring, so that the date according to modern reckoning would be early in 1054 and not 1055. In order to do this, he asserts that Guibert could not have been born in

---

at another (p. 70) as "scarcely half a year" (*annus ferme dimidius*). One should not expect precision in Guibert's use of the rare word *iduatus*, since he is indicating the size of reeds at a certain season, not an exact date.

[3]*Normannia,* XII (1939), 465–486, esp. pp. 477–478.

[4]*Ibid.*, p. 478.

[5]This is the view of Bourgin (p. iii) and of most other commentators.

[6]*Historia ecclesiastica,* ed. Le Prevost, III, 237, and V, 157.

1055, because Easter fell on April 16th in 1055 and Guibert says that he was baptized "about April 13th."[7] This reasoning is curious and unconvincing, since if Guibert was born shortly after the battle of Mortemer, and the battle of Mortemer occurred in early 1054 rather than in 1055, then Guibert must have been born the day before Easter in 1054; that is, on April 2nd. Dhondt's argument must then rest on his assumption that Guibert was baptized a few days after his birth. He fails to note, however, that Guibert refers to "that joyous day on which I was born and reborn" (p. 42), and one would expect a baby likely to die to be baptized immediately, as Guibert's account suggests he was.

Must one then accept that Dhondt, correct in rejecting the date of 1053 for Guibert's birth, was wrong in his date of 1054 for the battle of Mortemer, and that both the battle and Guibert's birth took place in 1055? While Dhondt's analysis provides no other evidence which forces us to eliminate early 1055 as a possible date for the battle of Mortemer, Guibert's statement about his birth is not evidence that it did occur in that year. The solution to this problem lies in separating Guibert's birth from the capture of his father by a long time, rather than a little. The phrase *nec longo post tempore fui* is in fact ambiguous. It can be read as saying "I was born a short time later," but that is not likely from the context. The point of Guibert's phrase is to explain why at this point in his story he does not use the word "mother," but refers instead to his father's wife. He avoids the word, he says, because he was not yet born, and was not for a long time after. This interpretation is only possible, of course, if Duke William released his father from captivity. But we know from another source that William did in fact ransom prisoners captured at Mortemer,[8] and Guibert's father must have been present at his birth, for Guibert says that his father was crushed with sorrow at his mother's difficult labor, and he later refers to the vow which his father made that he should then be offered to Mary as an oblate (pp. 41 and 44). As to the Latinity of the troublesome phrase, there is some re-

[7]Dhondt, "Relations," p. 478.

[8]Guillaume of Poitiers, *Gesta Guillelmi ducis Normannorum et regis Anglorum*, ed. Raymonde Foreville (Paris, 1952), p. 74

assurance in knowing that this interpretation was that of Mabillon, who was certainly excellently versed in monastic Latin.[9]

If we can reject the birth date of 1053 as unsubstantiated, and if we are not forced to place it a few months after the battle of Mortemer, then what is the most likely date? We have a *terminus ad quem* in the information that when Guibert began his studies at Saint-Germer, St. Anselm was still prior of Bec. Since Anselm was elected abbot of Bec shortly after August 26, 1078, and Guibert was at least twelve and probably thirteen when he entered Saint-Germer, he must have been born no later than 1066, and 1065 is a likely upper limit.[10] Besides saying that it was "a long time after" the clash between Henry and William, it is hard to be as certain about the *terminus a quo*. There is reason, however, to suggest that it should be placed in 1064. This conclusion is based on Guibert's statement that he received "all the sacraments of benediction" *(omnia benedictionum sacramenta)* from Bishop Guy of Beauvais, who became bishop in the fall of 1063 or early in 1064.[11] "All the sacraments of benediction" presumably includes the sacrament of baptism. As bishop of Beauvais, Guy could have been in Guibert's birthplace near Beauvais on the day before Easter; it is unlikely that he would have been there before he became bishop, since he was earlier dean of Saint-Quentin and then archdeacon of Laon.[12] The dates of Easter in the three years marked out by these limits are April 11, 1064, March 27, 1065, and April 16, 1066. In picking a date which is "about the Ides of April," 1065 is eliminated. As was said before, 1066 is quite unlikely, since it leaves so little time between Guibert's entry into Saint-Germer and the date when Anselm was elevated from prior to abbot that one wonders why Guibert would mention the distinction. Although it falls short of a desirable degree of certainty, April 10, 1064, seems the most likely date for Guibert's birth, with April 15, 1066, a possible, though remote, alternative.

Placing his birth a decade later than the usual estimate makes

[9]*Annales O. S. B.*, IV, 444: "Haec [the capture of Guibert's father] verò longè ante natum Guibertum accidisse testatur Guibertus ipse."
[10]See above, pp. 72 and 89; Eadmer, *The Life of St. Anselm*, ed. Richard W. Southern (Edinburgh, 1962), p. 44.
[11]Above, p. 74. Guy's predecessor died in September, 1063.
[12]*Gallia Christiana*, IX, 708–711.

better sense of other chronological indications in Guibert's story. In the first place, Guibert says that before his mother left him to enter Saint-Germer (which happened when he was twelve), she attempted to get a prebend for him in the local church. This occurred, he says, at a time when "the Apostolic See was making a fresh attack on married priests" (p. 51). This description would accurately apply to the pronouncements of Gregory VII's Lenten synod of 1074.[13] Secondly, a birth date of 1064 makes sense of Abbot Garnier's objection to Guibert's commenting on the Hexameron. It was not that Garnier was anti-intellectual, but simply that a youth under twenty was too young to comment on one of the most demanding parts of the Bible.[14] Thirdly, when Guibert described his speech before Pope Paschal in 1107, he referred to his *iuventus* (p. 154). While one can accept a man of forty-two alluding to his immaturity, such a statement seems inconsistent with Mabillon's birthdate of 1053. And lastly, as we shall see, Guibert was still writing in 1124 or 1125. While it is conceivable that Guibert was still an active abbot and author in his seventies, the inexorable odds of tables of longevity, medieval or modern, make a death date in his sixties more likely.[15] If 1064 is not established with certainty, it is still much more probable than the accepted date of 1053.

Although based on a fuller discussion of evidence, Mabillon's identification of Guibert's birthplace has been less widely accepted than his dating. Mabillon gave four reasons for thinking that Guibert was born in Clermont-en-Beauvaisis.[16] In the first place, Guibert says directly that his brother was *municeps* of the castle of Clermont, situated between Compiègne and Beauvais (p. 51). Secondly, an arm of St. Arnoul was preserved in the *oppidum* where he was born, and Mabillon points out that such a relic existed in his own day in the church of Notre-Dame of Clermont.[17]

[13]Augustin Fliche, *La réforme grégorienne* (Louvain, 1924–37), II, 136–141.
[14]See above, p. 91 and n. 14.
[15]For a recent consideration of aging, see Creighton Gilbert, "When Did a Man in the Renaissance Grow Old?" *Studies in the Renaissance*, XIV (1967), 7–32.
[16]*Annales O. S. B.*, IV, 497.
[17]Above, p. 226. What Mabillon did not know is that this relic had been given to the chapter of Clermont by the monks of Saint-Arnoul of Crépy-en-

Thirdly, Guibert says that there was a church dedicated to SS. Léger and Maclou below the town *(sub oppido)*, and in fact there is a church dedicated to St. Léger at Agnetz, a mile below the hill of Clermont.[18] And, finally, Guibert refers to the village of *Castanetum* as being about two *milliaria* from his town, and Catenoy is about that distance from Clermont.[19]

Guibert's first editor, Dom Luc d'Achery, thought that Guibert was born in Beauvais, other authors have suggested that he may have been born in Agnetz or Catenoy, and Bourgin raised the question and left it open.[20] The latest to discuss the matter in detail was Dr. Léon Dautheuil in his article "Où est né Guibert de Nogent?"[21] The answer to this question, in his opinion, is the hamlet of Autreville. Dautheuil usefully shows that *Castanetum* is Catenoy in the region of Clermont, and not a place near Beauvais.[22] But his determination of Autreville is simply mechanical; setting his compass for 3.4 kilometers, the distance he thought appropriate for *duo milliaria*, he marked out Autreville on the old

---

Valois in 1608 (see Oise, arch. dép. G 6377). All the same, it appears that a relic did exist at Clermont earlier. In his "Recherches historiques et critiques sur l'ancien Comté et les Comtes de Clermont-en-Beauvoisis," *Mémoires de la Société Académique . . . de l'Oise,* IX (1874), 56, n. 2, Eugène de Lépinois states that the arm of St. Arnoul was destroyed in the sack of Clermont in 1359. Unfortunately, Lépinois does not give his source. Presumably there was a relic of some sort, since the church was also named for St. Arnoul.

[18]Above, p. 227. Guibert liked to name other saints venerated at a church besides the one which provided the name; e.g., he refers to Saint-Corneille of Compiègne as the church of Notre-Dame and Saints Cornelius and Cyprian (p. 216). That we have now no record of the veneration of St. Maclou at Agnetz does not argue against the identification.

[19]Catenoy is about 7 kilometers from Clermont. The problem is to know how far Guibert considered two thousand paces to be. In another place (ed. Migne, t. 156, col. 564), he refers to the distance from Chivy to Laon as "interstitium ferme duorum millium," and that distance is 6 kilometers. Allowing for the imprecision expressed by *ferme*, the two measurements are reasonably close.

[20]To the reference given by Bourgin (p. ii), add Denis Simon, *Supplément à l'histoire du Beauvaisis. Pt. II. Le nobiliaire de vertu* (Paris, 1704), p. 50, who suggests that Guibert was a native of Catenoy or Agnetz.

[21]*Bulletin et Mémoires de la Société Archéologique et Historique de Clermont de l'Oise,* années 1933–37 (1938), pp. 28–35.

[22]Guibert says that *Castanetum* belonged to Bishop Guy of Beauvais; Dautheuil points out that Catenoy had once been the property of the bishops of Beauvais.

road from Compiègne to Beauvais. No text or remains, however, tell us that Autreville was an *oppidum,* that it had a relic of St. Arnoul, or that below it there was a church dedicated to SS. Léger and Maclou. Clermont, a hilltop fort and supporting community, fits the term *oppidum.* Beauvais, a true *urbs* or city, would be too important and, in any case, does not fit the other indications. There is no evidence that there was ever fortification at Autreville. Agnetz and Catenoy were suggested without reflection, for Guibert clearly says that these places were at a distance from his *oppidum.* No other candidates for the honor have been put forward. Bourgin points out that Rouen and Guise both had relics of St. Arnoul,[23] but this is beside the point, since neither fits the other qualifications, and Guibert himself mentions the relic at Guise as different from that at his birthplace. Only Clermont-en-Beauvaisis accords with all the information we have, and it accords very well indeed.

Once his birthplace is determined, we can turn to the question of Guibert's family. He tells us enough to suggest that his family was fairly highly placed on the social scale. His father, named Evrard, fought for King Henri against William the Conqueror; Bourgin concluded from this that he was a vassal of the king.[24] An uncle named Lisiard was an archdeacon of Beauvais (p. 117). Evrard of Breteuil, one of the great barons of the region, was his relative (p. 57). Countess Hèlisende of Eu was his *familiaris* and called him her son (p. 136). His grandfather had been the protector of Abbot Garnier of Saint-Germer (p. 77). Guibert's mother had dressed him so finely that he "seemed to equal the sons of kings and counts" (p. 68), and as a grown man Guibert presented himself as being on familiar terms with the higher nobility.

One must wonder, therefore, if Guibert was an immediate member of the family of Breteuil or that of the lords of Clermont. The answer is apparently not. There seems to be no way to fit him and a father named Evrard into the genealogy of the house of Breteuil without his being the brother of the Evrard of Breteuil whom he mentions, and that is highly unlikely from the way he writes of the man. There are no known Evrards or Guiberts in the family of the lords of Clermont, and in any case Guibert distin-

23P. ii.

24Above, p. 69; cf. Bourgin, p. iii.

guishes his relatives from the lord of Clermont by saying that they appealed to the *dominus oppidi* for a prebend for him.[25]

What we do know is that his brother was a *municeps* of Clermont and another relative was one of the *castri primores* (pp. 50 and 226). Presumably Guibert's family lived at Clermont and assisted in the defense of the castle as vassals of the lord of Clermont, the *dominus castrensis*. It was probably as a vassal of Renaud of Clermont that Guibert's father fought against Duke William, and we know from Ordericus Vitalis that Renaud of Clermont narrowly escaped capture at Mortemer. Since it was his father's nephew, rather than his brother, who was *necessarius* of the lord of Clermont, it is likely that his father was one of the younger brothers of the family, rather than the head of the household. These slight indications point to the conclusion that Guibert's father was the younger son of a noble family of Clermont which was itself subordinate to the lords of Clermont. His mother came from a distant region (p. 64), perhaps from near Saint-Germer or from Normandy itself, and her family may have been of somewhat higher standing than that of her husband.

In understanding Guibert's life and work, it is desirable to know not only his origin but something of his development and the progression of his thought. Although it is difficult to assign precise dates to most of his writing, it is possible to establish the following approximate chronological order.

1. Youthful erotic verse. Guibert says that he wrote verses, which he modeled on classical authors, anonymously or under an assumed name (p. 88). Unfortunately we have no way of attributing any specific surviving eleventh-century poems to Guibert.

2. *Liber quo ordine sermo fieri debeat.* This work, which was affixed as a preface to the commentary on Genesis, was written before Abbot Garnier retired from Saint-Germer; that is, before about 1084 (p. 91).

3. *Moralia in Genesim.* Guibert says that this work, begun before Garnier's retirement, was quickly brought to a conclusion when he was free from his abbot's authority (p. 91).

[25]Above, p. 51. On the early history of the lords of Clermont, see Lépinois, "Recherches critiques," IX (1874), 13–17; X (1875), 11–25.

4. *Epistola de buccella Judae data.* Written for Siffroi, prior of Saint-Nicolas-aux-Bois near Laon, this letter was composed after Guibert went to Nogent in late 1104. Since the major argument of the letter, which was written in response to a request, is mentioned in passing in the *Gesta Dei per Francos,* it is likely that the letter was composed first.[26]

5. *Gesta Dei per Francos.* This book was composed about 1108, since Guibert says it was written about two years after the death of Archbishop Manasses of Reims (September 18, 1106).[27]

6. *Tractatus de Incarnatione contra Judaeos.* This work was written at the request of Bernard, dean of Soissons, and therefore presumably after Guibert went to Nogent. Guibert tells of sending a copy of this work, "which I had written about four years before," to Guillaume the Jew at Saint-Germer (p. 136). If that reference means that he wrote it four years before the *Memoirs* (and not four years before he sent it), then it can be dated to about 1111. The alternative reading would place it even earlier.

7. *Monodiae (Memoirs).* This work can be dated fairly precisely to 1115. The first book was composed before the capture of Guillaume of Nevers in the fall of 1115 (p. 61). On the other hand, since it contains information about recent events at La Chartreuse, it is likely that it was written after Godfrey of Amiens returned from there, since Godfrey seems to have been accompanied by a monk of Nogent who could have given Guibert his information (p. 202). The final book recounts events which took place in the spring of 1115, and says that the siege of Le Castillon was still continuing (p. 206). According to Suger, that siege ended after two years, so 1117 is the absolute *terminus ad quem.*[28] But since the book treats Godfrey of Amiens, who died on November 8, 1115, as if he were still alive, it is likely that it was completed before the end of 1115 (p. 207).

8. "A little book in chapters on various meanings in the Gospels and the prophets, including some things from the books of Numbers, Joshua, and Judges" (p. 92). Guibert states in his *Memoirs* that

[26]Ed. Migne, t. 156, col. 527 (cf. Vatican ms. Regina lat. 235, fol. 56), and *Gesta Dei,* p. 126

[27]*Gesta Dei,* p. 219.

[28]*Vie de Louis VI le Gros,* ed. Henri Waquet (Paris, 1929), p. 178.

this work was uncompleted at the time he wrote; it has never been identified.

9. *Liber de laude Sanctae Mariae.* Since it refers to Bishops Barthélemy of Laon and Guillaume of Châlons, this work was written after 1113. Probably it was composed shortly after the Council of Reims in October 1119, for Guibert tells a story which he says Bishop Léger of Viviers had recently related to King Louis in the presence of Bishop Guillaume of Châlons; according to Ordericus Vitalis, the bishops of Châlons and Viviers were prominent spokesmen at this Council, which the king also attended.[29]

10. *Tropologiae in Osee, Jeremiam, et Amos.* The letter of dedication to St. Norbert places the completed work in 1121 or after, since Norbert settled in the region of Laon in 1121. It was probably written before he became bishop of Magdeburg in 1126.[30]

11. *Tropologiae in Abdiam, Jonam, Micheam, Zachariam, Joel, Nahum, Habacuc, et Sophoniam.* The letter of introduction to this work, addressed to Abbots Geoffroi of Saint-Médard and Alard of Florennes, makes clear that this commentary was written after the preceding one. Geoffroi became abbot in October, 1119.[31]

12. Abel Lefranc speculated that *De pignoribus sanctorum* was Guibert's last work, although he had no definite proof of it.[32] Although it is not possible to show whether it was written before or after the commentaries on the minor prophets, the approximate date of the work can be established. In this treatise, Guibert relates a miracle in which a child cried out in church that the priest celebrating mass was holding an infant in his hands, and says that this event occurred at Soissons last Easter.[33] By good fortune the same tale is told in the *Vita A* of St. Norbert.[34] Ac-

[29]Ed. Migne, cols. 570 and 572; cf. Ordericus Vitalis, *Historia ecclesiastica,* ed. Le Prévost, IV, 389. Bishop Léger was also known as Hatton, the name used by Ordericus; see Jacques Rouchier in Louis de Mas Latrie, *Trésor de Chronologie* (Paris, 1889), col. 1515.

[30]On Norbert's career see Godefroid Madelaine, *Histoire de saint Norbert* (3rd ed., Tongerloo, 1928).

[31]For the letter, see Mabillon, *Annales O. S. B.,* VI, 592; cf. *Gallia Christiana,* IX, 187.

[32]"Le traité des reliques," p. 287.

[33]Ed. Migne, t. 156, cols. 616–617.

[34]*Vita Norberti,* ch. XI, ed. Roger Wilmans, in *Mon. Germ. hist., Scriptores,* XII, 681.

cording to this version, in early December of the winter when Norbert came to Laon to learn French—that is, in late 1120—a woman of Soissons named Helwige came to the saint complaining that she was childless. Norbert predicted that she would have a child. She did, and named him Nicolas, after the feast being celebrated at the time. After Helwige's visit, the Council of Soissons, at which married priests were denounced, was held in early 1121, leading many to say that the host held by married priests at the altar was not the body of the Lord. Then when her son was five years old, says the *Vita,* Helwige took him to church and there he had his miraculous vision of the infant Jesus held in the hands of a married priest.

The information in the *Vita* places the boy's birth in 1121. While the five years may have been an error, it is unlikely that the event occurred when the boy was two and a half; that is, in 1123. "Last Easter" may have been in 1124, but it is more likely that it was in 1125, and it could possibly have been in 1126. The treatise was probably not written after that year, since it was dedicated to Abbot Eudes of Saint-Symphorien of Beauvais, whose death is dated in 1126.[35]

The date of the composition of *De pignoribus sanctorum,* probably about 1125, pushes hard on the date usually assigned to Guibert's death. The last dated document which refers to Guibert as alive is his testament, written in 1121.[36] D'Achery, Mabillon, and some other historians place his death in 1124, but this date is presumably only an estimate, since no evidence for this specific year is indicated.[37] The *terminus ad quem* is 1129, in which Guibert's successor at Nogent, Abbot André, appears as a witness.[38] Without further documentation, all that can be said about this date is that *De pignoribus sanctorum* was written about 1125 and that its author died within the next few years.

[35]*Dictionnaire d'histoire et de géographie ecclésiastiques,* VII, 258.
[36]Bourgin, p. xii, n. 5. Bourgin has misprinted 1122 for 1121.
[37]*Ibid.,* p. xvi, n. 1.
[38]Cartulary of Prémontré, Soissons, Bibl. mun, ms. 7, fol. 97v, printed in Migne, *Patrologia latina,* t. 156, col. 1127.

Appendix II

Emendations of the Latin Text

It is an interesting indication of national differences on the eve of World War I that while the French reviews of Bourgin's edition were uniformly favorable and suggested no corrections to his text, a number of German reviewers were quite critical of Bourgin's editing. The reviews which proposed specific emendations are: O. Holder-Egger in *Neues Archiv der Gesellschaft für ältere deutsche Geschichtskunde,* XXXIII (1907), 236–238; S. Hellmann in *Historische Vierteljahrschrift,* 2nd ser., XII (1909), 315–316; and E. R. Curtius in *Münchener Museum für Philologie des Mittelalters und der Renaissance,* II (1913), 205–210, reprinted in his *Gesammelte Aufsätze zur romanischen Philologie* (Bern and Munich, 1960), pp. 54–57.

In the preceding translation, I have made use of many of the emendations suggested by these reviewers and have added a few of my own. A list of all of the changes from Bourgin's text follows. The reader should, of course, also note Bourgin's own list of *corrigenda* on p. 251 of his edition.

p. 7, line 6: *minus* for *magis*
p. 9, line 2: *naturaliter* for *nataliter*
p. 14, line 3 of ch. V: *ludis* for *lupis*
p. 16, line 7: *nam* for *non*
p. 17, line 12 of ch. VI: *persulcaret* for *proculcaret*
p. 22, line 14: *alio* for *alii*
p. 25, line 5: comma after *provincias,* semicolon after *ignaras*
p. 33, line 3 of 3rd paragraph: *ceteris* for *certis*
p. 36, line 2 from bottom: *ingenua* for *ingenita*

p. 40, line 6: *temptamenta* for *temperamenta*
p. 42, last line: *latitudo* for *lassitudo*
p. 43, line 14: *exanimata* for *examinata*
p. 50, line 17: *pertusuris* for *partusuris*
p. 59, line 6: *perhibentur* for *prohibentur*
p. 67, line 3: *putabatur* for *putabantur*
p. 67, line 1 of 2nd paragraph: *quondam* for *quodam*
p. 68, line 6: *Suspicatus* for *Suspicatur*
p. 78, lines 2–3: *addidici* for *addidi ei;* line 11: *nolui* for *volui;* line 25: *volebam* for *nolebam;* last line: *dilatationem* for *dilationem*
p. 83, line 4: *acediosus* for *acidiosus*
p. 87, line 23: *in genibus* for *ingentibus*
p. 88, last line: *sacrilegos* for *sacrilegas*
p. 100, line 3 from bottom: *nedum* for *necdum*
p. 101, line 15: *ilico* for *illo*
p. 103, line 16: *sederat* for *sed erat*
p. 113, line 12: comma after *verbum;* line 13: *quia* for *Quia;* line 14: period after *contexere; Ipsa* for *ipsa*
p. 115, line 8: *perhibetur* for *prohibetur*
p. 116, line 17: *miserabili* for *mirabili*
p. 121, line 4, first word: *cum* for *eum*
p. 123, line 6 of 2nd paragraph: *noluissetis* for *voluissetis*
p. 131, line 2: *creaverat* for *crearat;* line 4 of 2nd paragraph: *dilatationem* for *dilationem*
p. 137, line 5 of ch. IV: *creaverat* for *crearat*
p. 155, line 18: *loquar* for *loquor*
p. 157, line 17: *miter ne* for *miterne*
p. 164, line 4 of 2nd paragraph: *nisi* for *si;* line 2 from bottom: period for question mark
p. 184, line 1 of 3rd paragraph: *exosum* for *Exosimi*
p. 192, line 3: [*h*]*odoeporicum* for *ode puricum*
p. 193, line 12: *verbosor* for *verbosior*
p. 212, line 7: delete *cum; cum sparsi* for *conspersi*
p. 218, last line of 2nd paragraph: *computruit* for *computuit*
p. 222, line 7: *pertusulum* for *pertulusum*

Bibliography

Extant Works by Guibert of Nogent in Approximate Chronological Order[1]

De virginitate, in Migne, *Patrologia latina,* t. 156, cols. 579–608.

Moralia in Genesim, ibid., cols. 19–338; contains *Liber quo ordine sermo fieri debeat,* cols. 21–32.

Epistola de buccella Judae data et de veritate Dominici corporis, ibid., cols. 527–538.

Gesta Dei per Francos, in *Recueil des historiens des croisades. Historiens occidentaux,* IV (Paris, 1879), 115–263.

Tractatus de Incarnatione contra Judaeos, ed. Migne, cols. 489–528.

De vita sua sive monodiarum suarum libri tres, ed. Georges Bourgin as *Guibert de Nogent: Histoire de sa vie,* Collection de textes pour servir à l'étude et à l'enseignement de l'histoire (Paris, 1907).

Liber de laude Sanctae Mariae, ed. Migne, cols. 537–578.

Tropologiae in Osee, Jeremiam, et Amos, ibid., cols. 337–488.

Tropologiae in Abdiam, Jonam, Micheam, Zachariam, Joel, Nahum, Habacuc, et Sophoniam. The introductory letter is printed by Jean Mabillon, *Annales Ordinis S. Benedicti* (Paris, 1703–39), VI, 639 [Lucca ed., VI, 592]. The complete work is in Paris, Bibl. nat., ms. lat. 17282, fols. 40–99v.

[1]For the order of the works, see above, pp. 236-239. The sermon *Sapientia vincit malitiam,* printed in Migne, *Patrologia latina,* t. 184, cols. 1031–1044, has often been attributed to Guibert. Dom Jean Leclercq shows that this ascription is false in "Les sermons synodaux attribués à Saint Bernard," *Revue bénédictine,* LXIII (1953), 292–309.

De pignoribus sanctorum, ed. Migne, cols. 607–680.

Works on Guibert of Nogent

This list does not include the numerous books and articles which deal with Guibert as part of a larger subject.

AMORY, FREDERIC. "The Confessional Superstructure of Guibert de Nogent's *Vita,*" *Classica et Mediaevalia,* XXV (1964), 224–240.

BOEHM, LAETITIA. *Studien zur Geschichtsschreibung des ersten Kreuzzugs. Guibert von Nogent,* Munich Diss. 27 July 1954. 243 pp. typed.

CHAURAND, JACQUES. "La conception de l'histoire de Guibert de Nogent," *Cahiers de civilisation médiévale,* VIII (1965), 381–395.

———. "Guibert de Nogent, chroniqueur laonnais (1053–1124)," *Mémoires de la Fédération des Sociétés d'Histoire et d'Archéologie de l'Aisne,* XII (1966), 122–131.

CLÉMENTEL, CHARLES. "Guibert, Abbé de Nogent," in *Histoire littéraire de la France,* X (1756), 433–500; new ed., Paris, 1868.

DAUTHEUIL, LEON. "Où est né Guibert de Nogent?" *Bulletin et Mémoires de la Société Archéologique et Historique de Clermont de l'Oise,* années 1933–37 (1938), pp. 28–35. Reprinted in *Bulletin religieux du diocèse de Beauvais,* 1953, pp. 453–454; 1954, pp. 31–34, as "Le neuvième centenaire de Guibert de Nogent."

DUMÉRIL, ALFRED. "Les mémoires d'un moine au XIIe siècle," *Mémoires de l'Académie des Sciences, Inscriptions et Belles-Lettres de Toulouse,* 9th ser., VI (1894), 1–22.

———. "Les 'Gesta Dei per Francos' de Guibert de Nogent," *ibid.,* 9th ser., VII (1895), 161–178.

GEISELMANN, JOSEPH. "Die Stellung des Guibert von Nogent (†1124) in der Eucharistielehre der Frühscholastik," *Theologische Quartalschrift,* CX (1929), 66–84, 279–305.

HALLENSTEIN, SUSE. *Nachbildung und Umformung der Bekenntnisse Augustins in der Lebensgeschichte Guiberts von Nogent,* Hamburg Diss. 12 Sept. 1935. 48 pp. typed.

HALPHEN, LOUIS. "Un pédagogue," *Comptes rendus de l'Académie des Inscriptions et Belles-Letters,* année 1939, pp. 558–599. Reprinted in his collected works, *A travers l'histoire du moyen âge* (Paris, 1950), pp. 277–285.

LANDRY, BERNARD. "Les idées morales du XIIe siècle. Les écrivains en latin. VII. Un chroniqueur: Guibert de Nogent," *Revue des cours et conférences,* année 1938–39, II, 343–361.

LEFRANC, ABEL. "Le traité des reliques de Guibert de Nogent et les commencements de la critique historique au moyen âge," in *Études d'histoire du moyen âge dediées à Gabriel Monod* (Paris, 1896), pp. 285–306.

MISCH, GEORG. "Die Autobiographie des Abtes Wibert von Nogent," *Deutsche Vierteljahrschrift für Literaturwissenschaft und Geistesgeschichte,* III (1925), 566–614. Expanded and reworked in:

———, *Geschichte der Autobiographie,* III, 2 (Frankfurt am Main, 1959), pp. 108–162.

MOLLARD, AUGUSTE. "Interprétation d'un passage du 'De Vita Sua' de Guibert de Nogent et correction d'une expression fautive," *Le Moyen Age,* XLII (1932), 32–36.

———. "L'imitation de Quintilien dans Guibert de Nogent," *ibid.,* XLIV (1934), 81–87.

MONOD, BERNARD. *Le moine Guibert et son temps* (Paris, 1905), which contains the substance of his earlier articles on Guibert.

SMALLEY, BERYL. "William of Middleton and Guibert de Nogent," *Recherches de théologie ancienne et médiévale,* XVI (1949), 281–291.

Index of Citations

Entries marked with an asterisk are possible sources but are not clearly identifiable as the basis for Guibert's choice of words. Guibert may, of course, have taken some of his quotations from *florilegia* or other authors; it is unlikely, for instance, that he was directly familiar with Tacitus's *Germania*.

Biblical Citations

Classical and Patristic

Proverbial Sayings

Canon Law

INDEX